CAMBRIDGE STUDIES IN ANGLO-SAXON ENGLAND

32

PARADISE, DEATH AND DOOMSDAY IN ANGLO-SAXON LITERATURE

CAMBRIDGE STUDIES IN
ANGLO-SAXON ENGLAND

FOUNDING GENERAL EDITORS
MICHAEL LAPIDGE AND SIMON KEYNES
CURRENT GENERAL EDITORS
SIMON KEYNES AND ANDY ORCHARD

Volumes published

1 *Anglo-Saxon Crucifixion Iconography and the Art of the Monastic Revival* by BARBARA C. RAW
2 *The Cult of the Virgin Mary in Anglo-Saxon England* by MARY CLAYTON
3 *Religion and Literature in Western England, 600–800* by PATRICK SIMS-WILLIAMS
4 *Visible Song: Transitional Literacy in Old English Verse* by KATHERINE O'BRIEN O'KEEFE
5 *The Metrical Grammar of 'Beowulf'* by CALVIN B. KENDALL
6 *The Irish Tradition in Old English Literature* by CHARLES D. WRIGHT
7 *Anglo-Saxon Medicine* by M. L. CAMERON
8 *The Poetic Art of Aldhelm* by ANDY ORCHARD
9 *The Old English Lives of St Margaret* by MARY CLAYTON and HUGH MAGENNIS
10 *Biblical Commentaries from the Canterbury School of Theodore and Hadrian* by BERNHARD BISCHOFF and MICHAEL LAPIDGE
11 *Archbishop Theodore: Commemorative Studies on his Life and Influence* edited by MICHAEL LAPIDGE
12 *Interactions of Thought and Language in Old English Poetry* by PETER CLEMOES
13 *The Textuality of Old English Poetry* by CAROL BRAUN PASTERNACK
14 *The 'Laterculus Malalianus' and the School of Archbishop Theodore* by JANE STEVENSON
15 *The Text of the Old Testament in Anglo-Saxon England* by RICHARD MARSDEN
16 *Old English Biblical Verse* by PAUL G. REMLEY
17 *The Hymns of the Anglo-Saxon Church* by INGE B. MILFULL
18 *Scenes of Community in Old English Poetry* by HUGH MAGENNIS
19 *The Old English Apocrypha and their Manuscript Source: 'The Gospel of Nichodemus' and 'The Avenging of the Saviour'* edited by J. E. CROSS
20 *The Composition of Old English Poetry* by H. MOMMA
21 *Trinity and Incarnation in Anglo-Saxon Art and Thought* by BARBARA C. RAW
22 *Heathen Gods in Old English Literature* by RICHARD NORTH
23 *'Beowulf' and Old Germanic Metre* by GEOFFREY RUSSOM
24 *Ælfric's Letter to the Monks of Eynsham* by CHRISTOPHER A. JONES
25 *The Intellectual Foundations of English Benedictine Reform* by MECHTHILD GRETSCH
26 *Apocryphal Gospels of Mary in Anglo-Saxon England* by MARY CLAYTON
27 *Representations of the Natural World in Old English Poetry* by JENNIFER NEVILLE
28 *Anglo-Saxon Gestures and the Roman Stage* by C. R. DODWELL
29 *Literary Appropriations of the Anglo-Saxons from the Thirteenth to the Twentieth Century* by DONALD SCRAGG and CAROLE WEINBERG
30 *Rewriting Old English in the Twelfth Century* by MARY SWANN and ELAINE M. TREHARNE
31 *Text and Picture in Anglo-Saxon England: Narrative Strategies in the Junius 11 Manuscript* by CATHERINE E. KARKOV

Paradise, Death and Doomsday in Anglo-Saxon Literature

ANANYA JAHANARA KABIR
Trinity College, Cambridge

CAMBRIDGE
UNIVERSITY PRESS

CAMBRIDGE UNIVERSITY PRESS
Cambridge, New York, Melbourne, Madrid, Cape Town, Singapore, São Paulo

Cambridge University Press
The Edinburgh Building, Cambridge CB2 2RU, UK

Published in the United States of America by Cambridge University Press, New York

www.cambridge.org
Information on this title: www.cambridge.org/9780521806008

First published 2001
This digitally printed first paperback version 2006

A catalogue record for this publication is available from the British Library

ISBN-13 978-0-521-80600-8 hardback
ISBN-10 0-521-80600-3 hardback

ISBN-13 978-0-521-03060-1 paperback
ISBN-10 0-521-03060-9 paperback

To my parents
Khairan Ara and Zuglul Kabir

We said: give thanks to me, and to your parents
Qur'an Sharif, 31:14

Contents

Preface

The Master and Fellows of Trinity College, Cambridge, have supported my research over the past six years, first in the form of an External Research Studentship and, from October 1997 onwards, through a 'Title A' Research Fellowship. I would like to express my deepest thanks and gratitude to this extraordinarily generous and stimulating institution, which allows its members to spend time in no better fashion than musing about interim paradises. There are other, more specific intellectual debts which I have incurred, and without which this book would never have been written, let alone conceived. I have been fortunate in those who have taught, inspired and guided me intellectually: Malcolm Godden, Simon Keynes, Michael Lapidge, Andy Orchard and Eric Stanley, and my teachers in Presidency College, Calcutta, who first taught me how to articulate my responses to the written word. The greatest pleasure in writing this book lies in being able to thank them all. I would also like to thank Rohini Jayatilaka for her kindness over the years, and Helen Dixon, Sean Miller, Jennifer Neville, Caitríona Ó Dochartaigh, Patrick Sims-Williams, Loredana Teresi, Tessa Webber and Charlie Wright for help, advice and speedy response to queries, often made with little preamble over email. My most fundamental debts are to my parents and my aunts, who, among other things, taught me how to love books and expand my horizons, my brother, for preventing me from taking myself too seriously, and my husband, Mrinal, for sharing with me the fun of intellectual pursuit and the nostalgia of self-imposed exile.

Abbreviations

ALW	*Archiv für liturgie-wissenschaft*
ASE	*Anglo-Saxon England*
ASPR	*The Anglo-Saxon Poetic Records*, eds. Krapp and Dobbie
BaP	Bibliothek der angelsächsichen Prosa
BeP	Beiträge zur englischen Philologie
CCSL	Corpus Christianorum, Series Latina
CMCS	*Cambrian [formerly Cambridge] Medieval Celtic Studies*
CSASE	Cambridge Studies in Anglo-Saxon England
CSEL	Corpus Scriptorum Ecclesiasticorum Latinorum
EETS os	Early English Text Society, original series
EETS ss	Early English Text Society, supplementary series
ES	*English Studies*
HBS	Henry Bradshaw Society
HE	Bede, *Historia Ecclesiastica*, eds. Colgrave and Mynors
JEGP	*Journal of English and Germanic Philology*
JMH	*Journal of Medieval History*
JTS	*Journal of Theological Studies*
LSE ns	*Leeds Studies in English*, new series
MÆ	*Medium Ævum*
MGH AA	Monumenta Germaniae Historica, Auctores Antiquissimi
MGH SRM	Monumenta Germaniae Historica, Scriptores Rerum Merovingicarum
MP	*Modern Philology*
MS	*Mediaeval Studies*
N&Q	*Notes and Queries*
NM	*Neuphilologische Mitteilungen*
PMLA	*Publications of the Modern Language Association of America*

PRIA	*Proceedings of the Royal Irish Academy*
RB	*Revue bénédictine*
RC	*Revue celtique*
RES	*Review of English Studies*
SC	*Studia Celtica*
SC	Sources chrétiennes
SettSpol	*Settimane di studio del centro italiano di studi sull'alto medioevo* (Spoleto)
SM	*Studi Medievali*
TPS	*Transactions of the Philological Society*
ZCP	*Zeitschrift für celtische Philologie*

No attempt has been made to regularise the orthography of Old English and Latin words such as *heofon*, *neornawang* and *paradisus* as and when they appear in different editions cited in the course of this book.

All citations of the Bible are taken from R. Weber, with B. Fischer and J. Gribimont, eds., *Bibla Sacra iuxta Vulgatem versionem*, 2 vols. (Stuttgart, 1975).

1

Between Eden and Jerusalem, death and Doomsday: locating the interim paradise

> If it is permissible to define literature, with a certain rhetorical flourish, as a mirror of society, it is nevertheless a more or less distorting mirror depending on the conscious or unconscious desires of the collective soul which is examining itself – depending, more particularly, on the interests, prejudices, sensibilities and neuroses of the social groups responsible for making the mirror and holding it up to society, or at least that part of society capable of seeing, that is, of reading. Fortunately, the mirror is also tendered to us as members of a posterity better equipped to observe and interpret the interplay of illusions.[1]

This book is about what I term the 'interim paradise', reflected in the mirrors of Anglo-Saxon literature. Its subject is the rarely noted conjunction of two much-discussed concepts: paradise, and the soul's condition in the interim period between death and Judgement Day. It also involves a methodological conjunction: the use of the techniques of literary analysis and source-study to trace the history of an idea in Anglo-Saxon England, and to understand, through that history, some of the processes of production and consumption of literature in this period.

Today, the interim period between death and Judgement Day is most commonly associated with the concept of purgatory, even as the word paradise evokes either the Garden of Eden, or a heavenly state of bliss after death. In Anglo-Saxon England, however, several texts refer to an 'interim paradise', or paradise as an antechamber to heaven, which houses, during the interim period, good souls and those assumed in the body. These literary witnesses diverge considerably in their description of this interim paradise,

[1] J. Le Goff, 'Peasants and the Rural World in the Literature of the Early Middle Ages (Fifth to Sixth Centuries)', in *Time, Work and Culture in the Middle Ages*, trans. A. Goldhammer (Chicago, IL, and London, 1980), pp. 87–97, at p. 88.

and in its function within the early medieval world-view. In other texts, vigorous denial of this signification of paradise itself signals an awareness of it. I interpret these scattered references as a particular 'interplay of illusions', a series of unpredictable distortions produced by the mirrors of literature. By tracing the evolution and transformation of the notions of the interim paradise through the Anglo-Saxon period, I follow these channels of distortions, and try to discover thereby 'the interests, prejudices, sensibilities and neuroses' which dictate the shape taken by the idea in specific groups of texts.

SEMANTIC EXCAVATIONS AND IDEOLOGICAL DEBRIS: THE MANY MEANINGS OF PARADISE

Why, unlike the Anglo-Saxons, do we no longer associate paradise with the interim period? This question is of immense relevance for both the subject and the methodology of this investigation. The unconscious imposition of our own, post-medieval preconceptions can result in blurred and conflicting explorations of early medieval ideas of paradise. To get around this problem, we need to excavate buried meanings of the term, and ask how and why these meanings were lost. This task involves acknowledging, even celebrating, the 'distorting factor' of the written word, the trick mirrors, which often furnish the only clue to ideas that have now vanished. But before attempting to thus 'interpret the interplay of illusions', we also need to overcome what Katherine O'Brien O'Keeffe has called 'the peculiar nature of human perception, which obscures the very categories of intellection through which we understand the world.'[2]

Recent scholarship in cultural history has developed a laudable sensitivity to the preconceptions a modern investigator necessarily brings, but must also shed, while grappling with the histories of religion, culture and literacy. Thus, in attempting to distinguish between the object and the methods of enquiry, Roger Chartier asks:

> Is 'popular' religion the religion practised by peasants, or by the dominated (as opposed to the dominating elite), or by the laity (as opposed to the clergy)? Our indecision in the face of such questions reflects the fact that historians have accepted as a definition of popular religion the one that the clergy themselves made. What theologians and pastors did in the Middle Ages, and more so under the Catholic Reformation, was dual: they defined a whole body of practices and beliefs

[2] O'Brien O'Keeffe, *Visible Song*, p. 9.

as contradicting legitimate Christianity and qualified as 'popular' the practices and beliefs they considered as superstitious. By adopting these distinctions historians have made themselves victims of an inherent ambiguity. The clergy's definition of superstition is always a compromise made between theological references, which since Saint Augustine have characterized superstitions by assimilating them within the category of idolatry, and the inventory of practices that embody these idolatrous beliefs in everyday life.[3]

These comments can be applied, *mutatis mutandis*, to the subject of the present investigation. The ideological burden of the term paradise, while perhaps not equal to that borne by fraught concepts such as magic or superstition,[4] has left a comparable residue of semantic and connotative confusion which has to be recognised before it can be accounted for.

During early Christianity, there existed various conceptual systems for discussing the life hereafter. Within these systems, terms such as 'paradise', 'third heaven', 'kingdom of heaven', 'bosom of Abraham', and 'place of refreshment' were interlocked in semantic interdependence. Competing groups both within and outside Christianity constantly shifted the use of the term paradise within these systems in order to change the meaning of the entire configuration and uphold the advantages of one belief-system over all others. In Scripture, apocrypha and exegesis, paradise could as easily refer to a celestial interim location as it could to the terrestrial Garden of Eden, and as frequently merge with heaven as it could be distinguished from it. Several of these senses of paradise survived into the early Middle Ages to enter new contexts and develop fresh, often unexpected, applications.

BEYOND HISTORY AND IDEOLOGY? SOME ASSUMPTIONS ABOUT PARADISE

Within theological scholarship, this semantic fluidity of the term paradise during early Christianity elicits, in general, two kinds of response.

[3] Chartier, 'Culture as Appropriation', p. 230.

[4] See, in this connection, K. Thomas, *Religion and the Decline of Magic: Studies in Popular Belief in the Sixteenth and Seventeenth Centuries* (Harmondsworth, 1971), its review by H. Geertz, 'An Anthropology of Religion and Magic I', *Journal of Interdisciplinary History* 6 (1975), 71–89, and the response by Thomas in 'An Anthropology of Religion and Magic II', *Journal of Interdisciplinary History* 6 (1975), 91–109. More recently, see E. Duffy, *The Stripping of the Altars: Tradition and Religion in England c. 1400–1580* (New Haven, CT, and London, 1992).

Investigations into any one of its meanings, most often 'the terrestrial paradise', sometimes accept unquestioningly and rather uncritically the existence of its alternative meanings, including its association with the interim state.[5] Alternatively, all interpretations of the term, other than those ultimately retained within the canonical books of the Bible and promoted by the Church itself, are refused validity, with the 'official' meanings of paradise being imposed upon documents which may bear witness to its earlier polysemy.[6] A recent exception is Charles Hill's investigation into the term *regnum caelorum* in early Christianity, where he examines the competing interpretations of this phrase within and outside chiliasm, or Greek millenarian thought.[7] By focusing on the close association of theology and polemics in the early Church, he reveals the interim state to be an ideologically charged concept within Latin Christianity's own processes of self-definition. Hill's conclusions make even more pressing the need for an investigation into the precise role played by the concept which we have isolated as the interim paradise, born out of these early polemics, but nourished by the early medieval imagination.

It would seem that such an investigation has been retarded by a reluctance to expose the arsenal of rhetoric deployed in the battle between heterodoxy and orthodoxy. Perhaps it is unreasonable to expect theologians to reveal as being implicated in historical change what theology considers as being sacramental and transcendental. But the transcendental appearance of terms such as paradise and heaven has beguiled even those claiming to analyse, from a non-theological point of view, the detail amassed through the primary research of theologians. Many an intellectual historian tackling these topics seems to have fallen prey to its emotive nature, producing fuzzy and impressionistic accounts based on convenient dichotomies and catch-phrases which appeal to the modern imagination.[8] The most seductive of such dichotomies is that between Eden, the 'earthly garden', and Jerusalem, the 'heavenly city'. Most modern discussions of paradise and heaven devolve around the opposition between these two groups of ideas, and some even postulate a phenomenological or psychic

[5] As seen, for instance, in Daniélou, 'Terre et paradis', Grimm, *Paradisus coelestis, paradisus terrestris*, and A. Stuiber, *Refrigerium interim*.

[6] As, for instance, by Ntedika, in *L'évocation de l'au-delà*, where he investigates in detail the meaning of the terms *paradisus*, *regnum caelorum* and *sinus Abrahae* within funeral liturgies.

[7] Hill, *Regnum Caelorum*.

[8] To take the most recent example, see Russell's *A History of Heaven*.

progression from one to the other.[9] A natural extension of this association is to see its secular parallels in versions of 'arcadia' and 'utopia'.[10] Also, in works that concentrate on either paradise or heaven, the other concept is often invoked in an ancillary or a synonymous manner, which underestimates both their complicated interrelationship as well as the need to acknowledge and possibly unravel it.[11]

These tendencies are fuelled by the modern understanding of paradise as either the earthly Garden of Eden or as a synonym for heaven. However, this understanding itself derives from the system promoted by theologians from Augustine onwards, and thus reflects the hegemony of mainstream Latin Christian ideology, which continues to structure so many of our 'categories of intellection'. Instead of asking why we conceive of paradise through certain categories and not others, therefore, modern writers often anachronistically impose these categories on to earlier periods. The survival and transformation of the interim paradise from early Christianity into the early Middle Ages is, if at all noted, dismissed in a brief paragraph or section – an inclination especially of studies which trace 'the history of paradise' or 'the history of heaven' over the *longue durée*.[12]

THE HISTORIAN, THE LITERARY CRITIC, AND 'THE HISTORY OF PARADISE'

Criticism of historians of the *longue durée* may seem unduly provocative within this introduction, given that one of the best known investigators of

9 See McClung, *Architecture of Paradise*, where he constructs an elaborate argument for an 'ascendancy of an architecture over a horticulture of paradise' whereby from the 'arcadian' paradise, vulnerable and unwalled, we move to 'compromised Edens, paradisal gardens to some degree assimilated to architectural phenomena like walls, temples and cities' (p. 7).

10 This connection is most marked in investigations into the concept of utopia, the historical predecessor to which is often seen as the idea of paradise; thus Manuel and Manuel, *Utopian Thought*, remark at p. 33: 'Paradise in its Judaeo-Christian terms has to be accepted as the deepest archaeological layer of Western utopia.' See also McClung, *Architecture of Paradise*, p. 2.

11 As demonstrated, for example, by McDannell and Lang, *Heaven: a History*, pp. 67–79, and Simon, *Heaven in the Christian Tradition*, pp. 204, 216 and 242.

12 As seen in Delumeau's *Une histoire du paradis*, 2 vols., I, pp. 37–57, where he discusses 'paradis comme un lieu d'attente' through a rapid review of documents, from Judaeo-Christian apocrypha to twelfth-century vision literature, which refer to paradise as an interim abode for souls.

interim eschatology, Jacques Le Goff, belongs squarely within this tradition of historical scholarship. Le Goff's pioneering study of the emergence of purgatory, which examines evidence ranging from Egyptian and Greek culture to that of thirteenth-century Europe, attempts to bridge the gaps between theology, the history of ideas and cultural history.[13] His two scholarly concerns – the *longue durée* and the study of *mentalités* – are representative of the *Annales* school of historiography,[14] which, in the past few decades, has produced and inspired some valuable and exciting 'alternative cultural histories' of medieval and early modern Europe.[15]

Like most historians of *mentalités*, Le Goff brings the historian's perspective to the study of mainly 'theological' sources such as exegesis, homiletic writing and liturgy. He concludes thereby that the social and cultural developments of twelfth-century Europe necessitated the development of the doctrine of purgatory, within a tripartite otherworld consisting of purgatory, heaven and hell, in order to describe the interim state of the soul. Unfortunately, the teleological emphasis of this argument produces an inevitable bias in his interpretation and choice of source material. In arguing for purgatory as a product of the high Middle Ages, Le Goff all but ignores early medieval witnesses to the conceptualisation of the interim condition as a pleasant as well as a penal location, as a paradise alongside a 'proto-purgatory', or a provisional hell. At the same time, his premises and assumptions lead him to interpret as four-fold divisions, the tripartite schemes present within earlier writings, and, conversely, four-fold divisions discernible in twelfth-century witnesses as tripartite.[16] This misrepresentation of interim eschatology before the twelfth century also leaves a vital question unasked: when and why did the idea of an interim paradise, separate from heaven, give way to the tripartite cosmology of purgatory, hell and a state equally well defined as either paradise or heaven?

Le Goff's methodology also provokes an important criticism, applicable to most cultural historians and historians of ideas, who work with written records such as visions of the otherworld, hagiography and homilies: in

[13] Le Goff, *Birth of Purgatory*.

[14] For an overview of the *Annales* school and its approach to history, see R. Chartier, *On the Edge of the Cliff: History, Language and Practices*, trans. L. G. Cochrane (London and Baltimore, MD, 1997), and P. Ricoeur, *Time and Narrative*, trans. K. McLaughlin and D. Pellauer, 3 vols. (Chicago, IL, and London, 1984), I, pp. 95–120.

[15] For some examples of such scholarship, see below, p. 73, n. 77.

[16] See below, p. 91, where this point is argued in greater detail.

charting the history of the interim state, he leaves little room for the effects of strictly 'literary' or aesthetic impulses. Historians of *mentalités*, consciously following in Le Goff's footsteps, have regularly drawn attention to *'les enjeux idéologiques'*[17] which lead to cultural compromises between elite and dominated groups in society, between literate and illiterate or between clergy and laity. Yet they have often overlooked the demands of form and content imposed by those cultural artefacts through which such compromises are articulated. Written texts, as one class of such artefacts, are not mere receptacles from which beliefs and ideas may be recovered in pristine form. Rather, they are moulds, which impress their shape and structure on the very concepts they preserve. Without this awareness, the analysis of ideas transmitted through the vehicle of literary texts remains incomplete.

The opposite problem prevails in investigations of similar texts undertaken within a 'literary' framework. A salient example is Howard Patch's influential compendium, where, like Le Goff, he examines centuries of imaginative writing and theological exposition, distributed amongst thematically ordered chapters.[18] An impressive amount of material is analysed thereby, but we are left with little idea of the intersections and connections between exegesis and vision, homily and poem, and of the ideological and political reasons promoting certain words, certain images, and even certain genres over others. On the other hand, literary critics who do attempt to place images and descriptions of paradise against a specific conceptual backdrop inevitably return to the standard dichotomy between Eden and Jerusalem.[19]

The temptation to associate the description of a city with Jerusalem, and that of nature with paradise, and to define one with the help of the other, is often implicit in literary discussions of paradise or ideal landscapes in the Middle Ages, as is inadvertently revealed by Paul Piehler's comment:

> Landscape symbolism of the Middle Ages or any other period is not easy to comprehend without some understanding of the basic psychic polarity of city and wilderness which naturally arises out of man's experience of his environment. It is this

[17] The phrase is Schmitt's, 'Les Traditions folkloriques', p. 10.

[18] H. R. Patch, *The Other World according to Descriptions in Medieval Literature* (Cambridge, MA, 1950).

[19] Note, for example, the observation of Pearsall and Salter, *Landscapes and Seasons*, p. 56: 'As the beginning and the end of man's quest for perfection, as Eden and as the Celestial Paradise, it [paradise] spanned all human history.'

polarity, moreover, that can provide us with an important clue to the nature of the attractive power of the *locus amoenus*.'[20]

Later in his argument, he qualifies the *locus amoenus* as the 'enclosed garden, park or paradise . . . intensely desirable, and situated either very remotely or behind inhibiting physical or psychic barriers'.[21] Piehler's statements also point to the scholarly reliance on alluring images such as the *hortus conclusus*, 'enclosed garden', or the *locus amoenus*, 'pleasant place', reflected in the numerous studies discussing the literary development of these images which originated in Scripture or patristic writings. However, very few studies actually consider the reasons why these images journeyed from one domain of thought to another, and the mutations they may have undergone in the process. One consequence of this approach is the failure to explain why many such images were not uniformly current throughout the Middle Ages. In Anglo-Saxon England, for instance, there is scarcely one description of an 'enclosed garden' as an ideal landscape,[22] or of the earthly paradise which bears the same resonances as in later medieval texts.

PARADISE IGNORED? THE TEMPTATIONS OF EVOLUTIONARY LITERARY HISTORIES

The absence of the Anglo-Saxon contribution from literary studies of paradise, heaven or the otherworld is also the by-product of an evolutionary model for literary history, which would consider all literary manifestations of a particular theme prior to the appearance of a work regarded as canonical as somehow unworthy of independent study and evaluation. Thanks to this subconscious 'Darwinism',[23] many such studies are conducted towards furthering our appreciation of Dante's *La divina commedia* and Milton's *Paradise Lost*.[24] The existence of these literary peaks has tended to dwarf all predecessors, which are then viewed as inferior precursors rather than works of independent merit. Accordingly, only those aspects of these concepts are examined which have doctrinal and psychological implications directly rel-

[20] Piehler, *Visionary Landscape*, pp. 72–3. [21] *Ibid.*, p. 77.

[22] Rather, the ideal landscape of Old English poetry is an open space, as I demonstrate in ch. 6.

[23] See, in this connection, G. Beer, *Darwin's Plots: Evolutionary Narrative in Darwin, George Eliot and Nineteenth-Century Fiction* (London, 1983).

[24] See, for instance, Evans, *'Paradise Lost'*, Russell, *History of Heaven*, and Le Goff, *Birth of Purgatory*.

evant to the work in question. The Anglo-Saxon contribution to later medieval concepts of paradise, heaven and purgatory is usually glossed over in a series of rather naive generalisations, such as those made by Evans while discussing the description of Eden in *Genesis A*:

> Clearly this is a far less sophisticated picture of the world's pristine innocence than that in the *Metrum in Genesim* or the *Alethia*. Living as he did in an environment more akin to the savage landscape of the *De Rerum Natura*, the eighth-century poet had little time for the refined delights of sight, smell, and sound elaborated in the Christian-Latin poems. His idea of perfection extended little further than climatic stability and the absence of bodily discomforts inflicted by Nature . . . the more primitive ideal of an amenable countryside.[25]

In their haste to reach Dante's *Paradiso*, it would seem, surveys of the idea of paradise within European literature symptomatically leap from patristic writings to the high Middle Ages.[26]

Unfortunately, this imbalance is reproduced, albeit unwittingly, within Anglo-Saxon scholarship. Numerous articles and larger investigations dealing with the concept of hell exist, but Anglo-Saxon ideas of paradise and heaven remain under-studied, perhaps because of the presupposition that the Anglo-Saxons were wholly preoccupied by the horrors and delights which awaited them after Doomsday.[27] The frequent comparison of Anglo-Saxon to Celtic conceptions of the afterlife, and Anglo-Saxon borrowing of infernal motifs and themes from Celtic sources, has led Anglo-Saxonists and Celticists alike to suppose that this dependence was true of Anglo-Saxon interim eschatology in general.[28] This assumption has obscured the importance of the interim paradise and the role played by Anglo-Saxon England

[25] Evans, *'Paradise Lost'*, pp. 148–9. In ch. 6 I suggest some other explanations for the absence of the 'refinements of sight, smell and sound' in Old English descriptions of paradise.

[26] As demonstrated, for instance, by Evans, *'Paradise Lost'*, and Pearsall and Salter, *Landscapes and Seasons*. This tendency is, of course, also found in more general studies such as McDannell and Lang's *Heaven: a History* and Delumeau's *Une Histoire du paradis*. Similar patterns within enquiries into early medieval representations of the natural world have been noted by J. Neville, *Representations of the Natural World in Old English Poetry*, CSASE 27 (Cambridge, 1999), p. 14.

[27] For an illustrative example of how such assumptions predicate further misinterpretations of Anglo-Saxon writings on the interim condition, see my comments on the works of Gatch, pp. 43 and 74 below. The pressure of Le Goff's work, and its corollary that all pre-Doomsday imaginings before the twelfth century must somehow foreshadow purgatory, could also have contributed to this prevailing impression.

[28] See below, p. 91.

in its development. Particularly misleading in this respect has been the perceived similarity between Anglo-Latin visions of the otherworld and the Celtic genres of the *immram* and the *echtrae*.[29] The few articles that do discuss heaven and paradise appear quite unaware of the existence of such a concept as the interim paradise, or the theological scholarship that could illuminate their enquiries somewhat by pointing to parallels in liturgy and in apocrypha.[30] The only holistic reconstruction of what an Anglo-Saxon might have imagined as transpiring between death and Doomsday is that of Patrick Sims-Williams's, who brings together vision literature, prayers, liturgy and apocryphal writings in his richly contextualised examination of the Vision of the Monk of Wenlock, as reported by Boniface.[31] Sims-Williams's overall focus is the cultural history of the western kingdoms of early Anglo-Saxon England, which provides an illuminating backdrop for this text, but which also confines his insights concerning the interim paradise to the period and area he is interested in surveying. Later vernacular literature, for instance, remains largely outside his scope, as does a detailed examination of the early Christian history of the interim paradise.

AIMS, ASSUMPTIONS AND METHODS OF THE PRESENT INVESTIGATION

From this survey of scholarship treating of both paradise and the interim condition, it is clear that largely methodological constraints have prevented the emergence of the interim paradise in Anglo-Saxon England as a subject of investigation. In the present investigation, accordingly, I have allowed myself the liberty of certain assumptions: that ideas do not move, transform or crystallise into images of their own accord, and that images or words are not primarily chosen for the sake of some essential 'beauty'. Rather, words, images and ideas are constantly reappropriated by writers to express their own agenda and world-view. I have tried to see in this 'interplay of illusions' some of the socio-cultural processes that dictated the flow of ideas from one group of texts to another, their translation into images and descriptions,

[29] See below, pp. 92, 109 and 177–8.

[30] See, for instance, the confusions between paradise and heaven in Tristram, 'Stock Descriptions', and Roberts, 'A Preliminary Heaven Index'. For further references to these articles, see below, pp. 146 and 153.

[31] Sims-Williams, *Religion and Literature*. His arguments are examined in greater detail below, pp. 95–6.

and the absorption of these into new ideas. In order to do so, I have turned to the conclusions of cultural historians of Late Antiquity and the early Middle Ages, as well as to the analyses of liturgical and devotional material by theologians and historians. But I have tried not to let these important perspectives detract from the caprices of that human impulse which may, for want of a clearer term, be called the 'aesthetic', and the subversive forces inherent in both the written word and its reception. It is in this interaction of use, ornament and pleasure that we must seek the genesis and development of particular concepts. If the production and consumption of literature is seen as a chain of reappropriations, where each text represents the articulation of a compromise between literary form and individual ideology, then the study of these reappropriations can tell us something not only about the particular concept under investigation but also the world which gave voice to it.

These assumptions underlie the choice of sources and their overall arrangement within this book. It attempts to bring together the 'literary', the 'cultural', and the 'theological' in analysing the Anglo-Saxon witnesses to the interim paradise, although the resultant methodology is by no means uniform throughout. It does not claim to provide an exhaustive survey, but a representative one. Both Latin and Old English texts from different literary genres are examined, not always chronologically, but in a manner that best illuminates the continual play of reappropriations shaping the concept of the interim paradise in this particular part of the early Middle Ages.

The following chapter introduces the background to Anglo-Saxon speculation on paradise and the interim state. Apocryphal descriptions are contrasted with Augustinian exegesis, to establish that an interim paradise, distinct from heaven, was developed in contexts which were deemed unorthodox by the formulators of Christian doctrine in the Latin West, who adopted and upheld the synonymy of paradise and heaven. I then show how Ælfric struggled between these conflicting legacies for Anglo-Saxon England, and ask why he should have been pressurised into devising various rhetorical compromises to accommodate them both. This question is partially answered in the third chapter, which examines several anonymous prose vernacular texts from the ninth and tenth centuries that freely develop various distinctions between heaven and an interim paradise. I suggest that not only are these anonymous writings the immediate target of Ælfric's objections to the interim paradise, but that they also indicate the divergent reappropriations of the same conceptual legacies by different authors.

The fourth chapter refines these suggestions by demonstrating how Bede and Boniface use the genre of the visionary journey to the otherworld – itself a product of the social circumstances of seventh-century Europe – to express late patristic modifications of Augustine's position on the interim state. The Anglo-Latin visions indicate that learned authority wished to retain rather than jettison the interim paradise, and that their resultant compromises actually sharpened the distinctions between paradise and heaven, largely through the literary exigencies of the visionary genre. In the fifth chapter, this ambivalence within Anglo-Saxon monasticism is re-examined through Anglo-Latin prayers from the eighth and ninth centuries, and the funeral liturgy likely to have been known in Anglo-Saxon England at this time. Within the contrasting vocabulary of these two groups of supplicatory material we see the private acceptance of the interim paradise within the monastic world-view on the one hand and its rejection within the public funeral rite on the other. However, evidence from the tenth century suggests that this particular form of monastic compromise was replaced by a stricter attitude towards the interim paradise in later Anglo-Saxon England.

The dialectic between systems of thought and their literary expression is further explored in the sixth chapter. The tension between the conflation of paradise and heaven on the one hand, and their distinction through the interim paradise on the other, is reflected in the different techniques employed by poets to describe paradise and heaven. The concluding chapter illustrates some consequences of these continuing dialectics. I argue for the reappropriation of *The Phoenix* by the author of an anonymous prose text in late Old English, and compare its description of the interim paradise with that of other late Anglo-Saxon texts and twelfth-century accounts of interim eschatology. I thereby suggest that the conceptual load of the interim paradise had become fragmented by the end of the Anglo-Saxon period. The altered significations which result open the way to its disappearance in the subsequent centuries and its replacement by newer schemes of the otherworld.

Mapping the concept of the interim paradise on to the contours of different Anglo-Saxon texts highlights the recurrence of certain features of the concept within certain literary environments, and their absence in others. These alignments demonstrate that the interim paradise was a necessary, influential and ideologically charged concept during the early Middle Ages, and within Anglo-Saxon England in particular. However, its changing fortunes also provide a unique angle from which simultaneously to view several ostensible oppositions – orthodoxy and heterodoxy, learned and popular sensibilities, Latin and the vernacular, prose and verse. I hope to review these oppositions as ongoing and intersecting cultural processes. But their lack of fit and non-congruencies can perhaps also shed light on the aporias of cultural history, and the pattern of compromises and reappropriations that modulate both the anarchy of the imagination and the discipline of dogma.

2

Assertions and denials: paradise and the interim, from the *Visio Sancti Pauli* to Ælfric

> Men ða leofostan Paulus se apostol ealra ðeoda lareow awrat be him sylfum þæt he wære gelædd up to heofonum. oð þæt he becom to ðære ðriddan heofonan. and he wæs gelæd to neorxnawange. and þær ða gastlican dygelnysse gehyrde and geseah. ac he ne cydde na eorðlicum mannum ða ða he ongean com. hwæt he gehyrde. oððe gesawe . . . Humeta rædað sume men. ða leasan gesetnysse. ðe hi hatað Paulus gesihðe. nu he sylf sæde. þæt he ða digelan word gehyrde. þe nan eorðlic mann sprecan ne mot.[1]

> Hwæt wille we eow swiðor secgan be ðisum symbeldæge. buton þæt maria cristes modor wearð on ðisum dæge of ðisum geswincfullum middanearde genumen up to heofenan rice . . . Gif we mare secgað be ðisum symbeldæge þonne we on ðam halgum bocum rædað þe ðurh godes dihte gesette wæron. ðonne beo we ðam dwolmannum gelice. þe be heora agenum dihte oððe be swefnum fela lease gesetnyssa awriton . . . dwollican bec ægðer ge on leden ge on englisc.[2]

[1] Ælfric, *Item in letania maiore, feria tertia*, Godden, ed., *Catholic Homilies*, p. 190: 'Beloved men, Paul the apostle, teacher of all peoples, about himself recorded that he was led up to the heavens, until he came to the third heaven, and he was led to paradise, and there heard and saw spiritual secrets, but when he returned, he did not reveal to any earthly men what he had heard or seen . . . How then do some men read those lying narratives which they call Paul's vision, when he himself said that he heard secret words which no earthly man should speak of?' Translations of Latin and Old English texts are mine, unless otherwise noted.

[2] Ælfric, *Assumptio sanctae Mariae virginis*, Godden, ed., *Catholic Homilies*, p. 259: 'What more shall we say about this feast-day, except that Mary, mother of Christ was on this day taken from this toilsome earth up to the kingdom of heaven? . . . If we should say any more about this feast-day than what we read in the holy books which were recorded through God's disposition, then we would be like those heretics, who through their own disposition or through dreams have composed many lying narratives . . . heretical books both in Latin and in English.'

Ælfric's attacks on the apocryphal stories about Mary's Assumption and Paul's vision of the third heaven exemplify his self-proclaimed and polemical brand of orthodoxy, which Anglo-Saxon scholars have often discussed.[3] It has nevertheless gone largely unnoticed that both *dwollican bec* which Ælfric rejects describe the afterlife in terms of a paradise quite distinct from the heavenly kingdom of Augustinian exegesis. The *Visio Sancti Pauli* distils into a potent otherworld the fluid meanings of paradise contained in diverse early Christian eschatologies, while the Assumption texts collectively known as the *Transitus Mariae* keep alive distinctions between paradise and heaven which Augustine seeks to merge. While Ælfric's own views on paradise are dependent on Augustine's ideas, he is also influenced, as we shall see, by later writers such as Julian of Toledo, Gregory and Bede, who attempt to bridge the gap between apocryphal descriptions of a post-mortem paradise, and Augustinian rejections of the same.

In this chapter, I introduce these successive responses to the conjunction of paradise and the interim between death and Doomsday, which pull Ælfric in contradictory directions. I thereby provide a background for his specific anxieties on this subject, as well as for the wider context of Anglo-Saxon speculations on paradise and the interim. In the ideas he rejects, and those he substitutes, Ælfric offers us a tantalising glimpse of the ideological issues at stake in Anglo-Saxon representations of paradise, and, accordingly, a useful starting-point for our larger investigation.

PARADISE AND THE THIRD HEAVEN IN THE *VISIO SANCTI PAULI*

The *Visio Sancti Pauli*, henceforth referred to in this chapter as the *Visio*, is the collective term for all the Latin versions of the Greek *Apocalypse of Paul*, composed around the third century, and translated into Latin, Coptic, Syriac and Arabic between the fourth and sixth centuries.[4] The different versions of the so-called Long Latin *Visio*, which preserve the entire Greek *Apocalypse*, were enormously influential in the medieval West, shaping

3 See, for instance, Godden, 'Ælfric's Saints' Lives and the Problem of Miracles', 83–100, Clayton, *Cult*, pp. 260–6, and Hill, 'Reform and Resistance', pp. 22–38.

4 For editions of the long and abbreviated versions see, respectively, Silverstein and Hilhorst, eds., *Apocalypse of Paul*, and Silverstein, ed., *Visio Sancti Pauli*. Details of dates and transmission history may be found in the introduction to each edition.

popular ideas about the afterlife even as their rambling contents were themselves whittled away into numerous abbreviated redactions that emerged throughout the medieval period. Both the long and several abbreviated versions were well known throughout the Anglo-Saxon period. Redactions IV, VI and XI arose in Insular circles, and Aldhelm's condemnation of the *Visio* appears to be directed towards a long version.[5]

The Long Latin *Visio* describes how Paul was transported to the third heaven and led through its different regions, pleasant and punitive, by an angelic guide.[6] In this, it is a direct response to Paul's guarded allusions to his translation into the third heaven and paradise in 2 Corinthians XII. 2–4:

Scio hominem in Cristo ante annos quattordecim, sive in corpore nescio, sive extra corpore nescio, Deus scit; raptum eiusmodi usque ad tertium caelum, et scio huiusmodi hominem, sive in corpore sive extra corpus nescio Deus scit; quoniam raptus est in paradisum, et audivit arcana verba quae non licet homini loqui.[7]

[5] Aldhelm, *De uirginitate*, in *Aldhelmi Opera*, ed. R. Ehwald, MGH 15 (Berlin, 1919), p. 256, where he mentions the detail of the golden boat in which Paul was ferried across the Acherusian Lake. As Silverstein points out in *Visio Sancti Pauli*, p. 6, this detail belongs to the description of paradise found in the Long Latin versions but omitted in most of the later redactions. Anglo-Saxon knowledge of a Long Latin version appeared confirmed by Willard's discovery of a fragmentary Old English translation of what seemed to be a Long Latin version ('The Address of the Soul to the Body', p. 958). In her edition of this translation, Healey describes its Latin source as similar but not identical to the St Gallen Long Latin version of the *Visio* (*Old English Vision*, pp. 25–28). I therefore cite from Silverstein and Hilhorst's edition of the St Gallen text later in this chapter, although the different Long Latin versions do not differ too greatly in the sections I discuss below. My preference for the St Gallen version is thus largely a matter of convenience, as are my own references to 'the Long Latin version', in seeming contradiction of the various long versions of the *Visio* available in the early Middle Ages and, indeed, to Anglo-Saxon England. The questions of which details were actually present in that version whose fragment survives in the Old English translation, and whether Aldhelm knew of yet another version, remain open, especially as Redaction XI of the *Visio* also mentions the golden boat, as discussed below, p. 55. For Redactions IV and VI see McNamara, *The Apocrypha in the Irish Church*, pp. 106–8, and Dumville, '*Fís Adamnán*', pp. 69–70.

[6] My focus in this book remains on the pleasant regions of the otherworld visited by Paul. For the impact of the punitive regions described in the *Visio* on early Christianity, see A. E. Bernstein, *The Formation of Hell: Death and Retribution in the Early Christian Worlds* (New York, 1993), pp. 292–313. The influence of the *Visio* on Insular conceptions of hell is discussed by Wright, *Irish Tradition*, pp. 106–74.

[7] 'I knew a man in Christ above fourteen years ago, whether in the body, I cannot tell, or whether out of the body, I cannot tell, God knows; such a person [was] caught up to the third heaven; and I knew such a man, whether in the body, or whether out of the body, I cannot tell, God knows; how that person was caught up into paradise, and there heard unspeakable words, which it is not lawful for a man to utter.'

Paul's statements, although cryptic, betray his familiarity with the tangled eschatologies of intertestamental apocalyptic, in which corporal ascent through multiple heavens and the transcendence of paradise both play an important role. The *Visio*, in seeking to disambiguate Scripture, depends on much the same network of beliefs, but its plethora of detail is perhaps even more confusing than the ambiguities of the 2 Corinthians reference.

The kaleidoscopic rapidity with which Paul is taken into the third heaven, and out of it, and back again, and the dream-like montage of different scenes, make it progressively difficult to distinguish the sights within the third heaven from those without, and to understand the relation of the many parts of the *Visio* to the whole. Precisely this descriptive richness, however, makes it a valuable repository of the major eschatological schemes that had accumulated by the third century. Images and ideas from orphism, millenarianism, Byzantine eschatology as well as intertestamental apocalyptic are wrenched out of their original context and compressed into the same space. Separating out these different strands in the fabric of the *Visio* gives us some insight into both their older significances and the newer meanings fashioned out of their juxtaposition by this author.

Underlying the *Visio*'s account of the third heaven is the concept of the visionary's ascent through multiple heavens. During the first few centuries AD, different religious groups of the eastern Mediterranean region – Neo-Platonic, Gnostic, Zoroastrian, Jewish and Christian – all divided heaven into several concentric regions, arranged in a hierarchy of increasing splendour, with God and his angelic court in the highest heaven.[8] The frequent emphasis on the third and the seventh heaven would derive from the fact that sequences of three and seven heavens were very common, although series of eight and nine heavens are also encountered.[9] Not only did the number of heavens vary in different belief-systems, but also their characteristics and functions. For instance, Gnostic cosmology describes the soul's purgation during its ascent through seven heavens, the lower of which are filled with instruments of punishment.[10] In Jewish pseudepigrapha, the seven heavens frequently provide a convenient framework for

[8] See, in this connection, Rowland, *Open Heaven*, pp. 78–83, Simon, *Heaven in the Christian Tradition*, pp. 8–14 and 41–3, and Stevenson, 'Ascent through the Heavens', p. 24.

[9] Apocalyptic texts which alter an originally different number of heavens to seven are discussed by Rowland, *Open Heaven*, pp. 81–2.

[10] See Stevenson, 'Ascent through the Heavens', p. 25, and *passim* for the discussion of the Irish 'Seven Heavens' apocryphon as a reflex of Gnostic cosmology.

the various cosmic and eschatological sights revealed to the visionary in question.[11]

At the same time, apocryphal texts written after the Fall of the Temple in 70 AD respond to growing messianic expectations by referring to an abode or garden of the elect and the righteous, prepared for the age to come. Unpopulated in the present age, it is only revealed to those visionaries translated in the body, such as Enoch and Elijah.[12] From these associations of the garden of the righteous with patriarchs preserved from death must have developed the penumbra of speculation on Enoch and Elijah's post-mortem fate that soon surrounded scriptural hints on the subject. In Christian texts such as *The Apocalypse of Peter*, the garden of the righteous is already populated and its occupancy extended to all the Old Testament patriarchs, often signalled by the trio of Abraham, Isaac and Jacob.[13]

The belief in a garden preserved for the righteous must also have raised questions about the relationship of this garden with the Garden of Eden. Indeed, apocryphal descriptions of the two locations are often confusingly similar, incorporating, for instance, identical lists of spice-trees.[14] Parallels between the beginning and the end of the world developed in Jewish apocalyptic mean that the paradise of Eden itself becomes increasingly transcendental and heavenly.[15] The earthly Garden either obtains a celestial counterpart, or is removed to a celestial location, and preserved alongside the heavenly Jerusalem until the coming of the Messiah.[16] Sometimes, the heavenly paradise of Eden is explicitly equated with the future reward of

[11] Although these references to the seven heavens can be vestigial, as in *The Apocalypse of Abraham*, chs. 19–22, in *Apocryphal Old Testament*, ed. Sparks, pp. 382–4. A clearer example is provided by *The Testament of Levi*, chs. 2–3, in *Apocryphal Old Testament*, ed. Sparks, pp. 526–7.

[12] As in *I Enoch*, ch. 32, *Apocryphal Old Testament*, ed. Sparks, p. 219, or *The Book of Jubilees*, ch. 4, pp. 23. The growth and diffusion of this theme is discussed by Milik, ed., *The Books of Enoch*, pp. 118–24. See below, pp. 179–85 for its Anglo-Saxon manifestations.

[13] See *The Apocalypse of Peter* (Ethiopic Version), ch. 16, in Elliott, *Apocryphal New Testament*, pp. 610–11.

[14] Cf. *I Enoch*, chs. 31–2 with *The Life of Adam and Eve*, ch. 43, in *Apocryphal Old Testament*, ed. Sparks, pp. 218 and 159 respectively.

[15] This development is traced by Russell, *Jewish Apocalyptic*, pp. 280–4, Rowland, *Open Heaven*, p. 382, and Simon, *Heaven in the Christian Tradition*, pp. 46–8. For its descriptive repercussions, see Himmelfarb, 'The Temple and the Garden of Eden'.

[16] See *IV Ezra*, ch. 8. 52, in *Apocrypha and Pseudepigrapha*, ed. Charles, II, pp. 597–8.

the righteous.[17] The verses from 2 Corinthians provide further evidence that speculation on the relationship between the garden of the righteous, the Garden of Eden and the multiple heavens had led to their being merged into the paradise of the third heaven even before the *Visio* chose to elaborate on it. But the *Visio* is the first text to make this association confidently and describe it at any length. In intertestamental apocrypha that definitely predate the *Visio*, the third heaven does not display any particularly paradisal characteristics.[18] On the other hand, the association of paradise and the third heaven is seen in works which are most probably themselves influenced by the *Visio*.[19]

The *Visio* states that on entering the third heaven, Paul reaches paradise, where he first encounters Enoch and Elijah (ch. 20). The disparate traditions about their translation into a heavenly abode or into the Garden of Eden appear to be combined here in their being placed in the paradise of the third heaven. Towards the end of the narrative, Paul re-enters this paradise, which is now defined as the place where Adam and Eve had erred, but which also houses all the other patriarchs and the Virgin Mary (chs. 45–51). The paradise of the third heaven is therefore identified with the Garden of Eden even while echoing Christian adaptations of the abode of the righteous into the present dwelling-place of Old Testament figures, as seen in the *Apocalypse of Peter*. Furthermore, there are indications that the third heaven is also where the souls of all the just dwell. Paul frequently asks about, and is shown, the souls of the just and of sinners exiting from their bodies (chs. 9, 13 and 14). Upon desiring to see the places of the just, he is brought to the gates of the third heaven (ch. 19). Later, the angel explains that 'haec est terra repromissionis . . . Animae autem iustorum cum exeunt de corpore, in hunc locum interim dimittuntur.'[20]

This statement appears related to the Byzantine belief that the souls of the just wait in paradise between death and Doomsday, while the souls of sinners similarly wait in a vestibule of Gehenna. This 'doctrine of delayed

[17] As in *The Syriac Apocalypse of Baruch*, ch. 51. 11–13, *Apocryphal Old Testament*, ed. Sparks, p. 871. [18] See *The Testament of Levi*, n. 11 above.

[19] Most notably *II Enoch*, ch. 5, in *Apocryphal Old Testament*, ed. Sparks, p. 331, and *The Testament of Abraham*, ch. 20, p. 421. For the influence of the *Visio* on these works, see Silverstein, ed., *Visio Sancti Pauli*, p. 3, and p. 93, n. 7.

[20] Silverstein and Hilhorst, eds., *Apocalypse of Paul*, ch. 21, p. 114: 'This is the land of counter-promise . . . The souls of the just, when they leave the body, are sent to this place for a while.'

retribution', articulated most strongly in the pseudo-Athanasian *Quaestiones ad Antiochum ducem*, remains current in Byzantine thought until the eleventh century.[21] Its rationale is that, prior to Doomsday, neither joy nor punishment can be absolute. Nevertheless, by being comfortably ensconced in paradise, the just are suitably provided for until they can gain complete happiness in heaven after Doomsday. Platonic influences led Origen to postulate a similar, but rather more curious scheme in his *De principiis*: between death and Doomsday, the souls of the just are instructed towards their future beatitude while continually ascending through a series of heavens, of which paradise is the lowest.[22]

Unlike these eschatologies, however, the *Visio* does not actually identify the abode of the just, the *terra repromissionis*, with the paradise mentioned earlier. Similarly, the soul's sojourn in the *terra repromissionis*, although clearly temporary, is not stated as ending with Doomsday. Instead, the narrative shades into an account of the Second Coming of Christ, when the promised land will become universally apparent. His saints will dwell here, and Christ will rule for a thousand years (ch. 21). At this point, the *Visio* starts resembling the language and ideas of early Christian millenarianism, which believed in the thousand-year long earthly reign of Christ and his saints during the period between the Second Coming and Doomsday. These connections become stronger when Paul describes what he sees next:

> Et circumspexi terram illam et uidi flumen currentem lac et mel. Et erant in litore illius fluminis arbores plantate plene fructibus. Unaqueque arbor erat afferens fructus duodecies in annum uarios et diuersos. Et aperui ostium loci illius et uidi omnem facturam dei. Et uidi ibi palmas cubitorum xxx, alias autem cubitorum x. Terra autem illa clarior erat sepcies argenti. Erant plene a radice usque ad summum, ordines decem milia ramorum fructuum super ramos. Vinee autem uites habebant x milia arbusta. In singulis autem uitibus x milia butriones et x milia racemi in singulis butrionibus; singule autem arbores ferebant milia fructuum.[23]

21 See Daniélou, 'Terre et paradis', pp. 448–50, and Wenger, 'Ciel ou paradis', pp. 560–3. For some iconographic representations of paradise and the afterlife in Byzantine architecture, see M. E. Frazer, 'Church Doors and the Gates of Paradise: Byzantine Bronze Doors in Italy', *Dumbarton Oaks Papers* 27 (1973), 145–62.

22 Crouzel and Simonetti, eds., *Traité des principes*, II, ch. 9. 6–7, pp. 407–13. Origen's eschatology is discussed by Hill, *Regnum Caelorum*, pp. 127–32.

23 Silverstein and Hilhorst, eds., *Apocalypse of Paul*, ch. 22, p. 116: 'And I looked around that domain, and I saw a river flowing with milk and honey. And on the banks of that river there were planted trees full with fruits. Each single tree was bearing fruits of

The river of milk and honey is biblical, but the images of marvellous fecundity reproduce almost verbatim the famous account of the earthly kingdom given by Papias and preserved by Irenaeus, the second-century millenarian, in his *Aduersus haeresibus*.[24]

Irenaeus, however, uses such images to characterise the period *after* the Second Coming. Prior to this, according to millenarianism, the souls of the just and indeed all of the dead would be detained in subterranean vaults in Hades, also identified with the bosom of Abraham into which Lazarus was taken (Luke XVI. 22).[25] Paradise would be closed to all but those few that had been translated in the body, although Tertullian also includes martyrs in this select company.[26] In this restriction of paradise to the corporally assumed, we see the close connections between messianic and millenarian ideas of the interim, also echoed in the idea that paradise would descend to earth upon the Second Coming.[27] The *prima resurrectio* (Apc XX. 5) would then take place. Humanity would be released from the vaults in shifts according to merit, with the saints first. The just would participate in the joys of the millennium until universal judgement on Doomsday and the second resurrection into the heavenly kingdom.

The severe exclusivity of the millenarians is rejected by the author of the *Visio*, along with the rather gloomy interim proposed for nearly all the just until the first resurrection and much of the millennium. Instead, the *Visio* transposes the extravagant millenarian images into the description of a present-day reality enjoyed by the souls of all the just. As the description

many different kinds twelve times a year. And I opened the portal of that place and I saw all the working of God. And there I saw palm trees of thirty cubits, yet there were others of ten cubits. Now that land was seven times brighter than silver. There were full from the root to top rows of ten thousand branches upon branches of fruit. Yet the vines of the vineyard had ten thousand plants. On each vine there were ten thousand bunches, and ten thousand clusters in each bunch. Furthermore, each tree bore a thousand fruits.'

24 Rousseau, Doutreleau and Mercier, eds., *Contre les hérésies, V*, ch. 33. 3, pp. 415–16; see also Hill, *Regnum Caelorum*, pp. 18–20.

25 For a stimulating and thorough analysis of millenarian beliefs about the interim, see Hill, *Regnum Caelorum*, pp. 1–40.

26 Waszink, ed., *De anima*, ch. 55. 5, p. 863: 'Tota paradisi clavis tuus sanguis est.' The reasons behind this stance are explored by Hill, *Regnum Caelorum*, pp. 24–8.

27 Hill locates these connections between messianism and millenarianism in specific 'pharisaic-apocalyptic' texts; see his *Regnum Caelorum*, pp. 41–63.

progresses, some cracks nevertheless appear in this appealing egalitarianism. The horticultural bounties of the *terra repromissionis* are for those chaste in marriage, but joys sevenfold greater await virgins and martyrs (ch. 22). To see these rewards, Paul and the angel cross the Acherusian Lake and enter the City of Christ:

Sol enim et xii porte erant in eam ornate omnem pulchritudinem [sic] et flumina quattuor circumibant. Et erat a limine ciuitatis flumen mellis et notus eius flumen lactus et flumen uini et de ore eius flumen olei. Et dixi angelo, 'Domine, quae sunt flumina haec circumientia ciuitatem hanc?' Et ait, 'Hec sunt quattuor flumina quę currunt sufficienter his qui in terris sunt, quorum nomina sunt haec: flumen mellis dicitur, id est, Fison, flumen lactis Eufraten et flumen olei Gion et flumen uini Tigris.'[28]

Each riverbank is populated by groups of prophets, infants, patriarchs and the humble. Inside the city, the increasing height of each wall and of the golden thrones within each gate, correspond to degrees of merit, which further subdivide the righteous (chs. 25–29).

The twelve walls and gates, and the images of gold and flashing light immediately recall the Heavenly Jerusalem of Revelation (Apc XXI. 10–20), as well as being more generally reminiscent of biblical and apocalyptic descriptions of the heavenly court. These images, along with the names of the rivers, have been interpreted as an attempt to christianise the 'orphic' features of the *Visio*'s otherworld.[29] However, the imagery has more than mere cosmetic significance. The rivers of paradise preserve continuity with the later reference to the Garden of Eden as well as the rivers of milk and honey seen earlier in the *terra repromissionis*, although the identifications suggested thereby are left implicit. At the same time, the City of Christ introduces a different set of images into the overall picture, with some very important conceptual repercussions.

[28] Silverstein and Hilhorst, eds., *Apocalypse of Paul*, ch. 23, p. 120: '. . . For there were the sun and twelve gates decorated in that complete beauty and four rivers encircled it. And there was a river of honey going from the threshold of the city, and south of it there was a river of milk and a river of wine, and out of the mouth of it a river of oil. And I said to the angel, "Master, what are these rivers which are encircling this city?" He replied, "These are four rivers which flow abundantly for those who dwell in this land, and whose names are these: the river of honey is called Phison, the river of milk, Euphrates, and the river of oil, Gihon, and the river of wine, Tigris. " '

[29] Casey, 'The Apocalypse of Paul', p 19.

The natural images of the *terra repromissionis* followed by the architectural images of the City of Christ create a descriptive correlative to the gradation of delights within the third heaven. The sequence of images belonging to separate conceptual categories, their distinction highlighted by the intervening Acherusian Lake, thus functions as a hierarchy where natural imagery is subordinated to the architectural. Furthermore, this hierarchy silently aligns itself to the associations of a garden with the paradise of Eden and a city with the heavenly Jerusalem, which cuts across the overall containment of paradise, the *terra repromissionis* and the city of Christ within the third heaven. From the *Visio* thus derive not only, as is well known, the gradation of punishment for sinners, but also the gradation of delights for the just, and its expression through images of nature and architecture. As we shall soon see, this conceptual interlocking of natural and architectural imagery was to have wide-ranging consequences on early medieval descriptions of paradise and heaven.

A related and equally important consequence is the *Visio*'s presentation of a composite paradise, celestial but distinct from the heavenly kingdom, and intimately connected with the immediate post-mortem fate of good souls. The *Visio* is thus the first witness to an elaborate interim eschatology, albeit unwieldy and confused, and is an early indication of the interdependence of the fate of the good and the bad in the working out of what would ultimately become the doctrine of purgatory. By combining various eschatological schemes and their attendant imagery into a picture of the interim state, the *Visio* is far more than a 'convenient precipitate' of early ideas on the afterlife;[30] it initiates a process that gathers momentum during the succeeding centuries alongside growing patristic acknowledgement of its influence.

PARADISE AS HEAVEN: AUGUSTINE'S DENIAL OF THE INTERIM STATE

Patristic references to the *Visio* come relatively late. Not until the early fifth century do we find the work condemned, somewhat predictably by Augustine.[31] Even so, his objections here seem directed against the basic contravention of Scripture represented by the *Visio* rather than the details of its contents. But elsewhere he does grapple with the very issues that

[30] *Ibid.*, p. 32. [31] Willems, ed., *In Iohannis evangelium tractatus cxxiv*, ch. 98. 8, p. 581.

prompted the composition of the *Visio*: the immediate post-mortem fate as posited in the diverse eschatologies of the first few centuries AD, the varying relationship of paradise and heaven in these schemes, and the meaning of Paul's words in 2 Corinthians within this context. Indeed, the same assortment of beliefs and speculations that find such benign acceptance in the *Visio* are comprehensively negated by Augustine in his *De Genesi ad litteram*. In the absence of an actual reference to the apocryphal work within this text, however, we might view Augustine's reaction here not as directly against the *Visio*, but as a circumspect parallel to its presentation of the third heaven and paradise.

De Genesi ad litteram is primarily devoted to the literal exegesis of the book of Genesis, balancing Augustine's earlier allegorical treatment of the same topic in *De Genesi contra Manicheos*. Its twelfth and final book pointedly departs from this agenda to discuss instead the problem of paradise and the third heaven posed by 2 Corinthians XII. 2–4 (ch. 1). A sophisticated exposition of these verses follows, developed out of some tentative ideas put forward by Ambrose in *De Paradiso*. Ambrose had introduced his treatise on the creation of Eden with a series of questions about the paradise into which Paul was translated, but had firmly cast these aside before commencing the task at hand.[32] He thus highlighted, but left unsolved, the problems created by Paul's reference to paradise and its possible relationship to other scriptural paradises. It is his disciple, Augustine, who set out to answer these questions in *De Genesi ad litteram*. The twelfth book attests to Augustine's drive to stabilise the meanings of paradise, the bosom of Abraham and the kingdom of heaven. His motivation appears two-fold: to correct what he perceived as being distortions of the true Christian message, and to bring, under one semantic umbrella, all scriptural references to the soul's condition after death.

Chapters 2 to 27 of *De Genesi ad litteram*, Book XII develop an elaborate theory of three sorts of visionary experience, the corporal, the spiritual and the intellectual respectively, which are then aligned to the three heavens of the Pauline reference (ch. 28). This theory of three visions provides an allegorical alternative to the multiple heavens described in both Gnostic and Jewish apocryphal works. The question of there being any further heavens beyond three is simply dismissed by Augustine as being too tedious, though he does entertain the possibility of increasing the kinds of visions to correspond to heavens numbering more than three (ch. 29).

According to Augustine, by the 'third heaven' Paul meant that he had

[32] Schenkl, ed., *De paradiso*, I, chs. 1–2, pp. 265–6.

been granted an intellectual vision, while 'paradise' indicated that the contents of the vision concerned the life forever that awaits us (ch. 28). As noted earlier, this extension of paradise to designate ultimate future happiness as well as a garden lost to mankind had already been made in Jewish apocalyptic, in tandem with the development of a celestial counterpart for the earthly Jerusalem. Of course, Augustine does not seek justification in Jewish apocalyptic writings for his very similar understanding of paradise, although his indebtedness to Jewish ideas is clearly evident in the example of the two senses of Jerusalem that he cites as an illustrative parallel to the earthly and heavenly paradises (ch. 28).

Augustine's grid of reference is the figural or typological exegesis developed by Philo, Origen and Ambrose to protect Scripture from the intellectually sophisticated scepticism of Christianity's many critics in the Hellenic world and in Rome.[33] The paradise of Eden has a corporal reality, but it may be understood also as a type or figure of both the present-day Church militant with all its saints, and the future Church triumphant, that is, the eternal life (ch. 28). The extension of paradise to the heavenly kingdom is here rhetorically validated through the reference to the heavenly Jerusalem, where, says Augustine, we shall enjoy a peaceful and unending abode after this exile (ch. 28). The typological application of paradise to both the Garden of Eden and the heavenly kingdom is a most important and influential exegetical manoeuvre, which was to cast a long shadow across medieval interpretations of paradise. But this move is merely the first step in Augustine's more ambitious enterprise of reconciling all the more contested references to the afterlife in the New Testament.

Later in *De Genesi ad litteram* XII, Augustine recapitulates the literal and allegorical meanings of paradise before turning to the relationship between the paradise of 2 Corinthians and the bosom of Abraham of the parable of Dives and Lazarus (Luke XVI. 19–26):

> Quanto magis ergo post hanc uitam etiam sinus ille Abrahae paradisus dici potest, ubi iam nulla temtatio, ubi tanta requies post omnes dolores uitae huius![34]

[33] For illustrative examples of such allegorical exegesis see *Philo, Supplement I: Questions and answers on Genesis, Translated from the Ancient Armenian Version of the Original Greek*, trans. R. Marcus (London and Cambridge, MA, 1961), Origen's *De principiis* and Ambrose's *De paradiso*.

[34] Zycha, ed., *De Genesi ad litteram*, XII, ch. 34, p. 430: 'How much more therefore can that bosom of Abraham also be called paradise after this life, where [there is] now no temptation, where [there is] so great a rest after all the sufferings of this life!'

This equation of the bosom of Abraham with paradise was a cornerstone of anti-millenarian exegesis from Origen onwards.[35] For Tertullian, who interpreted this parable in accordance with his belief that all the just are detained in Hades until the Second Coming, both Lazarus and Abraham are in hell.[36] Origen proposed instead that the bosom of Abraham was a region of repose in the upper part of hell, but until the Harrowing of Hell only; henceforth it was to be identified with paradise and the heavenly kingdom, where the patriarchs rescued from hell by Christ had been taken.[37] By adopting this interpretation, Augustine reiterates the anti-millenarian stance of a heavenly existence with Christ for all the righteous immediately after death. The added advantage of the Origenist position, which doubtless did not escape Augustine, was its rebuttal of apocryphal descriptions of the Old Testament patriarchs dwelling in a paradisal abode, culminating, of course, in the paradise of the third heaven described in the *Visio*.

Both in this passage and in the preceding chapter, Augustine takes Origen's polemic a step further by stating that even Lazarus and Abraham are in paradise rather than hell (chs. 33–34). Yet in his letter to Dardanus, Augustine relies heavily upon the infernal location of the bosom of Abraham before the Harrowing in order to interpret the meaning of Christ's promise to the Good Thief (Luke XXIII. 43).[38] The Good Thief begs Christ to remember him when he comes to his kingdom; Christ responds with *hodie mecum eris in paradiso*. Augustine reasons that the paradise which Christ had promised him could hardly be hell, which is, nonetheless, where Christ had descended into that day. If we identify paradise with the bosom of Abraham, a region of repose for the patriarchs in the upper part of hell, then Christ could have taken the Good Thief with him 'that day' to 'paradise', thus satisfying both temporal and spatial requirements of his promise.

Augustine concludes his argument in this letter with an exegetical *tour de force*: all problems of interpretation are solved if we simply take Christ's promise in an allegorical sense. If paradise allegorically means a happy state of existence, then to be with Christ is to be in paradise, and as Christ is everywhere, paradise is wherever he is (ch. 7). The same triumph of reasoning underlies the reference to the paradise of the Good Thief in *De Genesi*

[35] See Hill, *Regnum Caelorum*, p. 156.

[36] In Waszink, ed., *De anima*, ch. 55. 2–3, p. 862.

[37] See Hill's discussion of Origen, *Regnum Caelorum*, p. 139.

[38] Goldbacher, ed., *Epistulae*, no. 188, ch. 6, pp. 85–6.

ad litteram XII, with which Augustine consolidates the equation of paradise and the bosom of Abraham before returning to the original point of paradise and the third heaven:

quapropter animae illius latronis, cui dixit: hodie mecum eris in paradiso, non utique inferos praestitit, ubi poenae sunt peccatorum, sed aut illam requiem sinus Abrahae – non enim alicubi non est Christus, cum ipse sit sapientia dei adtingens ubique propter suam munditiam – aut illum paradisum siue in tertio caelo siue ubicumque alibi est, quo post tertium caelum est raptus apostolus, si tamen non aliquid unum est diuersis nominibus appelatum, ubi sunt animae beatorum.[39]

Thus Augustine's belief in the sameness of the post-mortem condition of the blessed, whatever it may be called in a given scriptural citation, is the rationale behind his entire discussion on paradise in *De Genesi ad litteram* XII. Christ's promise to the Good Thief is particularly useful from this point of view, as it patently indicated that Christ's kingdom is open to all the righteous, even a lowly thief, and not a thousand years later, but 'this very day'.[40]

The next chapter of *De Genesi ad litteram* XII appears to be a specific response to another argument against the immediate heavenly reward for all righteous souls, namely, the Byzantine doctrine of delayed retribution. Augustine says that the soul cannot be completely happy until its reunification with the body in the general resurrection (ch. 35). This point is a perfect rejoinder to the notion that the souls of the righteous cannot enjoy perfect happiness in heaven before Doomsday, and so are kept until then in a separate paradise. By insisting that happiness is necessarily incomplete until Doomsday, Augustine also takes care of this possible objection to his identification of paradise with the kingdom of heaven.

Yet Augustine has some difficulties in sustaining this position throughout his writings. In *De Genesi ad litteram* XII itself, he speaks of two spiritual realms, one of punishment and the other of peace and joy, where souls are

39 Zycha, ed., *De Genesi ad litteram* XII, ch. 34, p. 431: 'Therefore, for the soul of that thief to whom he said, "today you shall be with me in paradise", he certainly did not designate the lower regions where there are punishments of sinners, but either that repose of the bosom of Abraham – for there is not any place where Christ does not exist, since he is himself the wisdom of God, reaching out to all places on account of his purity – or he meant that paradise, whether it is in the third heaven or whether it is in some other place, to which the apostle was carried off after the third heaven, unless, however, where the souls of the blessed reside is some single place which is called by different names.'

40 For the absence of the Lucan exchange from millenarian discourse, and its corresponding usefulness for anti-millenarian exegetes, see Hill, *Regnum Caelorum*, pp. 156–7.

brought after death (ch. 32). Despite an accompanying qualification of the punishment as that of hell, it is not entirely clear whether these two spiritual realms are to be identified with hell and heaven respectively. A more definite reference to an interim state which is neither heavenly nor infernal is made in Augustine's *Enchiridion*:

> Tempus autem quod inter hominis mortem et ultimam resurrectionem interpositum est, animas abditis receptaculis continet, sicut unaquaeque digna est uel requie uel aerumna pro eo quod sortita est in carne dum uiueret.[41]

Indeed, this description of the interim condition is not so far removed from the graded suffering and delights meted out to souls in the *Visio*, although Augustine is careful to preserve his distance from such apocryphal works by leaving these 'hidden retreats' vague and undefined.[42]

The purpose of this rather compromising reference to the interim emerges in the discussion that follows. Augustine next asks whether the souls of the dead can benefit from the alms-giving and sacrifices of their living friends, earmarking three categories of souls for the purpose of discussion: those who are very good, and so will not need such help in order to be saved; those who have led such sinful lives that no manner of help can redeem them; and those in between:

> Est enim quidam uiuendi modus, nec tam bonus ut non requirat ista post mortem, nec tam malus ut ei non prosint ista post mortem; esta uero talis in bono ut ista non requirat, et est rursus talis in malo ut nec his ualeat cum ex hac uita transierit adiuuari.[43]

[41] Evans, ed., *Enchiridion*, XXIX, ch. 109, p. 108: 'Yet the time which has been set between the death of a man and the final resurrection holds the souls in hidden retreats, accordingly as each and every one is worthy either of peace or affliction as required by what it was assigned whilst it was dwelling in human flesh.'

[42] Augustine's vagueness here did not, however, escape reinterpretation in subsequent centuries, as we shall see in the course of this book. From the seventh century to the twelfth, different authors turn to the authority of this specific statement in order to justify their increasingly elaborate versions of interim eschatology, which are far from Augustine's original cautiousness. See, for instance, my later discussions of Julian of Toledo's *Prognosticon* and the *Tractatus de purgatorio Sancti Patricii*, pp. 44, 93 and 187 respectively.

[43] Evans, ed., *Enchiridion*, XXIX, ch. 110, p. 108: 'For there is a certain manner of living, which is neither so good as not to need those to not require those acts [alms-giving and the sacrifice of the mediator] after death, nor so bad that for it those acts might be of no use after death. There is, however, such a person in goodness so as not to require those acts, and again, such a man in evil so that not even by these can he be helped when he has left this life.'

In the opinion of Le Goff, Augustine differentiates here between two intermediate groups of souls, the *non ualde boni* and the *non ualde mali*, to parallel the fates of the *ualde boni* and the *ualde mali*, and to create a four-fold scheme which was reinterpreted as tripartite in the twelfth century.[44] However, Augustine's own words belie this claim. In the concluding lines of this chapter he employs only the three phrases *non ualde boni*, *ualde boni* and *ualde mali*; the phrase *non ualde mali* does not appear at all. Neither does he posit a functional difference between the *uiuendi modus nec tam bonus* and the *uiuendi modus nec tam malus*, who are affected equally by, and, indeed, are in equal need of, the prayers of the living.

Augustine thus describes here one intermediary group of souls, who are distinguished by the potential changeability of their fate after Judgement Day, and thus not from each other, but from the *ualde boni* and *ualde mali*, whose fates, in contrast, are decided immediately after death and forever.[45] For only this intermediate category of souls, then, can prayers make damnation more tolerable, if not obtain a complete remission of sins. It is obvious that without postulating an interim condition different from both the kingdom of heaven and the damnation of hell, Augustine cannot raise the issue of the possible benefits of intercession for the dead. These two chapters of the *Enchiridion* point to the functional connection between intercession and a non-heavenly, non-hellish interim, which, as we shall see presently, is developed through Late Antiquity and the Middle Ages.

However, Augustine himself modified this stance later. In his *De ciuitate Dei*, Book XXI,[46] Augustine's opinion on the efficacy of intercession and the possibility of a non-heavenly, post-mortem existence other than hell seems somewhat inconsistent mutually and internally, as well as with the ideas expressed in the *Enchiridion*. First, he denies that intercession and prayers could expiate sins after death (ch. 24). This change of heart appears

44 *Birth of Purgatory*, pp. 72–3.

45 That Augustine makes a three-fold rather than a four-fold division of souls in this passage is also suggested by Brown, 'Vers la Naissance du purgatoire', pp. 1248: 'Dans *l'Enchiridion*, son *Manuel de la foi chrétienne*, il dessinait, en formules lapidaires, une catégorie intermédiaire aux dimensions larges et aux frontières floues – la catégorie des *non valde mali*, des chrétiens qui sortent de ce monde ni "vraiment bons" – *valde boni* – ni "vraiment mauvais" – *valde mali* – mais, simplement, *non valde mali* – "pas vraiment mauvais".'

46 Dombart and Kalb, eds., *De ciuitate Dei*, II, chs. 24–6, pp. 789–99.

to have been provoked by various Neo-Platonic and laxist theories of salvation, which he systematically debunks.[47] Yet he also indicates, within the same chapter, that some sinners might be nevertheless saved after Judgement Day. Soon afterwards, however, he also admits, albeit extremely reluctantly, the possible existence of a purgatorial fire between death and Judgement Day (ch. 26). These prevarications and contradictions are perhaps necessitated by his anti-millenarian exegesis of Revelations in *De civitate Dei*, Book XX.[48] For Augustine, the millennium begins with the first resurrection, interpreted as baptism, after which all Christians participate in the Church, which is the kingdom of Christ (chs. 6–7). This kingdom includes both those who break the law and those who keep it, until the final resurrection sorts out the saved from the damned (ch. 9). The company of saints and the other righteous is therefore grouped together with all kinds of sinners until Judgement Day. Augustine's defensive exegetical position means that he cannot directly undo the seeming injustice of this scheme. However, some redress is provided by his later acceptance of a purgatorial fire for the cleansing of venial sins. Augustine thus appears to allow the interim state into his eschatology as long as it is infernalised through purgatorial flames, but he does not yield to its description as a pleasant place or as a paradise distinct from heaven. For him, the kingdom of heaven remains the only definitive place of rest, peace and joy after death.

Augustine's attempts to fix the semantics and pragmatics of the afterlife achieved mixed results in the succeeding centuries. His equation of the paradise of Eden with the heavenly city was a tremendous rhetorical success, but his proscription of all other meanings of paradise in the post-mortem context did not inhibit their continuing currency. As mentioned earlier, the *Visio* and its attendant ideas enjoyed increasing popularity, if not notoriety, through the Middle Ages. Furthermore, other apocryphal works sprung up and circulated, which also promoted distinctions between paradise and heaven in connection with post-mortem fate. One such group of apocrypha was that comprising the various narratives about Mary's death and post-mortem fate, which included the same Latin *Transitus Mariae* texts and their later Old English translations that Ælfric found so reprehensible.

[47] As argued by Le Goff, *Birth of Purgatory*, pp. 62–78.

[48] Dombart and Kalb, eds., *De ciuitate Dei*, II, chs. 6–7, pp. 706–19.

DEVELOPMENTS IN THE INTERIM: THE *TRANSITUS MARIAE* AND PARADISE

The early centuries of Christianity witnessed the emergence and rapid growth of a cult of Marian devotion that had its basis not so much in Scripture as in christological debates. New convictions about her special qualities as the mother of God, such as her virginity both *in partu* and *post partum*, led to growing popular desire to bestow on her an appropriate post-mortem reward.[49] From the fifth century onwards, therefore, and possibly earlier, apocryphal narratives describing the miraculous events surrounding Mary's death developed in Syrian, Greek, Coptic and Arabic before passing into the Latin West. These narratives, whose textual relationships and transmission history far surpass that of the *Visio* in complexity, diverge considerably in their descriptions of what happens to Mary's body and soul after her death. These and other differences of content do not map neatly on to their linguistic and doctrinal differences, thus retarding scholarly attempts to classify them into a definitive evolutionary sequence.[50]

In spite of these complexities, however, or perhaps because of them, the *Transitus Mariae* narratives provide valuable insight into the sharpening of the distinction between paradise and heaven from the fifth century onwards. In many early Syriac texts, Mary's body is taken to the paradise of Eden after her death, but she is subsequently restored to life in the same paradise. The resurrected Mary then opens her eyes to see 'the mansions appointed for the just' and 'the abodes of the righteous', before commencing her tour of the various heavens, that include the secret abode of Enoch and Elijah.[51] These particular narratives thus correspond to a stage when the abode of the righteous had been identified with the Garden of Eden in apocalyptic writings, but not yet assimilated into the multiple heavens scheme as in the *Visio*, or, indeed, associated with the abode of the translated patriarchs.

[49] See Clayton, *Cult*, pp. 2–8.

[50] For a thorough overview of previous scholarship on Marian Assumption apocrypha, which nonetheless remains tentative about the absolute benefits of any one possible evolutionary sequence over others, see Clayton, ed. and trans., *Apocryphal Gospels*, pp. 25–100, especially her comments on pp. 24–28. An earlier survey of Marian Assumption material is by Jugie, *La Mort*.

[51] See, for instance, the Syriac *Six Books*, in Wright, *Departure of My Lady Mary*, pp. 28–30, and the Syriac *History of the Virgin Mary*, in Wright, *Contributions*, p. 40. For a summary of the Syriac apocrypha, see Clayton, ed., *Apocryphal Gospels*, pp. 31–42.

However, the Ethiopic *Liber Requiei*, which in other ways closely resembles the Syriac material, clearly identifies its paradise with the third heaven, distinguishing it further from the seventh heaven which Mary sees later during her tour.[52] It thereby points towards the influence of the paradise of the third heaven that is described in the *Visio*, and that houses those assumed in the body, such as Enoch and Elijah, while remaining separate from heaven. Interestingly, the early sixth-century Greek text known as the *Pseudo-John*, which describes not Mary's corporal assumption but only the separation of her body from her soul, nevertheless emphasises in two ways the singularity of its paradise. Firstly, it does not define it as the Garden of Eden, and secondly, it marks its separation from heaven by specifying the latter as the destination of Mary's soul.[53] This text thus sees Mary's reward in the preservation of her body in paradise while her soul is taken to heaven. Conversely, certain Coptic homilies which emphasise, for polemical reasons, the corruptibility and humanity of Mary's body, transport her soul to heaven but leave her body decaying conspicuously at her tomb.[54]

According to Clayton, the separation of Mary's body and soul in the *Pseudo-John* represents a *cul-de-sac* of sorts within the developing *Transitus* tradition in the Latin West, which relied much more heavily on the sixth-century text known as the Greek *R*.[55] This text describes the reunification of Mary's body and soul, as do the Coptic texts, but, unlike them, it places her body in paradise until that moment. It also describes Mary's subsequent resurrection and corporal assumption into paradise rather than heaven, stating that the archangel Michael brings back her soul from an unspecified location and places it within her body in paradise. At the same time, it is not clear whether this paradise is meant to be a location different from or

52 Cf. *De transitu Mariae apocrypha Æthiopice*, ch. 132, ed. V. Arras, Corpus Scriptorum Christianorum Orientalium 342 (Louvain, 1973), p. 53: 'et adsumpsit nos in septimum coelum' and ch. 135, p. 55: 'ivit in paradisum et in tertio coelo steterunt.' For the relationship between the fragmentary *Syriac Obsequies* and the *Liber Requiei*, see Clayton, ed., *Apocryphal Gospels*, pp. 38–41, and for similarities between the *Obsequies* and the *Apocalypse of Paul*, p. 36.

53 Elliott, *Apocryphal New Testament*, pp. 701–8, at p. 708; see Clayton, ed., *Apocryphal Gospels*, pp. 30–31.

54 See Clayton, ed., *Apocryphal Gospels*, pp. 42–7, where she also argues that the feast of the Assumption developed out of doctrinal conflicts between different factions of the Coptic Church.

55 Edited and translated by Wenger, *L'Assomption*, pp. 210–41, and discussed by Clayton in *Apocryphal Gospels*, pp. 49–61. For the relationship of the Latin tradition to the Greek *R*, see *ibid.*, pp. 66–100.

synonymous with heaven. It is interesting, therefore, that the Latin texts stemming from this tradition seem to experiment with various means of clarifying the status of this paradise and its relationship with heaven within the specific context of Mary's post-mortem reward.

In the Latin version known as *Transitus A*, for instance, Mary's body lies in the tomb, but the soul is simply given by Christ to Michael, with no mention of its destination (chs. 20–1).[56] Christ then departs to the *regnum caelorum*. Three days later, on Christ's instructions, Mary's body is first translated to paradise. Michael then brings her soul here, once again from an unspecified place, and replaces it in her body; they remain in paradise while Christ returns to heaven (chs. 47–50). Similarly, in the various versions of the Latin text known either as *Transitus C* or *Transitus W*, Mary's body is taken to paradise, with some of the versions specifying that it is laid under the tree of life.[57] Angels then bring her soul to paradise, where the resurrected Mary seems to remain afterwards.[58] As in *Transitus A*, the soul's temporary abode is not specified, thereby avoiding the anti-climax of its return from heaven to paradise. In fact, paradise in *Transitus W* seems to coexist with the millenarian concept of an abode, separate from paradise, where the souls of the just are taken. Two speeches by Mary and Peter describe how the souls of the righteous are taken after death to the *locus iustorum* and the bosom of Abraham.[59] It is perhaps hinted, although by no means unambiguously, that Mary's own soul joins them here for the brief period between the transportation of her body to paradise, and the reunification of her body and soul – her corporal assumption – in that paradise.

Insight into an additional layer of complications is provided by the Latin *Transitus of pseudo-Melito*, which exists in two versions, *Transitus B1* and *Transitus B2*.[60] In *Transitus B2*, the older version from the fifth century, and said to represent the *pseudo-Melito* better than *Transitus B1*, paradise

56 Wenger, ed., *L'Assomption*, pp. 245–56.

57 Wilmart, ed., 'L'Ancien Récit latin', pp. 325–57. I follow Clayton's use of the term *Transitus W* in her most recent work, rather than *Transitus C*, which appears in all the older scholarship on this Assumption text.

58 See Wilmart, ed., 'L'Ancien Récit latin', notes, pp. 356–7.

59 *Ibid.*, chs. 5 and 21, pp. 328–9 and 341. Note here the echo of millenarian ideas, according to which paradise is reserved for the corporally assumed, and the bosom of Abraham for the remaining righteous. I return to this point, and to the speeches themselves, below, pp. 60–1.

60 For *B1*, see Tischendorf, ed., *Apocalypses Apocryphae*, pp. 124–36, and for *B2*, Haibach-Rheinisch, ed., *Ein neuer 'Transitus Mariae'*, pp. 63–87, reprinted by and cited from Clayton, ed., *Apocryphal Gospels*, pp. 334–43.

and heaven are used indiscriminately, almost as if the redactor wished to blur any distinctions between the two terms.[61] Keeping in mind the Augustinian discourse on equating paradise with heaven, and also the desire to retain paradise in a functional capacity discernible in other *Transitus* redactors, the synonymous use of paradise and heaven in *Transitus B2* could well be part of an orthodox veneer intended for his text by the author of the original *pseudo-Melito*.[62] While this decision suited the redactor of *Transitus B2*, it evidently did not appeal to that of *B1*. In marked contrast to *Transitus B2*, *Transitus B1* insistently dissociates the two locations, reserving paradise for the destination of Mary's soul and body, and heaven for the destination of Christ.[63] Only once, when the apostles ask Christ to translate Mary into heaven, is this pattern broken. Now, this request is identically couched in *Transitus B2*, and must therefore belong to the original *pseudo-Melito*.[64] While adjusting his source by reintroducing distinctions between paradise and heaven, therefore, the redactor of *Transitus B1* must have missed out this one reference to heaven made by the apostles.

Transitus B1 thus reinforces the connection between paradise and corporal assumption by making paradise the destination of both the soul *and* the assumed body of Mary. In *Transitus W*, as in the Greek *R*, paradise is the locus of assumption, but only by default, as it were, as a consequence of Mary's body being taken there first. In *Transitus B1*, however, this function of paradise is pre-empted by sending Mary's soul there before the assumption, instead of to heaven or to some unspecified place. *Transitus B1* and *Transitus B2*, two near-simultaneous redactions of the same Assumption text, thus register divergent reactions to the function of paradise as the abode of the corporally assumed; *Transitus B2* invalidates it by denying paradise a separate meaning from heaven, while *Transitus B1* reaffirms it through the opposite semantic process.

[61] See Haibach-Rheinisch, ed., *Ein neuer 'Transitus Mariae'*, chs. 7 and 17, in Clayton, ed., *Apocryphal Gospels*, pp. 338 and 343 respectively, and pp. 83–98 for the relationship between *pseudo-Melito*, *Transitus B1* and *Transitus B2*.

[62] Cf. Haibach-Rheinisch's argument in *Ein neuer 'Transitus Mariae'*, pp. 162–4, that *B1* preserves an originally sharper distinction between paradise and heaven, refuted by Clayton, *Apocryphal Gospels*, pp. 93–4.

[63] See Tischendorf, ed., *Apocalypses Apocryphae*, ch. 8, p. 130, lines 4–7 and ch. 17, p. 135, lines 19–25.

[64] Cf. *ibid.*, ch. 15, p. 135, and Haibach-Rheinisch, ed., *Ein neuer 'Transitus Mariae'*, in Clayton, *Apocryphal Gospels*, ch. 15, p. 342.

The Latin *Transitus* tradition thus reveals a growing self-consciousness about not only Mary's corporal assumption, as observed by Clayton,[65] but also the corresponding roles of paradise and heaven. From the earliest Syriac narratives, composed at the latest in the fifth century, to *Transitus W*, *B1* and *B2*, circulating by the seventh, the basic idea of a paradise separate from heaven is chiselled into its definite association with corporal assumption. Decreasing references to the tree of life in the *Transitus* texts also indicate that this paradise gradually gains an identity distinct from the Garden of Eden. It is interesting that exegetical concern over the *Transitus* narratives gathers momentum in tandem with their sharpening focus on Mary's post-mortem destination. Earlier exegetes such as Augustine, Jerome or even Gregory say nothing about the *Transitus Mariae*, possibly because the tradition had not yet developed, and also perhaps because the Church was still laying the groundwork for Marian doctrine at that stage. By the eighth century, however, Aldhelm and Bede express caution over the possibility of Mary's corporal assumption and her post-mortem destination.[66]

By the ninth century, furthermore, demand for 'official' disapproval of the Assumption narratives seems to have created its own supply; Ælfric, writing his Second Series Assumption homily, can cite works by Augustine, Jerome and Gregory in support of his objections against the *Transitus* texts. In this context, however, 'Augustine' refers to an Assumption homily by Ambrosius Autpertus which circulated under the name of Augustine, and 'Gregory' is probably Ildefonsus, who also wrote two homilies on the subject. 'Jerome', similarly, refers to the famous pseudo-Jerome letter, *Cogitis me*, composed probably by the Carolingian, Paschasius Radbertus, and translated copiously by Ælfric in his own Second Series Assumption homily.[67] These anachronistic attributions have of course been established as imposters only by modern scholarship. There was no question of Ælfric, or anyone else in the Anglo-Saxon world, doubting their authority. Yet, the proliferation of these texts, especially in the Carolingian milieu, points to a genuine need at this time for 'heavyweight' patristic opposition to the *Transitus* tradition. It must also be noted that the objections are directed not towards the feast of the Assumption, which by now was firmly entrenched in the liturgical calendar, but towards the contents of those very

[65] In Clayton, *Cult*, pp. 10–11.

[66] As established by Clayton, *ibid.*, pp. 14–19.

[67] See *ibid.*, pp. 20–4, pp. 242–3.

narratives which, although originally providing textual support for the feast, had soon developed an independent rationale and motivations contrary to other teachings of the Church.

As I have demonstrated above, one such consequence of the *Transitus* narratives was their contribution to beliefs about paradise and the afterlife discredited by Augustine. In fact, by the early Middle Ages, two opposing interpretations of paradise had developed, their polarity determined not so much by any intrinsic meaning of the term as by its use in contrasting bodies of texts. In Augustinian exegesis, extensively adapted for homiletic use and thereby disseminated by, for instance, Caesarius of Arles, paradise was the Garden of Eden, typologically equivalent to heaven.[68] In texts like the *Visio* and the *Transitus Mariae*, paradise was applied to a location distinct from heaven and increasingly understood as distinct from Eden, in order to work out a more detailed picture of the immediate post-mortem condition. The unorthodox associations of this interpretation of paradise could only have been strengthened by the inclusion of the *Visio* and the *Transitus* texts among the works listed as apocryphal by the Gelasian Decree.

The term paradise thus gains a curious double valency as the Middle Ages progress. Identified with the kingdom of heaven, it comes to represent an orthodox view on the afterlife; distinguished from the same, it becomes a repository of ideas and functions associated with texts clearly branded as apocryphal by those who defined and upheld orthodoxy. It is not corporal assumption *per se*, therefore, which appears to be Ælfric's main problem with the *Transitus* texts but also the corollary that such assumption is necessarily into paradise, a special abode separate from heaven. This belief, varyingly echoed in the Latin Assumption narratives, is confidently sounded in their two Old English adaptations, which Ælfric also castigates in his Second Series Assumption homily, cited at the beginning of this chapter. In the following chapter, we shall see how these two anonymous homilies on the Assumption engineer their sources in keeping with Anglo-Saxon developments in the idea of an interim paradise. Interestingly, Ælfric criticises nothing in his account of John's Assumption,[69] probably because there were no narratives that he knew of which specified that this assump-

[68] See, for example, the use of *paradisus* in Morin, ed., *Sancti Caesarii Arelatensis sermones*, homily VII, p. 38, homily CL, pp. 613–16, and homily CLI, p. 618.

[69] Clemoes, ed., *Ælfric's Catholic Homilies*, pp. 58 and 77. In this context, see Godden, 'Experiments in Genre', pp. 266–9.

tion was into paradise. As we shall see in the final chapter of this book, this lacuna had been filled by the end of the Old English period.

At the same time, the prevailing belief that Enoch and Elijah were assumed in the body into paradise leads Ælfric to expend not inconsiderable energy on clarifying the exact locus of their assumption:

> We rædað on þære ealdan æ, þæt tweges Godes men. henoh and helias wæron ahafene to heofonum butan deaðe. ac hi elcyað ongean þam deað. and mid ealle ne forfleoð; Hi sind genumene to lyftenre heofenan: na to rodorlicere. ac drohtniað on sumum diglum earde mid micelre strencðe lichaman and sawle. Oððæt hi eft ongean cyrron, on ende þisre worulde, togeanes Antecriste. and deaðes onfoð.[70]

What exactly does Ælfric mean by the adjectives *lyften* and *rodorlıc*, which Benjamin Thorpe translates as 'äerial' and 'ethereal' respectively? These adjectives are reminiscent of the terminology employed for the first and fourth heavens, *lyftlic* and *rodor*, in those Anglo-Saxon homilies drawing on the 'Seven Heavens' apocryphon.[71] However, to distinguish thus between the first and fourth heavens seems to be of little significance, unless we allow for the possibility that it might be deliberately misleading. By engaging his audience in this subtle distinction, Ælfric perhaps hopes to divert attention from the fact that, in the *Visio*, Paul encounters Enoch and Elijah at the gates of the third heaven, which, of course, is also the location of paradise. If this is indeed the case, it is ironic that he betrays, in the process, his acquaintance with another apocryphal series of multiple heavens. With the phrase *digel eard*, reminiscent of Augustine's *receptacula abdita* in *Enchiridion*, Ælfric himself retreats, and one imagines with some relief, into descriptive and semantic opacity.

LEXICAL PREVARICATIONS: ÆLFRIC AND THE INTERIM PARADISE

We can now appreciate better the significance and the connections of the citations with which this chapter began. In his Assumption homily for the

[70] Clemoes, ed., *Ælfric's Catholic Homilies*, p. 352: 'We read in the old law, that two men of God, Enoch and Elijah, were lifted up to heaven without death: but they await death and will by no means escape it. They are taken to the äerial heaven, not the ethereal, and continue in some secret dwelling-place with great strength of body and soul, until they shall return again, at the end of this world, against Antichrist, but shall receive death' (trans. Thorpe, ed., *Homilies of the Anglo-Saxon Church*, pp. 307–9).

[71] See Willard, *Two Apocrypha*, p. 7.

Second Series, Ælfric pointedly refuses to say anything more about the feast other than the fact that, on this day, Mary was taken *up to heofenan rice*. While the mechanics of the assumption are not elaborated upon, her destination is specified as the kingdom of heaven rather than as paradise. A pattern emerges when we examine the two visions of the otherworld which Ælfric substitutes for the *Visio*'s paradise of the third heaven. The first is the Vision of Furseus, taken from the *Vita Fursei* in preference to Bede's version of the same vision in the *Historia Ecclesiastica*; the second is Bede's own account of the Vision of Dryhthelm, also in the *Historia Ecclesiastica*.[72] Ælfric's translations, and the Anglo-Latin visions themselves, are analysed later in this chapter; here we need simply note that in neither vision does the term *paradisus* appear.

Ælfric's own references to paradise in his homilies reveal an awareness of the term's less than orthodox applications. *Neorxnawang*, the Old English equivalent of the Latin *paradisus*, appears only twenty-one times throughout his rather compendious output, and is almost always warranted by Scripture.[73] Within his homiletic and hagiographic writings, ten of these occurrences use *neorxnawang* to mean the Garden of Eden.[74] Two of the remaining references to *neorxnawang* are made within his citation of Paul's words in 2 Corinthians, with which he dismisses the 'lying words' of the *Visio*, and five other references are found in citations of Christ's promise to the Good Thief.[75]

Like Ambrose and Augustine, Ælfric probably saw in this promise the best scriptural basis for the equivalence between paradise and the kingdom of heaven. In the Second Series homily *In dominica palmarum*, the Good Thief becomes a type for all those who are saved through Christ:

Gemun ðu min drihten. þonne ðu mihtig becymst. to ðinum agenum rice. roderes wealdend; Se hælend him cwæð to. mid soðum behate. nu todæg ðu bist. on neorx-

[72] Godden, ed., *Catholic Homilies*, pp. 190–8, and *alia visio*, pp. 199–203. For the argument that Ælfric intended this sermon (*Catholic Homilies*, XX) and its two subsequent pieces as a complete sequence, see Godden, 'The Development of Ælfric's Second Series', pp. 211–12.

[73] Searches for these and other Old English words have been made with the help of Healey and Venezky, eds., *Microfiche Concordance*.

[74] Clemoes, ed., *Ælfric's Catholic Homilies*, pp. 181, 183, 240, 259 and 370, and Skeat, ed., *Lives of Saints*, I, p. 332.

[75] The Lucan references are in Clemoes, ed., *Ælfric's Catholic Homilies*, p. 506, Godden, ed., *Catholic Homilies*, pp. 46 and 146 and Skeat, ed., *Lives of Saints*, I, p. 424; for both Pauline references, see Godden, ed., *Catholic Homilies*, p. 190.

enawange mid me; þes sceaða gesælig. siðode to heofenum. and se oðer gewende. welhreaw to helle.[76]

At the same time, the terms *rice* and *heofonas* bracket *neorxnawang* both lexically and semantically, communicating that the post-mortem paradise is the same as the kingdom of heaven. In another instance, the quotation from Luke ostensibly advocates deathbed confession and last-minute penitence, but once again, Ælfric equates *rice*, *neorxnawang* and *ece lif* even while making this hortatory point.[77]

Furthermore, the Augustinian equation of heaven, paradise *and* the bosom of Abraham is also adopted by Ælfric. In the *Life of St Martin*, the dying Martin tells the devil that he is about to be received into the bosom of Abraham.[78] Ælfric appears to deviate from his Latin source in adding that this location is the kingdom of heaven.[79] Similar identifications are made in another, anonymous, Old English version of the *Life of St Martin*,[80] and also by Ælfric himself in his earlier account of Martin's life, written for the Second Series.[81] However, of all these versions, both anonymous and Ælfrician, only Ælfric's second *Life of St Martin* concludes with a further reference to Martin's soul being received into paradise. The references to Abraham's bosom and the kingdom of heaven are thus used as an opportunity to reiterate the synonymy of these terms with *neorxnawang*. This difference between Ælfric's two *Lives of St Martin* thus suggests his growing anxiety over the connections between paradise, the kingdom of heaven and the bosom of Abraham.

[76] Godden, ed., *Catholic Homilies*, p. 146: '"remember [me] my Lord, ruler of heaven, when you come in glory to your own kingdom." The saviour said to him, "In truth I promise, now today you will be in paradise with me." This blessed thief went to the heavens, the other cruel one to hell.' [77] Skeat, ed., *Lives of Saints*, I, p. 424.

[78] Skeat, ed., *Lives of Saints*, II, p. 304.

[79] J. Fontaine, ed., *Sulpice Sévère: vie de Saint Martin* I, SC 133 (Paris, 1967), ch. 17, p. 342: 'Quid hic, inquit, adstas, cruenta besta? Nihil in me, fumeste, reperies: Abrahae me sinus recepit.'

[80] Of the anonymous *Life*, three versions exist: as Blickling XVII and Vercelli XVII, and in Junius 85/86, fols. 62–81. Both the Blickling and the Vercelli homilies lack this section, but the Junius homily uses the phrases *Abrahames bearm* and *heofonlic ham*; see Scragg, ed., *Vercelli Homilies*, pp. 307–8, and A. S. Napier, 'Notes on the Blickling Homilies', *MP* 1 (1903), 303– 8, at p. 308.

[81] Godden, ed., *Catholic Homilies*, pp. 296–7. For the relative chronology of Ælfric's works, see P. A. M. Clemoes, 'The Chronology of Ælfric's Works', in *The Anglo-Saxons: Studies in their History and Culture Presented to Bruce Dickins*, ed. P. A. M. Clemoes (London, 1959), pp. 212–47.

Ælfric provides the doctrinal basis for the identification of paradise, the kingdom of heaven and the bosom of Abraham in another Second Series homily, *Dominica in septuagesima*.[82] He first combines the parable of the vineyard with Christ's promise to the Good Thief in order to support the identification of paradise with the kingdom of heaven. If the Good Thief enters the kingdom of heaven before the apostles, it is like the labourer who entered the vineyard at the eleventh hour and still collected his farthing; moreover, the apostles, like the complaining labourers, had doubted Christ, whereas the thief had intuitively trusted him.[83] The implications of the kingdom of heaven being the destination promised to the Good Thief are explored further in this homily through certain statements about the post-mortem fate which Ælfric makes by again picking up the term *neorxnawang*. As an example of those who have toiled even longer before getting their farthing, Ælfric refers to the patriarchs under the old law who remained in the bosom of Abraham before Christ opened the *neorxnawanges fæsten* through his death, and took them to the kingdom of heaven. This reference to the gates of paradise reminds us of the Garden of Eden, closed to post-lapsarian man, and encourages the typological extension of that paradise to the post-mortem one.

In this homily, moreover, Ælfric follows Augustine in placing the bosom of Abraham in hell before the Harrowing, and in heaven afterwards. This shift in location is alluded to in Ælfric's description of Doomsday later on in the homily, when he refers to Abraham, Isaac and Jacob in the kingdom of heaven. Thus on one level, the homily describes the fate of the patriarchs before and after the Harrowing, whereby, like the labourers in the vineyard, different groups of people receive their reward after different lengths of time. But on a deeper level, the rhetoric conveys the sameness of this reward for all those saved by Christ and the concomitant equivalence of paradise, heaven and the bosom of Abraham after the Harrowing of Hell. Comparison with the patriarchs also allows Ælfric to insist that all those who live righteously under the new law can receive this post-mortem reward immediately after death.

[82] Godden, ed., *Catholic Homilies*, pp. 41–51.

[83] The scribes of manuscripts F (Cambridge, Corpus Christi College 162) and M (Cambridge, University Library, Ii.4.6) apparently desired an even stronger identification of heaven and the *neorxnawang* promised to the Good Thief than that provided by Ælfric himself. In F, *neorxena wange* is erased, and *heofenan rices myrihðe* substituted, while in M, *neorxena wanges* is glossed as *heofonan rices myrhðe* (Godden, ed., *Catholic Homilies*, p. 46, note to line 137).

In Ælfric's writing, therefore, paradise is firmly associated with the locations of heaven and the bosom of Abraham, and, through this association, with a battery of scriptural citations, to convey precisely the opposite of what a reader might extrapolate from the *Visio* and the *Transitus Mariae*: the synonymy of paradise and heaven in the context of the soul's fate after death. Within this lexical strategy, the phrase *Abrahames wunung* plays a significant role. Ælfric consistently renders *sinus Abrahae* as 'Abraham's dwelling-place' rather than 'Abraham's bosom', preferring *wunung* (abode, dwelling-place) as a translation for *sinus* rather than its more literal equivalents, the Old English nouns *bearm* and *fæðm*.[84] Apart from the St Martin homilies and the homily *Dominica in septuagesima*, Ælfric uses *Abrahames wunung* only three times.[85] But a glance at his other uses of *wunung* reveals that this choice of term is carefully premeditated.

Wunung collocates three times with *neorxnawang* as the Garden of Eden. In *De initio creature*, Ælfric says that God made man so that he would earn the *wununga on heofenan rice*, and so brought him into *neorxnawang*.[86] Similarly, the devil approached Adam and Eve in *neorxnawang* when he realised that they would earn the *wununga on heofenan rice*.[87] A more direct association is seen in the *Hexameron*. Here, Eden is termed *paradise*, *neorxnawang* and *wynsumu wunung*; we also have a later *paradise* where the *lifes treow* grows.[88] In fact terms such as *heofonan rice*, *heofonlic*, *ece lif* and *upplic* are the most common collocates of *wunung* in Ælfric's writings, especially in the context of the soul's reward after death.[89]

The metaphoric and literal force of *wunung* gives it a useful ambivalence, which Ælfric exploits by repeatedly applying it to heaven, the bosom of Abraham and the Garden of Eden. He casts thereby a lexical net through which he can bring together these various terms and contain the meaning

84 For homiletic uses of *Abrahames bearm*, see n. 80; *Abrahames fæðm* occurs only once in the Old English corpus, in Napier, ed., *Wulfstan: Sammlung*, p. 238, to be discussed below, p. 58.

85 In Clemoes, ed., *Ælfric's Catholic Homilies*, pp. 226 and 367, and Pope, *Supplementary Series*, p. 794.

86 Clemoes, ed., *Ælfric's Catholic Homilies*, p. 12.

87 *Ibid.*, p. 183.

88 S. J. Crawford, ed., *Exameron Anglice, or the Old English Hexameron*, BaP 10 (Hamburg, 1921), pp. 65, 66–7 and 71.

89 In Clemoes, ed., *Ælfric's Catholic Homilies*, *wunung* appears in this lexical environment on pp. 193, 211, 225, 247, 327, 332, 370, 377, 398, 429, 434, 477, 482 and 520. Comparable occurrences in Godden, ed., *Catholic Homilies* are on pp. 46, 251, 296, 319 and 339. Similarly, see Pope, ed., *Supplementary Series*, pp. 206, 342, 435, 555, 558, 572 and 625.

of the most problematic term of all – *neorxnawang* as a non-heavenly post-mortem abode. In Ælfric's hands, however, *wunung* also operates in a subtler manner. A telling instance is his use of the term in his Assumption homily for the First Series:

> [O]n his Fæder huse sindon fela wununga: soðlice we gelyfað þæt he nu todæg þa wynsumestan wununge his leofan meder forgeafe; Godes gecorenra wuldor is gemetegod be heora geearnungum.[90]

Unlike the apocryphal Assumption narratives and their vernacular translations, which he castigates here as well, Ælfric sees Mary's reward not in her corporal assumption into paradise, but in her glorious spiritual assumption into the most pleasant *wunung* within Christ's house. We are prepared for this statement by an earlier reference to Mary's destination being the *heofonlicere wununga* (p. 437). The *wynsumeste wunung* also recalls Ælfric's frequent description of *neorxnawang*, the Garden of Eden, through the paranomastic collocation of *wynsum* and *wunung*.

This description of Mary's post-mortem fate differs considerably from that given in his Second Series Assumption homily. There, it should be recalled, Ælfric simply says that Mary was taken up to the kingdom of heaven, to share, by implication, the fate open to all righteous individuals immediately after death. Here, in contrast, heaven is presented as having different compartments of varying quality, to which people are assigned places according to their merit. In support of this idea, Ælfric deploys the Johannine quotation *in domo patris multae mansiones sunt* (Io XIV.2). By translating *mansio* as *wunung*, he harnesses the power of Scripture through both form and content. In his only other homiletic citation of this verse, Ælfric uses *wunung* in a similar manner. In the First Series homily *Dominica III post pentecosten* he refers to the *heofonlice wununga* which we should all hope to attain, before stating that 'in my father's house are many dwelling-places' (*fela wununga*, p. 350), which are allocated to us in accordance with our strengths and deeds. The preceding homily contains the phrase *heahfæderes wunung Abrahames* while recounting the parable of Dives and Lazarus, and concludes with a reference to the *wunung* on Christ's eternal kingdom (*rice to ecum life*, p. 338). Again, the collective impression is of a heaven whose

90 Clemoes, ed., *Ælfric's Catholic Homilies*, p. 434: '[I]n his [Christ's] Father's house are many dwellings: therefore we believe that he now today gave to his mother the most pleasant dwelling. The glory of God's chosen is measured by their deserts' (trans. Thorpe, ed., *Homilies of Ælfric*, p. 447).

many dwelling-places enable the functioning of a post-mortem meritocracy.

It thus seems that Ælfric's insistence on the uniformity of post-mortem reward is a response specific to the term *neorxnawang*. In fact, he seems to be playing a rather clever game, equating paradise and the kingdom of heaven through the very word, *wunung*, which he uses elsewhere to paint a more elaborate picture of the afterlife. One such discussion *wunung* initiates is in the Supplementary Series homily, *Sermo ad populum in octavis pentecosten dicendus* (Pope XI).[91] This, Ælfric's most detailed description of the interim between death and Doomsday, is also supremely evasive, its circumlocutions and digressions testimony to his anxieties rather than his convictions about the subject.

Ælfric first states that psychopomp angels bring the souls of good men to dwelling-places appropriate to their deeds (*wununge be heora gewyrhtum*, p. 424). He avoids discussing the gradation of reward implied thereby, broadening the focus instead to cover categories of sinners as well as the righteous. Thus, the good are taken to dwell with God (*mid Gode*, p. 424), those not completely good are sent to tortures (*to witum*, p. 424) to be cleansed until they are ready for release, and hardened sinners are detained forever in hell. This tantalising passage has enabled scholars like Gatch to hail Ælfric as the Anglo-Saxon pioneer of purgatorial doctrine, even as it has been ignored – unsurprisingly – by Le Goff in his argument for purgatory as a twelfth-century phenomenon.[92] Gatch's observation could have perhaps held true if Ælfric had stopped here. By *witu*, he does indicate a temporary punishment by fire, which cleanses venial sins and is clearly separate from the Doomsday conflagration. Ælfric even describes the mechanisms for the soul's release from this fire: individual deeds, masses and alms offered by living relatives and intercession by those already with God.

However, Ælfric muddies the waters by introducing a fourth category of good souls taken to rest (*to reste*, p. 424), the relationship of which to the other three locations remains vague. Even as those who go to hell can never leave it, the souls in rest are never subjected to torture. This reassurance, while implying that *rest* is not equivalent to heaven, points to it being a temporary abode of repose parallel to *witu*. Ælfric thus suggests that there

[91] Pope, ed., *Supplementary Series*, pp. 415–47, at pp. 424–30.

[92] Gatch, *Preaching and Theology*, p. 101, and Le Goff, *Birth of Purgatory*.

are two categories of souls whose interim fate differs from their final one, but divulges no more about this state of *rest*.

Ælfric's reticence can be accounted for by comparing Pope XI with its major sources, Julian of Toledo's *Prognosticon*, written in the early eighth century, and Ælfric's own excerpts from the *Prognosticon* preserved in the manuscript Boulogne-sur-Mer 63, fols. 1–10.[93] Julian's compendium recycles earlier patristic opinion, especially that of Augustine, Gregory and Isidore, to satisfy growing medieval interest in both final and interim eschatology.[94] The latter topic is discussed in the second book, within which paradise plays a prominent and interesting role. Julian begins by citing Isidore's contention that there are two paradises, one terrestrial, where Adam and Eve lived, and the other celestial, where good souls rest, awaiting Doomsday:

> Unus est terrenus, ubi primorum hominum corporaliter uita extitit: alter coelestis, ubi animae beatorum statim ut a corpore exeunt transferuntur, atque digna felicitate laetantes, expectant receptionem corporum suorum.[95]

This idea, which echoes the Byzantine doctrine of delayed retribution, should probably be attributed to the Byzantine milieu of parts of seventh-century Spain.[96] The citation reappears in Ælfric's excerpts in Boulogne-sur-Mer. Julian then adds a qualification most important for the history of

[93] See Raynes, 'MS. Boulogne-sur-Mer 63 and Ælfric'. The apparatus to Pope XI presents the correspondences between the *Prognosticon*, the 'Boulogne Excerpts' and the Old English text, while the excerpts are printed in full by Gatch, *Preaching and Theology*, pp. 134–46, with a preceding discussion, pp. 129–33.

[94] Julian's sources are discussed by Madoz, 'Fuentes teologico-literarias', and Hillgarth, 'Fuentes de San Julián de Toledo'. For the *Prognosticon*'s dissemination and the Insular role therein, see Hillgarth, ed., *Sancti Iuliani opera*, pp. xxiv–xlv. I retain the title *Prognosticon* rather than *Prognosticum*, preferred by Hillgarth, as Gatch and other Anglo-Saxon scholars use the former. For a fuller discussion of this section of the *Prognosticon*, see below, pp. 93–4.

[95] Hillgarth, ed., *Prognosticon*, II, ch. 1, p. 44: 'One is the earthly paradise, where the first men lived life corporally, the other is the celestial, where the souls of men, on leaving their bodies, are transferred, and where, moreover, rejoicing in worthy happiness, they await the reception of their bodies.' For the original statement by Isidore, see his *Differentiarum libri II*, II, ch. 12. 32, Patrologia Latina 83, ed. J. P. Migne (Paris, 1844–65) col. 75 A-B.

[96] See, in this connection, Diaz y Diaz, 'España visigótica del siglo VII', pp. 841–2, and Hillgarth, 'Fuentes de San Julián de Toledo', pp. 100–6.

the interim paradise: the celestial paradise is for those good souls who are not fully perfect.[97] This specification, although not excerpted by Ælfric, is unlikely to have been missed by him.

However, neither statement about the interim paradise within the *Prognosticon* finds its way into Pope XI, in which Ælfric otherwise relies heavily on Julian's material, both directly and mediated through his own excerpts. The clear conjunction of paradise and the interim condition seen in Julian's *Prognosticon* is thus deliberately obscured by Ælfric, possibly because he is all too mindful of its apocryphal, non-Augustinian resonances. Why then does he admit to an interim eschatology at all, especially as elsewhere he appears to gloss over this possibility by equating paradise with heaven? In any case, his attempts to avoid the term paradise, but retain its function as a place of temporary repose are shot through with unresolved ambiguities. Apart from terminology, in fact, there appears little difference between his accounts of the *fela wununga* and the graded rewards of the *Visio*.

A comparison between what Ælfric accepts and what he disallows is best enabled by the item entitled *alia visio*, appended to the homily where he denounces the *Visio Sancti Pauli*. In the homily itself, Ælfric provides the Vision of Furseus as a respectable alternative to the *Visio*. As the former largely describes places of punishment, it is not of immediate relevance to the present discussion, but we should note that it is actually remarkably similar to the punishments detailed in the *Visio*.[98] Under the rubric *alia visio*, Ælfric then translates the vision of Dryhthelm from the *Historia Ecclesiastica*, obviously as another trustworthy account of the otherworld which Bede had sanctioned. Dryhthelm visits two places of punishment and two places of rest and bliss, led by an angel who explains these sights to him. The significance of the four-part otherworld, and its connections to

[97] Hillgarth, ed., *Prognosticon* II, ch. 2, pp. 44–5 and, more clearly, in ch. 10, p. 49; these statements are supported by, rather tantalisingly for this investigation, a reference to the lost work of Julianus Pomerius, *De animae natura dialogus*. In *Prognosticon* II, ch. 9, Julian even cites Augustine's *Enchiridion* XXIX, ch. 109 (see n. 42 above) in preparatory support of the celestial interim paradise.

[98] As Gatch notes in passing, *Preaching and Theology*, p. 218, n. 50. Indeed, from this and other visions reported by Ælfric, discussed pp. 69–75, Gatch concludes that Ælfric's dependence on (Augustinian) ideas of the Church as the kingdom of heaven gives his interim eschatology a lucidity absent from anonymous homilies treating of the same topic. These observations are quite different from the arguments advanced here and consolidated below, p. 74, that Ælfric, unlike the anonymous homilists, is more encumbered than freed by his Augustinian legacy.

Julian's interim eschatology, will be explored in chapter 4. Here, however, some points specific to Ælfric are noted.

Bede describes the first place of rest as a flowering, fragrant and light-filled *campus* or plain (*HE*, V, ch. 12). To render this into Old English, Ælfric uses highly evocative vocabulary:

Se engel me lædde þærrihte to eastdæle on miccles leohtes smyltnysse into anre byrig. þærbinnan wæs swyðe smeðe feld and brad. mid blowendum wyrtum and grennysse eal afylled. and mid beorhtran leohte þonne ænig sunne scinende.[99]

The words *smyltnys*, *grennys* and *blowende* strongly recall descriptions of ideal landscapes and paradise in Old English poetry.[100] None of them appear in the corresponding description from the earlier vernacular translation of the *Historia Ecclesiastica*.[101] Ælfric also replaces the *murus* of Bede's account with *burg*, a word most frequently applied to heaven in Old English poetry.[102] Remembering Ælfric's desire to provide a substitute for the *Visio*, it is interesting that its sequence of natural and architectural imagery is altered in his picture of a stronghold enclosing a meadow. Further, the connotations of the vocabulary used align Ælfric's description to the typological identification of heaven and paradise.

These suggestions are consolidated through Ælfric's strategic deployment of *wunung* within the angel's interpretation of the meadow:

þeos wynsume and ðeos blostmbære stow. is ðæra sawla wunung ðe on godum weorcum geendodon. and swa ðeah næron swa fulfremede þæt hi ðærrihte moston into heofenan rice.[103]

This use of *wunung* is itself in keeping with Ælfric's use of *wunung* for the Johannine *multas mansiones*; the *Old English Bede* uses *wunenes* instead.[104] Moreover, the collocation of *wynsum* and *wunung*, which reappears in the

[99] Godden, ed., *Catholic Homilies*, p. 201: 'The angel then led me directly to the east in the tranquillity of a great light, into a stronghold. Inside was a truly level and broad meadow, with blossoming plants, and completely filled with greenness, and with light brighter than any shining sun.' [100] For which, see below, pp. 142–7.

[101] Miller, ed., *Old English Bede*, I, p. 430.

[102] As I point out below, pp. 147–50. The significance of Ælfric's choice of vocabulary in this description is discussed on pp. 159–60.

[103] Godden, ed., *Catholic Homilies*, p. 202: 'This pleasant and blossom-bearing place is the dwelling-place of those souls who died in good deeds, but nevertheless were not so perfect that they could immediately enter the kingdom of heaven.'

[104] Miller, ed., *Old English Bede*, I, p. 430.

angel's later assurance that these *wynsuman wununge* will be Dryhthelm's post-mortem abode, is, as we have seen, elsewhere applied by Ælfric to the Garden of Eden. The frequent use of the plural form of *wunung* ties in with his references to the *fela wununga* in his Assumption homily for the First Series and in Pope XI, even while leaving unspecified which one of these pleasant abodes will be assigned to Dryhthelm himself.

Ælfric thus modulates Bede's description of a shining meadow to distinguish it from an interim paradise such as that suggested in the *Visio*, and to recall instead the paradise of Eden, typologically subsumed within the heavenly kingdom. At the same time he incorporates the meadow into his own double-edged scheme of 'many dwelling-places'. As Bede, unlike Julian of Toledo, does not himself use the term paradise in the Vision of Dryhthelm, Ælfric's fastidiousness may seem excessive. But nearly two centuries lie between Bede and Ælfric, ample time for beliefs to strengthen and develop. Moreover, Bede's Anglo-Latin vision must have been less accessible to the lay populace, relatively speaking, than Ælfric's vernacular translation, aimed specifically as an antidote to his audience's interest in unorthodox ideas.

But why does Ælfric not jettison altogether the idea of an interim abode for the good, instead of struggling to camouflage its apocryphal roots? A clue to this puzzle lies in Ælfric's reiteration of the influence of alms, masses and intercession on the interim state. This idea, hesitatingly enunciated by Augustine, is vigorously promoted by Gregory the Great. In Gregory's *Dialogi*, Book IV, several reports of otherworldly visions convey the importance of these external factors for the fate of souls in the afterlife.[105] The Vision of Dryhthelm follows this trend. Souls in the first place of punishment, translated as *witnungstow* and *witu* by Ælfric, can be released through prayers, mass and intercession. Another illustrative story from the *Historia* is that of Ymma, also translated by Ælfric and added to the *alia visio* of Dryhthelm under the rubric of *Hortatorius sermo de efficacia sanctae missae.*[106]

Ælfric clearly recognises and highlights the connections between Gregory and Bede. His translation of The Vision of Dryhthelm concludes with the observation that other visions of *witnungstowa* and *halgena wununga* are available in the *Dialogi,* whereby we learn of the help the living can render the dead. The story of Ymma, the captive soldier whose bonds burst

[105] For a detailed analysis of Gregory's visionary otherworld, see below, pp. 78–82.

[106] *HE*, IV, ch. 31, pp. 401–5; Godden, ed., *Catholic Homilies*, pp. 204–5.

through the power of the mass, is aptly chosen as the next item, and Ælfric ends the *Sermo* with another reminder that 'se halga papa Gregorius awrat on ðære bec dialegorum. hu micclum seo halige mæsse manegum fremode.'[107] For Ælfric, then, descriptions of interim abodes of repose *and* torture are invariably accompanied by an emphasis on rites and beliefs that knit Church and laity into an interdependent whole. That this juxtaposition is organic rather than accidental will be demonstrated in the course of this book.

This chapter began with Ælfric's condemnation of apocryphal texts, and attempted to map this reaction on to a long history of contrasting interpretations of paradise and the interim condition. In the process, more questions have been raised than answered, but certain facts have come to light: Ælfric wishes to emulate Augustinian exegesis concerning paradise, but the undertow of later exegetical trends continually deflects him towards opposing beliefs which he nevertheless decries. This struggle is registered in various strategies of compromise, such as his definition of the pleasant interim abode as *rest* and *wunung* rather than *neorxnawang*, and its description as a shining meadow, but one within a stronghold. In the next chapter, these discrete observations emerge as part of a pattern where paradise, corporal assumption, the interim state and the shining meadow are intricately linked, and which, when examined, reveals an equally close mesh of compromise and circumlocution criss-crossing its reverse side.

[107] Godden, ed., *Catholic Homilies*, p. 205: 'The blessed Pope Gregory narrated in his book of Dialogues how the holy mass helped a great many.'

3

Old hierarchies in new guise: vernacular reinterpretations of the interim paradise

> Let us leave to learned culture, and to its historians, a clarity of meaning and a crisp set of boundaries . . . For us there is the play of culture, the priest who heals by using 'superstitious' remedies, the carnival and its inversions, the almanac with its predictions (itself a form of play), and the 'man of signs' descended from astrology. Meanings are prolific.[1]

This chapter examines the conjunction of paradise, the interim state and corporal assumption within several anonymous Old English prose texts: the 'Three Utterances' and 'Theban Legend' homilies, the homilies on Mary's Assumption, and the different versions of the *Life of Margaret*. Two Latin texts which display similar concerns about the interim condition are also examined here: *Transitus W*, which is the source for one of the Assumption homilies, and Redaction XI of the *Visio Sancti Pauli*. In the previous chapter, I pointed to Ælfric's anxieties surrounding this very conjunction; these anonymous texts and their Latin sources and affiliations will now enable us to locate precisely the focus of Ælfric's objections and also to discern the contours of a sensibility different from his. Through this analysis, I aim to place the concept of the interim paradise within the arena of 'the play of culture', while considering whether appreciation of such 'play' can proceed only after demarcating the boundaries of 'learned culture and its historians' as strictly as is suggested in the citation above.

The texts in question, all of the type Willard branded long ago as 'ecclesiastical fiction',[2] satisfy popular curiosity about the afterlife by drawing on millenarian and apocryphal motifs such as those transmitted through the *Visio*. Long cut loose from their original ideological moorings, and unhindered by any authorial preoccupations with doctrinal niceties, these ideas merge and mutate in the vernacular texts with little regard for theological

[1] D. Hall, 'Introduction', *Understanding Popular Culture*, ed. Kaplan, pp. 5–18, at p. 16.
[2] Willard, *Two Apocrypha*, p. 2.

consistency. The result is an ill-defined cosmology which situates paradise and heaven in a shifting hierarchy, often paralleled by a similar hierarchy between two infernal regions. In these writings, then, paradise itself becomes an alternative location for descriptions and functions that more orthodox viewpoints would banish from heaven. What literary and cultural implications can we extrapolate from these writings, and how may we situate them alongside Ælfric's views on the interim paradise? These are the questions which are addressed in this chapter.

HIERARCHIES BETWEEN PARADISE AND HEAVEN: THE 'THREE UTTERANCES' HOMILIES

The expression of the soul's interim fate through a hierarchy between paradise and heaven best emerges in two anonymous homilies, one written for Rogationtide from Oxford, Bodleian Library, Hatton 114 and a Lenten item from Oxford, Bodleian Library, Junius 85/86.[3] Both homilies draw upon the so-called 'Three Utterances' exemplum, which describes the fate of two souls, one good and the other bad, immediately after death.[4] The bad soul, upon being led out of the body by devils, utters three statements about the grim and hellish sights it sees. The devils inform it that worse is in store. Similarly the good soul, while being led out by angels, utters three statements about the wonderful sights it sees; the angels reply that better is yet to come.

These neat parallels and contrasts undoubtedly contributed to the popu-

[3] Edited by Bazire and Cross, *Rogationtide Homilies*, pp. 121–3, and Luiselli Fadda, *Nuove omelie*, pp. 7–31, respectively. For details of dates and provenances of manuscripts cited containing Old English prose, see Scragg, 'Corpus of Vernacular Homilies'.

[4] First described by Willard, *Two Apocrypha*, pp. 34–6, who prints, on pp. 37–57, parallel versions of the exemplum from the Hatton and Junius homilies (then as yet unedited), a Latin sermon from Paris, Bibliothèque Nationale, Latin 2628, previously printed by L. Dudley, *The Egyptian Elements in the Legend of the Body and Soul* (Baltimore, MD, 1911), pp. 164–5, an Irish version from *Liber Flauus Fergusiorum*, ed. and trans. Marstrander, 'The Two Deaths', and another anonymous Old English homily from Cambridge, Corpus Christi College 302 and London, British Library, Cotton Faustina A. ix. This last homily, although entitled *be heofonwarum and be helwarum*, describes, through an intriguing combination of the 'Three Utterances' exemplum and the 'Seven Heavens' apocryphon, the fate of the bad soul only. For a full discussion of this text and its sources, see L. Teresi, 'Mnemonic Transmission'.

larity of the 'Three Utterances' exemplum, but what is remarkable is the strong Insular role played in its manuscript tradition. Apart from its Old English witnesses, one Irish and at least thirty Latin versions exist, many of which occur in manuscripts of Insular or Hiberno-Latin origin, or travel with Hiberno-Latin items.[5] However, the Hatton and Junius homilies differ from the Irish and most Latin versions in their obvious attempts to map the exemplum onto ideas of an interim paradise. Their independent readjustments of the exemplum to fit this specific context resulted in some interesting divergences even while confirming a shared desire to make these changes.

The Junius 'Three Utterances' homily incorporates the terms paradise and heaven into the utterances themselves:

> Seofon siðum heo bið beorhtre þanne sunne, and þa halgan Godes ænglas hie lædað to Paradysum and þanne cwyð seo saul to ðam ænglum þe hie lædað: 'Eala, micel is ðeos blis þe ic on gelædad eam.' Ond þanne andswergeað hire þa ænglas and cweðað: 'Mare blis þe is on heofonum gegearwad.' Ond þanne seo saul eft cweð: 'Micel is þes þrym þe we on syndan.' Ond þanne andswergeað hiere þa ænglas and cweðað: 'þu cymest ful ær to maran þrymme'. Ond þanne cwyð seo saul þriddan siðe: 'Mycel is þis leoht þe ic on eam.' Ond þanne andswergeað hiere þa ænglas and hie cweðað: 'þu gemetst mare leoht mid Gode.'[6]

Each utterance describes one aspect of paradise – bliss, glory and light – while conveying that its wonders are superseded by those in heaven, where the soul may also see God face to face. The two locations are thus differentiated qualitatively. A spatio-temporal distinction is also implied through

[5] For the Irish version, see n. 4 above. Some of the Latin versions have been edited as follows: from Paris, Bibliothèque Nationale, Latin 2628, and from Oxford, University College 61, Willard, 'Latin Texts', in a parallel edition at pp. 150–64; from the Homiliary of Toledo, London, British Library, Additional 30853, along with the identification of five other manuscripts, R. Grégoire, *Les Homéliaires du moyen âge*, pp. 224–5; from Vatican, Biblioteca Apostolica, Pal. lat. 220 and 212, McNally as Sermon I, *'In nomine Dei summi'*, pp. 134–6. See also Wright, 'Apocryphal Lore and Insular Tradition, at pp. 134–5.

[6] Luiselli Fadda, ed., *Nuove omelie*, pp. 19–21: 'It [the good soul] is seven times brighter than the sun, and the holy angels of God lead it to paradise and then the soul says to the angels who lead it: "Lo, great is this bliss to which I have been led." And then the angels answer it and say: "Greater bliss is prepared for you in heaven." And then the soul again says: "Great is this glory which we perceive." And then the angels answer it and say: "You will very soon come to greater glory." And then the soul says for the third time: "Great is this light which I am in." And then the angels answer it and say: "You will meet greater light with God."'

the fact that the soul is led first to paradise, although it is not stated exactly when it would leave paradise for heaven.

The Junius homily's use of *paradisus* derives from its immediate source, which was established some years ago as being a Latin sermon in the ninth-century manuscript, Munich, Bayerische Staatsbibliothek, Clm. 28135.[7] This latter sermon is itself the only Latin 'Three Utterances' text in which the good soul enters *paradisus*. In the other Latin 'Three Utterances' sermons, the terminology at this point is either *tabernacula sanctorum* or *tabernacula iustorum*.[8] The 'tabernacles' are retained within the Junius and Clm. 28135 homilies, but only *after* the third utterance is completed. While escorting the good soul to its greater glories, the angels chant 'eadig eart ðu sawl, ðu name Gode eardunge in ðinum huse.'[9] This vernacular rendering of the *Beatus quem elegisti* chant, which appears in the Latin source, and includes the phrase *inhabitauit in tabernaculis tuis*, translates *tabernaculum* as *eardung*, a well-attested practice in psalter glossing.[10]

It thus seems that in the Junius homily and its immediate source, the belief in the good soul's entry into paradise immediately upon death, and heaven only sometimes afterwards, leads the homilists to redefine the *tabernacula sanctorum* or *tabernacula iustorum* as *paradisus*. As both these homilies

[7] See Wack and Wright, 'A New Latin Source'; for the detail of *paradisus*, see p. 190: 'Et sancti angeli qui ducunt eam †ad paradysus quo dicitur.† Et dicit anima, "Magna est laetitia." Et respondent angeli, "Maiorquę erit tibi apud deum." Et iterum dicit anima, "Magna est magestas in qua sumus." Et dicunt angeli, "Maiorque erit tibi apud deum." Et tertia dicit anima, "Magna [*sic*] est lumen." Et respondent angeli, "[. . .] apud deum."' I am grateful to Professor Wright for confirming to me this reading of Clm. 28135.

[8] McNally, '*In nomine Dei summi*', p. 136: 'Deducimus te ad tabernacula sanctorum carens iniustorum habitationibus'; Willard, 'Latin Texts', from Paris, Bibliothèque Nationale, Latin 2628, and Oxford, University College 61 respectively, p. 156: 'Deducimus te ad tabernacula sanctorum carentia iniustorum habitatione', and 'Deducimus te ad tabernacula iustorum.'

[9] Luiselli Fadda, ed., *Nuove omelie*, p. 21: 'Soul, you are blessed: through God you took tabernacles [abodes] into your house.' (For the equivalent Latin in Clm. 28135, see Wack and Wright, 'A New Latin Source', p. 190). *Eardunge* could represent either the singular or plural form; Fadda, in her facing-page Italian translation, renders it as singular: 'Beata sei tu, o anima, tua hai approntato una dimora per Dio nella tua casa'. However, I have translated it as the latter to correspond with the plural of *tabernacula*. Of course, a conceptual equivalence between a plural sense of 'abodes' or 'tabernacles' and the singular one of 'paradise' then needs to be posited.

[10] See Healey and Venezky, eds., *Microfiche Concordance*, fiches 147–73; on *eardung* and *eardungstow* as psalter glosses for *tabernaculum*, see Gretsch, *Intellectual Foundations*, pp. 90–1.

draw on a distinctive, abbreviated Hiberno-Latin version of the 'Three Utterances',[11] their shared desire to articulate ideas of an interim paradise through the 'Three Utterances' exemplum seems to be Insular, perhaps even Anglo-Saxon, in origin. In fact, this belief might be seen as one of the underlying motivations of the abbreviated tradition itself, in which the 'Three Utterances' are no longer used to express a difference between the soul's going-out journey and its destination, but are reworked instead into a contrast between the present joys of the interim paradise with the greater glories which await in heaven.

In light of this connection between Insular transmission circles and the abbreviated tradition of the 'Three Utterances', it seems significant that the other Old English 'Three Utterances' homily preserved in Hatton 114 should also refer to the good soul's sojourn in an interim paradise. Since the Hatton homily lies outside the abbreviated tradition of the Junius homily and its Latin source, its reference to paradise is embedded not within the 'Three Utterances' themselves, but within a concluding statement. First, we get the utterances of the good soul, in both Latin and Old English, and the corresponding replies given by its psychopomp:

Đonne cweð seo sawul þus, 'Magna [sic] est lumen huius letitię.' 'Eala, hwæt! þis is mycel leoht and ðis syndon fægere geferan!' Hire þonne andswariað þa englas and ðus cweþað, 'Leohtre þe is toward þonne þu gesihst Godes beorhtnesse and his engla, and þin ansyn bið to heora ansyne ecelice gestaðelod.' Đonne cweð seo sawul oðre siþe, 'Magna est uius [sic] lętitia.' Đæt is, 'Eala, hwæt! þis is mycel bliss!' Đonne andswariað hyre þa englas and cweþað, 'Mare þe is toward þonne þu gesihst engla blisse, þa ðe cumað ongean mid mycelre blisse and songe.' And hi þonne mid heora gegyrlan ymbfoð þa sawle swyðe hwite and beorhte. Đonne cweð seo sawul þriddan siðe þus, 'Dulce est iter ad Dominum. Eala, hwæt! þis is swete siðfæt on to farenne and swyðe wynsum!' Hyre þonne þa englas andswariað and cweþað, 'Đe is mycele mare toward and wynsumre þonne we ðe gelædað to þæra soðfæstra eardinge.'[12]

[11] By Wack and Wright, 'New Latin Source', pp. 198–202. This claim was substantiated by their discovery of a florilegium in Vatican, Biblioteca Apostolica Vaticana, Pal. lat. 556, written in Anglo-Saxon script, containing a series of triads listing the three best and three worst things, verbally very close to the details in Clm. 28135; see 'New Latin Source', pp. 196–8. The 'third best thing' named in this triad is, significantly enough, 'paradisus cui dicitur [ducitur] et expectatio regni caelestis' ('New Latin Source', p. 197).

[12] Bazire and Cross, eds., *Rogationtide Homilies*, p. 123: 'Then speaks the soul in this manner: "Great is the light of this bliss. Lo! This is a great light and these are bright ways!" The angels then answer it and say: "More light awaits you when you see God's brightness

This reference to the *soðfæstra eardinge* corresponds to the terminology of the 'Three Utterances' homilies outside the abbreviated tradition: *tabernacula sanctorum* or, even closer, *tabernacula iustorum*.[13]

What is not present in those Latin homilies, however, is the clarification which immediately follows the 'Three Utterances' in the Hatton homily:

Đonne gelædað þa englas þa sawle in þone wuldorlican gefean neorxnawanges, þær heo forð wunað and ricsað mid Godes þam gecorenan, buton ælcum yfelum and earfoðum a oð ende, þær restað haligra manna sawla oð domesdæg.[14]

This statement is a manifestation of the same desire which we see in those homilists working within the abbreviated 'Three Utterances' tradition: to define the good soul's destination as paradise, and also mark out thereby the differences between this paradise and heaven. As I noted earlier, the Junius homily uses the 'Three Utterances' exemplum to underscore the hierarchy between paradise, to which the good soul is led first, and heaven, the more glorious place which it will enter only later and at some unspecified point in time. In the Hatton homily, the qualitative distinction between the two locations does not emerge as sharply as does the temporal. Its concluding clause 'until Doomsday' makes clear that this paradise is an interim abode for both 'God's chosen' and 'the souls of holy men', distinct from their post-Doomsday existence in heaven. The earlier removal of the qualification *ad dominum* from the Old English translation of the third utterance further suggests that those detained in this paradise must wait until Doomsday for

footnote 12 (*cont.*)
and his angels, and your countenance is eternally placed alongside theirs." Then says the soul a second time: "Great is this bliss." That is, "Lo! This is great bliss!" Then the angels answer it and say, "Greater [bliss] awaits when you see the bliss of the angels, when they come towards you with greater bliss and song." And they then envelop the soul with robes truly white and bright. Then says the soul as follows: "Sweet is the journey to the Lord. Lo! This is a sweet and truly pleasant journey to travel on!" Then the angels answer it and say, "Much more [sweetness] and pleasure awaits you when we lead you towards the tabernacles [abodes] of the righteous."' For the translation of *eardinge* as a plural form, see n. 9 above.

13 For *earding* as an infrequent variation on *eardung*, see Healey and Venezky, eds., *Microfiche Concordance*, fiche 136, and below, p. 68, for its appearance in a similar context.

14 Bazire and Cross, eds., *Rogationtide Homilies*, p. 123: 'Then the angels lead the soul into the glorious joy of paradise, where it henceforth dwells and rules with God's chosen ones, without any evils and sufferings always until the end, there where the souls of holy men rest until Doomsday.'

their encounter with God. By the same token, the retention of the phrase *Godes beorhtnes* in the vernacular rendering of the first utterance suggests that the Hatton homilist did not successfully adjust all the details of the exemplum to alter the focus of its original comparison.

REDACTION XI OF THE *VISIO SANCTI PAULI* AND THE 'THREE UTTERANCES'

What prompted the Hatton and Junius 'Three Utterances' homilists to insist on these distinctions between paradise and heaven? Some clues are provided by Redaction XI of the *Visio Sancti Pauli*. Dwyer, who brought this version to light some years ago, remarked on its importance as one of the few abbreviated redactions of the Long Latin *Visio* which preserves anything of Paul's visit to paradise in the third heaven.[15] However, Redaction XI, preserved in a manuscript written in Anglo-Saxon script in the early ninth century and exhibiting several 'Irish symptoms',[16] does more than retain these sections of the *Visio*; it brings them up to date, as it were, with current ideas about the interim state of the good soul, in a manner which is, furthermore, strikingly similar to the Old English 'Three Utterances' homilies. These affiliations make Redaction XI an invaluable index to changing beliefs about the interim paradise, even as its Insular origin adds to the argument, already adduced from the 'Three Utterances' homilies, that these beliefs thrived in, and were most probably shaped by, the Insular milieu itself.[17]

Redaction XI begins with an echo of 2 Corinthians XII. 2–4, into which is inserted the detail of the golden boat from the Long Latin *Visio*:

> Scio hominem raptum usque ad tertium caelum. In naui aurea erant quasi tres angeli hymnum dicentes ante me, uere siue in corpore siue extra corpus nescio, Deus scit.[18]

[15] Dwyer, 'An Unstudied Redaction', pp. 122–3. [16] Wright, 'Redaction XI', p. 34.

[17] In fact, Wright, 'Redaction XI', argues for its specifically Irish origin. The implications of these Irish affiliations will be addressed in greater detail below, pp. 108–9.

[18] Dwyer, 'An Unstudied Redaction', p. 128, ch. 1: 'I know a man caught up until the third heaven. It seemed there were three angels in a golden boat, singing a hymn, before me, truly, whether in his body, or whether out of it, I do not know, God knows.' For the golden boat of the Long Latin *Visio*, see Silverstein and Hilhorst, eds., *Apocalypse of Paul*, ch. 22, p. 120; for the significance of this detail for arguments concerning Aldhelm's knowledge of a possible Long Latin version of the *Visio*, see p. 16 above, n. 5.

The author then describes sinners hanging from leafless trees in front of the gates of the city of paradise (*portae ciuitatis paradisi*, ch. 3), and numerous other means of torturing the wicked, including graded immersion in a fiery river, at least some of which are presumably also taking place in front of these gates (chs. 3–8). The focus next shifts, rather suddenly, to five wise virgins in paradise, as radiant as the sun and wearing golden crowns and clothes as white as snow (*candida erant sicut nix*, ch. 9). Finally, two sections describe the abode of the saints (*locus sanctorum*, ch. 10) and the punishments of the impious (*poenas impiorum*, ch. 11) respectively. The description of the latter is targeted towards the fate of five virgins who were obviously less wise than those five described so glowingly in an earlier section. These parallels and contrasts between the fates of the good and the impious recall, of course, the 'Three Utterances' homilies, and the similarity is carried through further in the terminological and syntactic juxtapositions of their divergent fates. In the Latin 'Three Utterances' homilies, including the one preserved alongside Redaction XI, the adjective *carens* is used to bring together, within the same sentence, the opposing concepts of the *tabernacula sanctorum* and the *locus impiorum*.[19] Redaction XI uses syntax in a very similar manner to sharpen the contrasts between the fate of the righteous and that of the impious: 'hii sunt homines qui . . . nec fuerunt in numero sanctorum sed impiorum'.[20]

In its relatively streamlined conception of the interim state of souls, Redaction XI comes much closer to the schematic otherworld of Bede's *Vision of Dryhthelm* than to the haphazard wanderings of Paul described in the Long Latin *Visio*.[21] The two concluding sections contain other, even more noteworthy differences between the Long Latin *Visio* and this particular redaction. The angel commands Paul to follow him to the *locus sanctorum* (ch. 10) which, later, is also described as the *locus iustorum* (ch. 11) – a term which appears in the comparable section of the Long Latin version (ch. 19). However, as I noted in an earlier chapter, the Long Latin *Visio* also describes the paradise within the third heaven as the *terra repromissionis*, where souls of the just (*iustorum*) are sent for a 'while' (*interim dimittuntur*, ch. 21).[22] Redaction XI renders this explication thus:

19 See n. 8 above.

20 Dwyer, 'An Unstudied Redaction', p. 126, ch. 5: 'These are the men who were . . . not within the numbers of the saints but the impious'; see also the later juxtaposition of 'poena impiorum et locus iustorum' (ch. 9, p. 129).

21 A point which will be returned to in the next chapter, p. 109.

22 See above, p. 19.

Interrogaui et angelum: domine, domine, quis est locus iste? Respondit mihi angelus: ipse est locus sanctorum, ibi habitabunt usque ad diem resurrectionis. Et clause sunt porte paradisi usque ad diem iudicii; in manu petri et pauli claue sunt regni celorum.[23]

While in the Long Latin *Visio*, it is never quite clear whether the boundaries of the third heaven, paradise, *locus iustorum* and *terra repromissionis* completely overlap or merely intersect at some points, Redaction XI tightens the association of paradise and the abode of the righteous through the repetition of *locus sanctorum* within the angel's reply. Moreover, as in the Hatton 'Three Utterances' homily, and unlike the Long Latin *Visio*, the qualifications 'until the day of resurrection' and 'until the Day of Judgement' specify exactly how long this interim sojourn is to be. The assertions that the 'gates of paradise' are closed until the Day of Judgement', and the keys to the 'kingdom of heaven' are in the hands of Peter and Paul, emphasise further the duration of the interim period and the separation of paradise and heaven – by the locked gates – until Doomsday.

The thematic, descriptive and lexical similarities between Redaction XI and the 'Three Utterances' exemplum were obviously perceived by the compiler of the manuscript in which Redaction XI is preserved. This manuscript, Vatican, Biblioteca Apostolica, pal. lat. 220, also contains the sermons *In nomine Dei summi* – one of which is a Latin 'Three Utterances' text.[24] While it should be noted that this particular version of the 'Three Utterances' does not redefine its *tabernacula sanctorum* as *paradisus*, its coexistence within the same manuscript as Redaction XI demonstrates how older beliefs could be read and reinterpreted in the light of more recent ones. Just as the authors working in the abbreviated 'Three Utterances' tradition incorporated a newer hierarchy between the interim paradise and heaven into the original comparison between the soul's journey and its destination, another author abbreviated and reinterpreted the Long Latin *Visio* to convey the same idea. In fact, a neat partner to the manuscript pairing of Redaction XI and the *In nomine Dei summi* 'Three Utterances' sermon is

[23] Dwyer, 'An Unstudied Redaction', p. 128, ch. 10: 'And I asked the angel: "Lord, lord, what is that place?" The angel answered me: "That is the abode of the saints; they dwell there until the day of resurrection. And closed are the gates of paradise until the Day of Judgement; in the hands of Peter and Paul are the keys to the kingdom of heaven."'

[24] As pointed out by Wright, 'Redaction XI', p. 35. The 'Three Utterances' sermon in question is edited by McNally, '*In nomine Dei summi*', pp. 134–6.

the presence of one of the Old English 'Three Utterances' homilies in Junius 85/86, a manuscript which also contains, sandwiched between two parts of the work known as *An Address of the Soul to the Body*, a unique Old English translation of part of the *Visio*.[25]

It thus appears that the author of Redaction XI chiselled the idea of the *terra repromissionis* contained within the Long Latin *Visio* in order to express an interim otherworld with sharper spatio-temporal contours, another manifestation of which is seen in the hierarchy between paradise and heaven within the Old English 'Three Utterances' homilies. But from where did this hierarchy itself emerge? The full answer must wait until the following chapter. Here, it should be noted that, within millenarian thinking, a similar hierarchy existed between the bosom of Abraham, the interim abode for all the just, and paradise, reserved for those assumed in the body. This hierarchy, and vestiges of its underlying eschatology, had evidently been transmitted to Anglo-Saxon England, as we may deduce from its reappearance in a somewhat unexpected context. An anonymous homily from Oxford, Bodley 343, and edited as Homily XLVI by Napier, alludes to the 'Three Utterances' as well as to the bosom of Abraham while referring to distinctions between the fate of souls before and after Doomsday.[26] While the bad soul shall remain immersed up to his lips in a fiery river until Doomsday (p. 236), the good soul will be, not in paradise, but in *Abrahames fæðmum oð domes dæg* (p. 238).

This lone occurrence of the phrase *Abrahames fæðm* within the vernacular corpus and the particular context of its usage suggest that the millenarian hierarchy was restated at some point as a hierarchy between paradise and heaven, under influence of concurrent beliefs regarding the interim paradise. Another phenomenon may be seen as a by-product of this process. While some Old English texts redefine the millenarian *sinus Abrahae* as

[25] According to Willard, 'Address of the Soul to the Body', pp. 958–9, fols. 3r-11v containing the *Visio* were accidentally misbound between fols. 2v and 12r-17r, which contain *The Address of the Soul to the Body*. Healey, in *Old English Vision*, pp. 4–6, disagrees with Willard to conclude instead that this arrangement represents 'an intelligent piece of compilational art'. See also pp. 9–16.

[26] Napier, ed., *Wulfstan: Sammlung*, pp. 235–8. In fact, the 'Three Utterances' exemplum most probably developed from the account of the bringing forth of souls given in the *Visio Sancti Pauli*, with Napier XLVI representing an early stage in this process. See Willard, *Two Apocrypha*, pp. 74–7, 'Address of the Soul to the Body', p. 976, and Ostheeren's notes to Napier, ed., *Wulfstan: Sammlung*, p. 532.

paradise, others retain the millenarian (and apocryphal) function of paradise as the abode of those assumed in the body. Coexistence can only lead to further conflation; not unexpectedly, certain texts appear to interpret *neorxnawang* as simultaneously housing both righteous souls *and* those assumed in the body.

MARY, MARGARET AND CORPORAL ASSUMPTION INTO PARADISE

This lexical conflation of two, originally separate, locations can be seen in an anonymous Old English homily on Mary's Assumption, which exists in two versions, within the Blickling Homiliary and in Cambridge, Corpus Christi College 198.[27] This homily combines two Assumption narratives, *Transitus W* and *Transitus B2*.[28] Scholars have offered two reasons for its rather garbled amalgamation of these two quite divergent accounts of the Assumption – the homilist's desire to describe Mary's end in the fullest detail possible, and his need to clarify the ambivalences and reconcile the contradictions within the *Transitus* narratives available to him.[29] To these reasons we may add a third, evident in the homilist's reiterated use of *neorxnawang*: his attempt to create a vernacular Assumption narrative more in keeping with popular Anglo-Saxon conceptions of the interim paradise than either Latin text he had before him.

Before examining the Old English homily, we need to remind ourselves of what each *Transitus* text has to say about paradise, heaven and the different phases of Mary's corporal assumption. *Transitus B2*, it should be recalled, seems to blur distinctions between paradise and heaven by using

[27] The Blickling version appears as No. XIII in Morris, ed., *Blickling Homilies*, while the Corpus 198 version of the homily has been most recently edited by Clayton ed., *Apocryphal Gospels*, pp. 239–314. I cite the latter in preference to the older edition by Morris, for the same reasons as she chooses it for her base text: 'F [Corpus 198] . . . has almost as good – or as bad – a text as B[lickling], has some novelty value and is complete' (p. 241). To these reasons we may add the usefulness of the new edition itself as well as its detailed commentary. To facilitate cross-referencing, however, I continue to refer to the Assumption homily in question as Blickling XIII.

[28] Willard, 'On Blickling Homily XIII' and 'Two Accounts of the Assumption'.

[29] Clayton, 'Blickling Homily XIII Reconsidered', pp. 26–9, and Clayton, *Cult*, pp. 10–11 and 232–3; for an updated version of these arguments, see her *Apocryphal Gospels*, pp. 144–7.

both terms indiscriminately within the text, in contrast to *Transitus B1*, which distinguishes between heaven, always associated with Christ in that text, and paradise, where Mary's soul and body are taken.[30] Likewise, in all the versions of *Transitus W*, paradise is where her body is preserved and where her soul is finally brought in order to be reunited with its body; paradise is also where the resurrected Mary appears to remain thereafter.[31] However, where is her soul sent in the brief period between her death and her resurrection? While *Transitus W* resembles other *Transitus* narratives in refraining from a categorical answer to this question, an answer appears to be hinted at within two speeches it contains, and which provide interesting support for some of the hypotheses advanced at the close of the previous section of this chapter.

The first speech, made by Mary before her death, refers to a set of beliefs remarkably similar to the 'Three Utterances' exemplum:

> Et hoc notum uobis facio ut sciatis quia homo, quando iubetur ut exeat de corpore, occurrunt illi duo angeli, unus iustitiae et alter iniquitatis. Et si inuenerit angelus iustitiae in illo homine opera iusta et bona, gaudens et exultans deducit animam illius ad locum iustorum. Et tunc deflet angelus ille iniquitatis, quia nihil de operibus suis potuit inuenire in eo. Quodsi ergo angelus ille malitiae inuenerit opera sua mala in homine illo, gaudens et exultans adsumit secum quos nequiores scit. Et sic gaudentes deducunt animam illius ad locum penarum. Et angelus iustitiae tristis recedit.[32]

As in the 'Three Utterances' texts, this passage contrasts the soul of a just man to that of a impious one, the actions of a just angel to those of an iniquitous one, including the rejoicing of one party at the expense of the other,[33] and the terms *locus penarum* and *locus iustorum*, along with the standard fluc-

[30] See above, p. 34. [31] See above, p. 33.

[32] Wilmart, ed., 'L'Ancien Récit latin', ch. 5, pp. 328–9: 'And this I make known to you so that you may know, because there come to man, when he is commanded to take leave of his body, two angels, one of righteousness and the other of evil. And if the angel of righteousness should have found in that man good and right works, rejoicing and in exultation he leads his soul to the place of the righteous. And then the other angel, that of evil, weeps because he could find nothing of his own works in him. So now if that angel of wickedness should have found out his own wicked deeds in that man, rejoicing and in exultation he brings with him those whom he knows to be more wicked. And thus rejoicing they lead the man's soul to the place of punishments. And the angel of goodness goes sadly away.'

[33] Although in the 'Three Utterances' exemplum, the corresponding psychopomps are a host of angels and a host of demons, rather than a single representative of each group.

tuation between *iusti* and *sancti*.[34] A later speech by Peter reaffirms this set of beliefs:

Nam cum uenerit dies uocationis unicuique nostrum, ut transeat de hoc corpore, qui digni sunt ibi erunt ubi sunt patriarchae Abraham, Isaac et Iacob. Cum enim fuerit ingressus, mors mittetur foras. Qui uero in peccatis suis uocatus fuerit de corpore, et uiderit locum iustorum, dicet: Patiens esto, domine, donec exorem pro peccatis meis. Mors uero immissa non permittit, quoniam completum est tempus eius, et statim inducitur in locum tormentorum. Si autem boni aliquid fecerit, gaudet et exultat. Nam primum cum recesserit anima de corpore, ducitur ab angelis ante dominum. Et post haec unaquaeque anima secundum actum suum conlocatur, si bene fecerit, in sinu Abrahae; si autem peccatrix fuerit, in locum tormentorum erit.[35]

Thus *Transitus W* not only attests to the general 'Three Utterances' type scheme, including the soul's appearance in front of the heavenly court prior to being sent off to either punishment or reward, but also replicates the standard contrast between the place for the righteous and the place of torments and punishments which circulates within the 'Three Utterances' texts. Furthermore, its definition of the *locus iustorum* as the *sinus Abrahae* points, as does Napier XLVI, to the survival of a millenarian-like eschatology in which the corporally assumed were taken to paradise, and the souls of all the other righteous retained in the bosom of Abraham.

Turning now to Blickling XIII, we realise that many of the changes introduced by the homilist were geared towards the redefining of these older eschatological schemes. First, the homilist describes what happens to Mary's soul immediately after her death:

[34] See Wilmart, ed., 'L'Ancien Récit latin', p. 328, n. 5.

[35] *Ibid.*, ch. 21, p. 341: 'For when there will come the day of calling for each one of us, that the soul [lit: 'it'] passes out of this body, those who are worthy will be there where are the fathers Abraham, Isaac and Jacob. For when there will be the entrance, death is sent out of sight. However, he who has been called from his body in the midst of sins, and will see the place of the righteous, will say: "Be patient, Lord, until I have done penance for my sins." Now death, once entered upon, does not allow this since the man's time is finished, and at once he is led into the place of torments. If, however, he has done something good, he rejoices and is jubilant. For when the soul departs from the body, it is led by the angels before the Lord. And after this every individual soul is placed according to his behaviour – if it has done well, in the bosom of Abraham; if, however, it has been a sinner, it will be in the place of torment.'

Ond Drihten bead ðæm wolcnum þæt hie eodan on neorxnawange and ðær asetton ðære eadigan Marian saule.[36]

This statement translates the conclusion of *Transitus W*, but with one alteration: it renders the *corpus* of the original as *saul*.[37] Through this change, the Blickling homilist states that Mary's soul goes to paradise between her death and her corporal assumption, a clarification which we have seen is lacking in both *Transitus W* and *Transitus B2*. As in the Old English 'Three Utterances' homilies, the interim location of the righteous soul in Blickling XIII is thereby understood as *neorxnawang*.

At the same time, the homilist sees this same *neorxnawang* as where Mary's body is later assumed. To describe Mary's corporal assumption into paradise, the homilist translates the conclusion of *Transitus B2*, which he renders more emphatic through an additional comment emphasising the physicality of the assumption:

Ond Drihten cwæð to ðæm englum, 'Singað nu and onfoð minre meder on neorxnawange.' Ond ða apostolas on heora mægene hofon Marian lichoman up mid wolcnum ond hine ða asetton on neorxnawanges gefean.[38]

[36] Clayton, ed., *Apocryphal Gospels*, ch. 49, p. 268: 'And the Lord bade the clouds that they should go to paradise and set down there the soul of the blessed Mary.' As Michael had actually been ordered to receive the soul in ch. 25, Clayton finds the text unclear as to where Mary's soul is before this moment of Christ's commanding the clouds to take it to paradise (pp. 146–7). While it is undeniable that the text glosses over this fact, however, it is also clear that at this particular point, her soul is quite unambiguously brought into paradise. That this abode is where God and his chosen also dwell (ch. 49) need not entail, as Clayton suggests, 'a seeming identification of paradise and heaven' (p. 147). The homilist could have retained a detail from *Transitus W* which, it should be remembered, probably subscribed to the older, millenarian scheme where paradise was indeed the abode of God's elect, but in which the number of the elect was restricted to the corporally assumed.

[37] In *Apocryphal Gospels*, pp. 144–5, Clayton appears to retract her earlier claim ('Blickling XIII Reconsidered', p. 27), that the Old English homilist was working from a version of *Transitus W* which had already changed 'body' to 'soul.' No such version has been discovered, and *corpus*, in fact, appears in all three manuscripts collated by Wilmart which preserve the passage in question ('L'Ancien Récit latin', p. 357). These include the ninth-century G (St Gallen, Stiftsbibliothek, 732), which Clayton herself considers to be the closest to the Blickling homily ('Blickling XIII Reconsidered', p. 29, and *Apocryphal Gospels*, p. 144). It thus seems unnecessary to postulate the existence of an immediate source which had already made the alteration to 'soul', and Clayton's own editorial work now suggests 'a source which had been altered [by the Old English homilist]' (*Apocryphal Gospels*, p. 145).

[38] Clayton, ed., *Apocryphal Gospels*, ch. 52, p. 270: 'And the Lord said to the angels: "Sing now, and receive my mother into paradise." And the apostles in their power raised

Using both conclusions, therefore, the homilist not only describes fully both stages of the assumption[39] but also emphasises that paradise is the destination for Mary's soul as well as for her body.

Blickling XIII thus provides clear evidence of how two different functions of the interim paradise could be subsumed into a single location. In the other Old English Assumption homily, preserved within the marginalia of Cambridge, Corpus Christi College 41,[40] and a faithful translation of *Transitus B2*, a minor divergence from its source indicates that this homilist too, perhaps, understood *neorxnawang* as an interim rather than an eternal location.[41] While translating Christ's promise that Mary would be taken up to paradise by the celestial host, he leaves out *Transitus B2*'s qualification of this abode as the *receptacula vitae aeternae*:

Ac astih ofer þinre reste and þone gedefan ende þines lifes gefyl, forðon ðin bideþ se heofonlica camphad þæt he ðe inlædeþ in neorxnawonges gefean.[42]

Moreover, he adds a completely new statement that the apostles would come down from paradise to help with the assumption, thus augmenting the text's already numerous references to *neorxnawang*:

Nu todæge hi beoð genumene of neorhxnawonges gefean and her to ðe cumað.[43]

Mary's body up into the clouds and set it down in the joys of paradise' (trans. Clayton). This assumption is anticipated earlier in the narrative: 'Ond þa apostolas togon hie up and hie gesetton on þæm fægran neorxnawange' (ch. 15, p. 254). In 'Blickling XIII Reconsidered', pp. 32–3, Clayton ascribes this anticipatory comment to the author's eagerness to emphasise the corporal assumption, but note once again the accompanying repetition of the term *neorxnawang*, as well as the physical implications of the verb *teon*.

39 As noted by Clayton, 'Blickling XIII Reconsidered', p. 29.

40 Edited by Grant in *Three Homilies*, pp. 18–31, and more recently by Clayton in *Apocryphal Gospels*, pp. 213–36. I cite her edition as she has identified its source as *Transitus B2*, which 'means that it is possible to be much more accurate in discussing how the Latin is handled in this translation and also that deficiencies in the text can be identified with some degree of certainty.' (Clayton, ed., *Apocryphal Gospels*, p. 213, and pp. 141–4 for its dependence on *Transitus B2*).

41 Although this is not the contention of Clayton; see *Apocryphal Gospels*, p. 144.

42 Clayton, ed., *Apocryphal Gospels*, ch. 7, p. 222: 'But get on to your bed and complete the fitting end of your life because the heavenly army awaits you that it may lead you into the joys of paradise' (trans. Clayton).

43 *Ibid.*, ch. 2, pp. 216–18: 'This very day they will be taken from the joys of paradise and will come here to you' (trans. Clayton).

Also, *neorxnawang* remains the destination of the assumed body (ch. 17). Thus, while the Corpus 41 homily does not bring out the dual role of *neorxnawang* as clearly as does Blickling XIII, it nevertheless furnishes an additional target for Ælfric's polemical stance towards the association of corporal assumption and the interim paradise.[44] If this association was as strong in the Anglo-Saxon period as his objections indicate, its very presence in the Corpus 41 homily would have overridden the ambiguities it had inherited from *Transitus B2* and encouraged the reader or audience to interpret *neorxnawang* as an interim paradise, distinct from heaven.

This identification of corporal assumption with paradise also underlies certain divergences between the two Old English versions of the *Life of Margaret*, preserved in Cambridge, Corpus Christi College 303 and in London, British Library, Cotton Tiberius A. iii.[45] The story of Margaret's imprisonment and execution by the Roman prefect Olibrius was widely disseminated in Western as well as Eastern tradition, where she is called Marina. While the Corpus 303 *Life* belongs to the mainstream Western tradition (the 'Mombritius' or *Ia* tradition), the Tiberius A. iii *Life*, with affinities ultimately with the Greek version known as the *Passio a Theotimo*, represents a subsidiary tradition (either the 'Casinensis' or *Ib* tradition, or possibly even the 'pre-Mombritius' tradition which is the common original of both *Ia* and *Ib*).[46] These wider differences are reflected in the endings of each text. In the mainstream Latin texts, either the soul or the body of Margaret is borne heavenwards by angels after her execution, and the Corpus 303 *Life* opts for the former. The Tiberius A. iii *Life*, following the

[44] See above, p. 36.

[45] Clayton and Magennis, eds., *Old English Lives*, pp. 152–71, and 112– 39 respectively.

[46] For these different traditions underlying the two Old English versions, see Clayton and Magennis, eds., *Old English Lives*, pp. 7–18 and 42–51. For the Greek and Latin traditions, see p. 6 and pp. 7–23 respectively. For texts belonging to the *Ia* tradition, see B. Mombritius, ed., *Sanctuarium seu Vitae Sanctorum* II, 2nd edn (Paris, 1910), pp. 190–6, B. Assmann, ed., *Angelsächsische Homilien und Heiligenleben*, BaP 3, repr. with a supplementary introduction by P. A. M. Clemoes (Darmstadt, 1964), pp. 170–80, and P. Piper, ed., *Nachträge zur älteren deutschen Litteratur von Kürschners deutscher National-Litteratur*, Deutsche National-Litteratur 162 (Stuttgart, n. d.), pp. 334–46. A collated version from Paris, Bibliothèque Nationale, lat. 5574 and Saint-Omer, Bibl. Mun., 202, is printed by Clayton and Magennis as Appendix 2, *Old English Lives*, pp. 191–223. The subsidiary *Ib* tradition is edited by the Benedictines of Monte Cassino in *Bibliotheca Casinensis* II (Monte Cassino, 1873–94), pp. 3–7, and printed by Clayton and Magennis as Appendix 3, *Old English Lives*, pp. 224–34.

tradition of the Greek *Passio*, states that angels bear upwards only the severed head of the saint – possibly a somewhat bizarre compromise between the unorthodoxy of a complete corporal assumption and the tameness of a merely spiritual one.[47]

But even this partial corporal assumption produces an almost knee-jerk reference to paradise in the Tiberius A. iii *Life*:

And þus singende hi hit gesætton on neorxnawonge.[48]

This destination of Margaret's head recalls the similar insistence in the vernacular Assumption texts on Mary's corporal assumption into paradise. The connection between the assumed head and paradise is also preserved in the entry for Margaret within the *Old English Martyrology*, which is another witness to the Anglo-Saxon familiarity with a tradition otherwise rare in the medieval West:[49]

Ond ða ne wæs hire heafad no on eorðan gemeted, ac is wen þæt englas mid him hit læddan to Godes neorxnawonge; se lichoma elles is geseted on Antiocha ceastre.[50]

However, the reverse of this correspondence appears in the Corpus 303 *Life*, where Margaret's spiritual assumption is into the kingdom of heaven, not paradise:

And ures Drihtnes ænglas þider comon and þa sawla underfengon and heo on heofone rice gebrohton. And nu hi is mid Gode and mid eallum his halgum, and þær hi wunað nu and æfre wunian sceal in ealra worulda woruld a butan ende.[51]

47 Cf. the similar fluctuations between 'body' and 'soul' in the various versions of the *Transitus Mariae*, identified by Clayton, 'Blickling XIII Reconsidered', pp. 27–9.

48 Clayton and Magennis, eds., *Old English Lives*, ch, 23, p. 136: 'And thus singing they placed it [the head] in paradise' (trans. Clayton and Magennis). This specification occurs in Version *Ib*, and thus probably derives from the immediate source of the Tiberius *Life*: 'Accendentes uero adduxerunt caput eius in paradyso' (Clayton and Magennis, eds., *Old English Lives*, ch. 23, p. 233). The Greek *Passio* merely says that the angels bring the head 'to the Lord'; see Usener, ed., 'S. Marinae', fols. 140v- 140r, p. 45.

49 Clayton and Magennis, eds., *Old English Lives*, p. 56.

50 G. Kotzor, ed., *Das altenglische Martyrologium* II, Bayerische Akademie der Wissenschaften, Phil. -hist. Klasse, Abhandlungen n. s. 88, (Munich, 1981), p. 144: 'And then her head was not encountered in this earth, but it is believed that angels took it with them to God's paradise; the body is otherwise buried in the city of Antioch' (trans. Kotzor).

51 Clayton and Magennis, eds., *Old English Lives*, ch, 23, p. 170: 'And our Lord's angels came there and received the soul and brought it to the kingdom of heaven. And now she is with God and with all his saints and she dwells there now and will dwell world without end for ever and ever' (trans. Clayton and Magennis).

As most Latin texts representing the mainstream Latin tradition leave the soul's destination undefined at this point,[52] the joint insistence upon the kingdom of heaven and Margaret's soul appears to be a rejection of the same connection between corporal assumption and paradise that the Tiberius A. iii *Life* so readily articulates. In the Corpus 303 *Life*, the emphasis on the seamless continuation of the 'now' into 'forever' could represent an additional refutation of belief in an interim state for the righteous until Doomsday.

This contrasting use of paradise and the kingdom of heaven is extended throughout the two Old English texts with a consistency unique to them.[53] In the Tiberius A. iii *Life*, Margaret warns her executioner that he would not share her future joy in *neorxnawong* if he flinched at beheading her (ch. 22). The Corpus 303 *Life* incorporates *heofene rice* within the same warning (ch. 22). Neither the Greek nor the various Latin versions demonstrate such concern about maintaining parity between this celestial location and the one to which Margaret's head, soul or body is brought.[54] The Tiberius A. iii *Life* also refers to paradise within the speech of a dove which appears to Margaret in a vision during her incarceration. This dove foretells that angels would come and bear her head to *neorxnawong* (ch. 20). This statement is not found in the Corpus 303 *Life*, although in other Latin texts, the dove refers to the 'palace of the heavenly kingdom',[55] while the Greek *Passio* uses the phrase 'tabernacle of Christ' (fol. 138r). Thus the Tiberius A. iii *Life*, unlike the other versions, uses the dove's speech to specify the actual manner in which Margaret would be rewarded, in terms of both method and location. Later in the Tiberius A. iii *Life*, the dove refers again to paradise while describing the life awaiting Margaret:

[52] For instance, the Saint-Omer version simply says, 'Tunc descendentes angeli cum uirtutibus tollentes corpus beatae Margaritae in gremio suo ascenderunt super nubem' (Clayton and Magennis, eds., *Old English Lives*, ch. 23, p. 216).

[53] These deliberate changes in the Corpus 303 *Life* bear out the conclusions of Clayton and Magennis, who are 'unwilling to dismiss all peculiarities in the Old English as going back to a Latin intermediary' (*Old English Lives*, p. 65; see also p. 62).

[54] In the Greek *Passio*, Marina tells her executioner that he will not share with her the 'kingdom of heaven' (Usener, ed., *Acta S. Marinae*, fol. 140v, p. 45). In the Saint-Omer text, the phrase *paradiso Dei* appears (*Old English Lives*, eds. Clayton and Magennis, ch. 23, p. 216). Version *Ib* does not contain this exchange between Margaret and her executioner, which furnishes another direct link between the Tiberius *Life* and the Greek *Passio*.

[55] As in the Saint-Omer version; see Clayton and Magennis, eds., *Old English Lives*, ch. 20, p. 214.

Ac þær biþ sib and lufu and soþfæstnesse and blis and gefean, and nænig on neorxnawonge mare gemetod mid meder ealra Gescippendes nimþe þreo fæmnan.[56]

The latter half of this sentence is underlined by a later scribe, and, according to Clayton and Magennis, 'clearly caused difficulties, as it is marked out for cancellation'.[57] This statement is found nowhere else in the tradition, though the subsequent reference to Thecla and Susanna occurs at this point in various versions. This unique insertion of the term *neorxnawong* prior to the names of two virgins could indicate a desire to clarify Margaret's reward as that paradise which houses other virgin martyrs as well as Mary, whose corporal assumption was probably also accepted by the author.

Furthermore, the dove's initial address in the Tiberius A. iii *Life* refers to Abraham, Isaac and Jacob as those who share Margaret's reward (ch. 25). The names of these three patriarchs reappear only in the *Passio a Theotimo*, but as an extension of the phrase 'bosom of Abraham' (fol. 136r). While the omission of the 'bosom' is in keeping with what increasingly appears as a general Anglo-Saxon reluctance to use this phrase, the retention of the names points to a dwelling-place whose inhabitants include the patriarchs, virgins and Mary. Not unexpectedly, these are the categories of the righteous described as inhabiting the paradise of the third heaven in the *Visio Sancti Pauli*. It should also be recalled that in the Hatton 'Three Utterances' homily, too, the interim paradise is inhabited by the saints and the elect.

Nevertheless, no temporal qualification such as the Hatton homily's *oð domesdæg* differentiates paradise from heaven in either the homilies on Mary's Assumption or the Tiberius A. iii *Life*. Can we then claim that the paradise of the corporally assumed is considered to be distinct from heaven, or is even an interim location? The answer lies in the necessity of emphasising this distinction in the texts concerned. The 'Three Utterances' homilies distinguished between the two locations in order to inspire penitence.

56 Clayton and Magennis, eds., *Old English Lives*, ch. 20, p. 189: 'But there is peace and love and righteousness and bliss and joys, and none in paradise may experience more meetings with the mother of all creation than the three virgins.' This statement is included by Clayton and Magennis, not in their edition of the Tiberius *Life*, but in what they term its 'A Text', and print as Appendix 1, pp. 181–90; this represents the text of the Tiberius *Life* without the numerous scribal accretions and changes that they register in their edition proper.

57 Clayton and Magennis, eds., *Old English Lives*, pp. 146–7, n. 59. See this note also for a discussion of the grammatical and logical difficulties presented by the sentence as it stands.

In the Assumption texts and the Tiberius A. iii *Life*, however, there is no functional need to make this distinction. At the same time, the divergent terminology of the two *Lives* confirms that the fact of corporal assumption itself, even a partial one, signified that the paradise evoked thereby is distinct from heaven. *Neorxnawong* is repeatedly used in the version that describes the assumption of the head, while the version that describes the spiritual assumption insists on using *heofene rice*. As Corpus 303 is the later manuscript,[58] it is not impossible that its author knew the Tiberius A. iii *Life*, and wished to avoid its association of paradise and corporal assumption. A more likely possibility is that the choice of terminology reflects later developments in Anglo-Saxon England concerning the intercessory role of martyrs within the hierarchy of paradise and heaven.[59]

There is, however, one place in the text of Corpus 303 which hints at a very different understanding of Margaret's end. Addressing her persecutors fairly early on in the narrative, Margaret declares that God grants all those who pray for him a place in *paradise eardingstow*, a phrase which the recent editors and translators render as 'dwelling in paradise'.[60] *Eardingstow* seems to represent a combination of *eardungstow*, one of the more frequent glosses on *tabernaculum*, and *earding*, which is not only a less frequent form of *eardung* but the very form which appears in the phrase *soðfæstra earding*, used within the Hatton 'Three Utterances' homily to describe the interim paradise.[61] It thus seems possible to read the phrase *paradise eardingstow* as 'paradise [that is] the tabernacle'. Furthermore, this reference can be seen as bringing together both the idea of *tabernacula iustorum/sanctorum*, as seen in most of the Latin 'Three Utterances' homilies, and the redefinition of this phrase as 'paradise' within their two Old English counterparts.

The Corpus 303 *Life* thus provides some acknowledgement of that very same paradise of good souls and the corporally assumed which it elsewhere tries to overwrite, although this acknowledgement does seem puzzling in the light of its otherwise scrupulous substitution of the kingdom of heaven for paradise. It is not impossible that the source of the Corpus 303 *Life* also had either *paradisus* or *tabernaculum* at this point,[62] and that the Old English

58 See Scragg, 'Corpus of Vernacular Homilies', pp. 243 and 248.

59 For which see below, pp. 127–32 and 184.

60 Clayton and Magennis, eds., *Old English Lives*, ch. 9, p. 158, with translation on p. 159.

61 See above, p. 53.

62 See Appendices 2 and 3, ch. 9, Clayton and Magennis, eds., *Old English Lives*, pp. 200 and 227 respectively.

author either retained it by mistake, or decided to let slip in a single reference to the interim paradise, especially as it was masked somewhat by the Latin *paradisus* rather than Old English *neorxnawang*. Whatever his reason, this exception seems to prove the rule that, with regard to the interim paradise, the Corpus 303 *Life* takes up a stance diametrically opposed to that seen in the Tiberius A. iii *Life*; the former's inexplicable deviation from its own practice is matched by the fact that this entire statement is absent from the latter.

HIERARCHIES BETWEEN PARADISE AND HEAVEN: THE 'THEBAN LEGEND' EXEMPLUM

That at least the scribe of each manuscript perceived the defining characteristic of the version he had chosen is confirmed in an unexpected way. The same scribe who copied the Margaret *Life* in Corpus 303 filled a blank space in the manuscript with an item rubricated *De inclusis*.[63] This brief passage contains a version of the so-called 'Theban Legend', a highly popular exemplum without any direct Latin source, which circulated widely in anonymous Old English homilies.[64] In the legend, a captive devil relates to an anchorite first the horrors of hell and then the wonders of heaven. Within the latter account, Corpus 303 includes a standard homiletic reference to Adam's expulsion from Eden:

> þurh deofles swicdom and Adames gemeleaste we wæren æt frumþe ut of Paradis ascofene and on þas wrecceworld asænd þe we nu on wuniað. þærfore nabbe we her nane fæstlice stede ne langsume æþele, ac we gelomlice geherað and dæghwamlice geseoð to hwam se eorðlice dæl and se mænnissce gecynde gewurðan sceal.[65]

However, this passage is a sanitised substitute for the wildly fanciful account of paradise which reappears in all other versions of the 'Theban

63 For the identification of the scribal hand, see Scragg, 'Corpus of Vernacular Homilies', p. 243, and also Clayton and Magennis, eds., *Old English Lives*, p. 93. The item is printed by Scragg under the siglum H as part of his apparatus to Vercelli IX in Scragg, ed., *Vercelli Homilies*.

64 For the textual interrelationships of these homilies, see Scragg, ed., *Vercelli Homilies*, pp. 151–7.

65 *Ibid.*, Apparatus to Vercelli IX (H), pp. 182–4: 'Through the devil's treachery and Adam's carelessness we were in the beginning cast out of paradise and sent into this world of exile, which we now dwell on. Therefore we have here neither a steadfast home nor a long-lasting native land, but we repeatedly hear and daily see what the earthly lot and the human race must needs become.'

Legend', and which conveys far better its basic idea: even if any man had free and continuous access to the pleasures of paradise, he would readily forfeit these for the joy of one night in heaven.

Even as Corpus 303's reworking of the 'Theban Legend' is aligned to its presentation of Margaret's spiritual assumption into heaven, so, coincidentally, does Tiberius A. iii preserve the original description of the Theban Legend's paradise alongside its account of Margaret's corporal assumption into paradise. In fact, although the Tiberius A. iii 'Theban Legend' appears to be, in Scragg's words, 'a late and brilliant reworking' of an earlier version found in Vercelli IX and Bodley 340 and 342, the description of paradise remains unchanged in all these homilies:[66]

> þeah þær sy eal smætegylden mor æt sunnan upgange on neorxnawange, and se oferhlifige ealle iorðan, and se man mote sittan swa dyre swa cynebearn ofer ðam gyldenan more, and hæbbe Salemanes wlite and wisdom, and him sie eal middangeard on geweald geseald, mid ðam gestreonum þe geond ealne middangeard syndon, and him sy ælce niht niwe bryd to bedde gelæd and sio hæbbe Iunone wlite, Saturnes dohtor, and ælc stan sy gylden, and ealle þa streamas hunige flowen, and him þonne ne sie ofer eorðan nænig wiðerbreca, and þeah þe him syn ealle sundercræftas and wuldorsangas in gesamnode, and þeah þe hiene ealle frefran, and him sien ealle swetnessa to gelædde mid þam fægerestan gestreonum, and him þonne sy singal sumor butan ælcre onwendednesse, and he mote alybban butan sare, and þonne gif he wære ær ane niht on heofona rices wuldre, þonne forlete he þ*æt* he ær on þyssum wuldre gelyfede, þe ic ær bisæde, ofer þ*æt* heofena rice þe he ær on wæs þa ane niht, and he eft ne mote to heofena rices wuldre.[67]

66 As reflected in Scragg's apparatus to Vercelli IX, which collates all the versions. It will thus be convenient to cite the passage from here rather than from the earliest edition of the 'Theban Legend' by Robinson, 'The Devil's Account of the Next World'. Robinson's contention that Tiberius A. iii preserves the earliest version of the 'Theban Legend' is refuted by Scragg, in 'The Devil's Account Revisited'.

67 Scragg, ed., *Vercelli Homilies*, pp. 180–2: 'Even if there were a mountain all of beaten gold at sunrise in paradise, and it towered over all the world, and a man might sit on that golden mountain as proudly as a royal child, and have Solomon's glory and wisdom, and the power of the entire world were given to him, with all the treasures which are there in the world, and each night a new bride were led to him to bed, and she would have the splendour of Juno, Saturn's daughter, and every stone were golden, and all the streams flowed with honey, and he would have no enemy upon the earth, and even though all special powers and glorious songs came together in him, and though they all comforted him, and all sweetness and joys were led to him, along with the fairest of treasures, and then perpetual summer without end were there for him, and he were to live without pain, yet if he had previously spent one night in the glory of the heavenly kingdom he would

As Charles Wright has examined in detail the sources underlying this description, I shall focus only on those aspects salient to this investigation.[68] The basic descriptive element, the mountain which towers over the earth could refer to the belief, variously dispersed, that the Garden of Eden was situated on a high mountain.[69] In Vercelli IX, however, paradise is not located on this mountain; rather, the mountain is itself located *in* paradise. Furthermore, its description as 'golden', repeated in the later comment, 'each stone may be golden', and the accent on treasures all recall the visions of *I Enoch*,[70] while the streams flowing with honey echo the *Visio*.[71] Into this tissue of apocryphal commonplaces are woven details of unchanging summer, and life free from illness or enmity, which belong to the *locus amoenus* topos of classical literature utilised by Christian Latin poets to describe Eden.[72] Like the classical *locus amoenus* and its Christian Latin counterpart, the paradise of the 'Theban Legend' is located at the eastern fringes of the world, as indicated by the reference to sunrise in *æt sunnan upgange*.

The hypothetical quality of the entire construct, which is emphasised through the continuous use of the subjunctive mode, perhaps mitigated its apocryphal content and ensured its survival in collections like the Vercelli Book, where all the other homiletic references to paradise are in the context of the standard patristic equation between Eden and the heavenly Jerusalem.[73] It is thus significant that Vercelli IX is the only version of the 'Theban Legend' which goes on to describe heaven in any detail, evoking eternal life shared with the Trinity and other celestial inhabitants. The typical homiletic conclusion which it thereby appends to the 'Theban

give up that which he experienced before in this world which I have described, for that heavenly kingdom where he had been previously, even if he could not [experience] again the glory of the heavenly kingdom.'

68 Wright, *Irish Tradition*, pp. 207–14.

69 For a useful summary of these views, see B. Bischoff and M. Lapidge, eds., *Biblical Commentaries from the Canterbury School of Theodore and Hadrian*, (Cambridge, 1994), pp. 440–1. See also Wright, *Irish Tradition*, p. 209, especially notes 110–12.

70 In fact, as Wright notes in *Irish Tradition*, p. 209, n. 110, the connection between Enoch, a golden mountain and treasures reappears in a twelfth-century text, the *Pantheon* of Geoffrey of Viterbo; this point is discussed in more detail below, p. 179.

71 See Sparks, ed., *The Apocryphal Old Testament*, p. 207, p. 213, and my citations of the *Visio*, pp. 20 and 22.

72 See Curtius, *European Literature and the Latin Middle Ages*, pp. 195–200. I return to the *locus amoenus* topos below, pp. 81 and 142.

73 See Scragg, ed., *Vercelli Homilies*, pp. 145, 147, 198, 223, 240, 273 and 317.

Legend' could be an attempt to bring it more in line with those concepts of paradise and heaven sanctioned by Church authority. The 'Theban Legend' was also perceived as unorthodox by the compiler of Cambridge, Corpus Christi College 198, who recopied a later version of Bodley 340 and 342, while replacing its 'Theban Legend' piece with a post-Epiphany homily from Ælfric's Second Series.[74]

Even as the 'Theban Legend' provides fascinating insight into alternative conceptions of the otherworld, therefore, the varied responses it evoked in homilists and compilers indicate a general awareness of the less than orthodox paradise it describes. As a random assortment of half-remembered biblical, apocryphal and poetic details, its *neorxnawang* was recognised as being different from Eden, as, for instance, by the compiler of Corpus 303. At the same time, the unwavering descriptive focus on paradise in all other versions of the 'Theban Legend' points to a greater interest in that location rather than in heaven, whose delights it ostensibly conveys. The comparison between paradise and heaven itself appears to derive force from not merely the inexpressibility topos, but also from a hierarchy between the two regions. A similar hierarchy informs the description of hell in the 'Theban Legend', where hideous tortures are described only to illustrate that those experienced in hell proper are unspeakably worse. The structure underlying the 'Theban Legend' thus resonates remarkably well with the system of parallels and contrasts undergirding the 'Three Utterances' homilies. There, it should be recalled, the good soul and the bad were both told by their respective psychopomps that their present experiences and sensations would be immeasurably magnified in heaven and hell. In fact, the Irish version of the 'Three Utterances' actually places the exemplum within a framework of the 'Theban Legend', testifying to their close thematic links.[75]

No such overt attempt to tap into a common cosmology is seen in the Old English homilies using the 'Theban Legend.' Its paradise appears to be terrestrial, while that of the 'Three Utterances' is celestial. The 'Theban Legend' neither makes temporal distinctions between paradise and heaven, nor describes it as a post-mortem abode. What is nevertheless important is its presentation of a paradise, qualitatively subordinated to heaven, descriptively distinct from both the heavenly Jerusalem and the Garden of Eden, potentially capable of merging with the interim paradise which housed

[74] *Ibid.*, p. 152. [75] Marstrander, 'Two Deaths', p. 120.

righteous souls until their transfer to heaven after Doomsday, and which could, on occasion, welcome those assumed in the body.

UNORTHODOX PARADISES: POPULAR SENSIBILITIES AND THE PLAY OF CULTURE

The vernacular texts examined in this chapter thus prove fertile ground for the flowering of those associations and significances which Ælfric tries to suppress through his uses of *neorxnawang*. Ælfric's own struggles with the concept of *rest* in Pope XI, or his modulation of Bede's image of a meadow in translating the Vision of Dryhthelm, appear as his attempts to straightjacket the same shifting hierarchies and fluid cosmologies which coexist within anonymous vernacular prose. We can now come to a somewhat different conclusion about the confusion and inconsistency about the interim which Gatch persistently ascribes to these prose writings, often to offset his own arguments for Ælfric's theologically sound lucidity.[76]

Recent historians of medieval and early modern culture have shown how a change in methodological perspective can coax historical records into surprising eloquence, and illuminate areas of enquiry often dismissed as opaque.[77] This discussion has aimed to provide a similarly alternative perspective on anonymous vernacular witnesses to the interim state, especially as compared to Ælfric's treatment of the same topic. Gatch rightly points out that the theological framework inherited from Augustine dictates Ælfric's presentation of the interim state.[78] But, as I have demonstrated in the previous chapter, it is the very desire to mould concepts of the interim state into this confining framework, or press them into the service of mass

[76] A line of thought clearly discernible in Gatch's various writings; see especially his 'Anonymous Old English Homilies', pp. 124–8, 146–51 and 160–4, where the words 'confusion', 'ambiguity' and 'inconsistency' are frequently employed to describe the mentality of the anonymous homilists. See also his repeated comparisons between Ælfric and the anonymous homilists in *Preaching and Theology*, especially pp. 57–65, and his remarks on early medieval interim eschatology in *Death: Meaning and Mortality in Christian Thought and Contemporary Culture* (New York, 1969), pp. 91–3.

[77] See C. Ginzburg, *The Cheese and the Worms*, trans. J. and A. Tedeschi (Harmondsworth, 1982), where he traces the development of unorthodoxy in a miller's world-view through the documents of his trial during the Inquisition, and E. Le Roy Ladurie, *Montaillou: Cathars and Catholics in a French Village, 1294–1324*, trans. B. Bray (Harmondsworth, 1980), which reconstructs from similar legal documents the shape taken by Cathar heresies within medieval village society.

[78] See above, p. 45, n. 98.

and intercession, that causes Ælfric to prevaricate and disguise the ideas of paradise that he covertly subscribes to.[79] Contrary to Gatch's opinion, Ælfric's ideas allow only that oblique glance into the interim condition that typifies what Peter Burke describes as the learned voice of self-imposed authority.[80] In contrast, the semantic polyvalency gained by the term *neorxnawang* in anonymous prose writings reveals that, freed from pressures to conform to or elucidate doctrine, its meanings splinter, multiply, and gain descriptive richness in unexpected ways. Often, such independent development of different meanings of *neorxnawang* is facilitated through their usefulness for particular genres. The 'Theban Legend' and the 'Three Utterances' exempla are used in homilies for the penitential season, while the concept of an abode for those assumed in the body appears in hagiographic narratives. Semantic polyvalency is further encouraged through such variegated emphasis on different aspects of paradise, and highlighted when different genres inhabit the same manuscript, as in Tiberius A. iii.

Whether the resultant agglomeration of ideas on the interim state is interpreted as inelegant cacophony or stimulating atonality depends, of course, on individual critical perspective. To return to Hall's words, with which I began this chapter, one can either castigate or celebrate the 'marvellously ambivalent' within popular sensibility.[81] Nevertheless, at the apparent risk of begging the question, we must now ask whether the opposition between the 'popular' and the 'learned' is entirely justified in the context of Old English literature.

It may be argued that, unlike later periods of European literary culture, Anglo-Saxon England yields too little information about audience, author or authorial intent for us to map confidently the extant writings onto cultural dichotomies such as 'popular' and 'learned'. Moreover, as such Cartesian dualities are largely a creation of modern scholarship, they would seem to be imposed only anachronistically on to the culture of pre-modern Europe. Here, however, Chartier's reinterpretation of such dichotomies in terms of ongoing processes of appropriation proves particularly apt.[82] If we consider the labels 'popular' and 'learned' not as *a priori* cultural categories, but rather as characterising different techniques of cultural reappropriation, then the texts examined here can be usefully described as 'popular' in their

[79] See above, pp. 45–8.

[80] Burke, *Popular Culture*, pp. 23–64 and 77–87. For a modification of this view, see below, p. 76.

[81] See above, n. 1.

[82] Chartier, 'Culture as Appropriation', pp. 229–53.

use of received ideas of the interim paradise, even as Ælfric can be seen as a 'learned user' of the same concepts. In fact, the form taken by these ideas in the anonymous prose writings, and the nature of the texts themselves, together help define the sensibility that we may, for want of a better word, call 'popular', but which is nevertheless shared, as what we may term 'common cultural stock', by monastic and clerical authors and the laity whom they address. In this context, it is interesting that the vernacular texts which articulate unorthodox ideas of paradise are composed for Rogationtide, the feast-days of immensely popular saints, and Lent – all occasions of communal participation in processions, feasting and fasting.[83] As is regularly observed in connection with similar socio-cultural events such as Carnival, these are the moments most susceptible to exchange of ideas between different social groups and for the breakdown of conceptual inhibitions.[84] In retrospect, it comes as no surprise that Ælfric chooses a Rogationtide homily to express his concerns against the *Visio*, even as he provides his own version of events for the Feast of the Assumption in both the First and the Second Series of Catholic Homilies.

Ultimately, Ælfric and the anonymous writers are both mediators between the clergy and the lay audience, differing in their divergent attitude towards models prescribed by ecclesiastical authority as grounded in patristic discourse. Ælfric sees himself as a member of this establishment, ideologically committed to impose and perpetuate these models.[85] Yet his own confusions mirror the Janus-faced position of such self-appointed guardians of orthodoxy and learning, whose continued participation in the very world-view they seek to correct has received increasing attention in recent scholarship.[86] At the other end of the scale are nameless clergy, composing and preaching texts that, through creative appropriation of those same

[83] For the Old English poetic representation of feasting, see now Magennis, *Images of Community*, pp. 35–59, and, for a more general medieval perspective, C. Walker Bynum, *Holy Feast and Holy Fast: The Religious Significance of Food to Medieval Women* (Berkeley and Los Angeles, CA, and London, 1987).

[84] For instance, see Burke, *Popular Culture*, pp. 179–204. The *locus classicus* of such discussions is, of course, M. Bakhtin's *Rabelais and his World*, trans. H. Iswolsky (Bloomington, IN, 1984).

[85] As demonstrated by Hill through her analysis of Ælfric's authorial persona, 'Reform and Resistance', pp. 18–20, which nonetheless stops short of explaining his frequent *failure* to live up to this persona.

[86] See Hall's overview of such scholarship in 'Introduction', pp. 15–16.

models, inhabit the ever-present space between prescription and belief. Moreover, as Chartier comments, 'the determination to impose cultural models does not guarantee the way in which they are received and used'.[87] Later homiletic compilations mix even more startling descriptions of the interim paradise with Ælfric's Rogationtide substitutes for the *Visio*, thereby rejecting his caveats regarding unorthodoxy as well as such reappropriation of his work.[88] A full discussion of these compilations and their significance as the final stage of a literary and cultural process must wait, however, until the concluding chapter of this book.

The final chapter also returns to what I have tried to highlight more generally here: how ideas about the interim paradise proliferate in anonymous prose texts to fulfil, in their unrestrained multifacetedness, the pragmatic and imaginative needs of author and audience alike, and to lend these texts an ingenuous candour quite the opposite of Ælfric's writings. In between these ends of the spectrum, other genres and authors from Anglo-Saxon England represent various compromises regarding the interim paradise, which enable us to refine and extend the observations made here. In the remainder of the book, we shall see how unconscious pressures of literary form couple with conscious ideological manoeuvres of writers, so that compromise itself becomes the vehicle of reappropriation. Accordingly, the next chapter reveals how the hierarchy between paradise and heaven encountered in the anonymous vernacular texts is schematised within the mediating spaces of early medieval monasticism and the otherworld of Anglo-Latin visions.

87 Chartier, 'Culture as Appropriation', p. 235.
88 See Hill, 'Reform and Resistance', pp. 20–46.

4

Description and compromise: Bede, Boniface and the interim paradise

> Transmission is not a term which should be understood in a mechanical sense. What was handed on were not merely books but ideas which, being alive, change and are changed in the historical worlds they successively penetrate.[1]

In the second chapter, I discussed Ælfric's response to the Vision of Dryhthelm in Bede's *Historia Ecclesiastica*. I now return to the Vision of Dryhthelm and another Anglo-Latin vision of the otherworld which preceded the *Historia Ecclesiastica* by just fourteen years – that experienced by a monk of the Monastery of Wenlock, and recounted by Boniface in a letter written to Abbess Eadburg in 716 or 717 AD.[2] Both visions describe a remarkably similar otherworld, in which two regions of punishment mirror two pleasant regions. This four-part otherworld is a more schematised and visually charged presentation of the same hierarchies between an interim paradise and heaven on the one hand, and two infernal regions on the other, which inform the 'Three Utterances' homilies from at least a century later.

In this chapter, I investigate how and why these visions incorporate the concept of an interim paradise into their four-part otherworld, and the reciprocal impact of the literary form of the vision on the interim paradise. This close interaction of theological and literary interests is achieved through several stages of reappropriation, or the transmission and transformation of ideas, which I recover through analysis of the framework, structure and imagery of both visionary otherworlds. The similarities and differences between the two visions raise questions about their interrelationship, even as they shed light on each author's technique of reappropriation.

The framework of each Anglo-Latin vision affiliates it to the visionary

[1] Hillgarth, 'Preface', *Visigothic Spain, Byzantium and the Irish*, p. viii.

[2] Tangl, ed., *Bonifatius-Briefe*, Letter 10, pp. 8–15. The evidence for the date is reviewed by Sims-Williams, *Religion and Literature*, pp. 243–4.

genre that had evolved in the preceding century.[3] At the same time, their four-fold otherworld results from the use of this genre to articulate late patristic discourse on interim eschatology, as best represented by Julian of Toledo's *Prognosticon futuri saeculi*, Book II. In the actual description of two pleasant regions, images from the otherworlds of Gregory the Great and the *Visio Sancti Pauli* are converted by Bede, and, less successfully, by Boniface, into ideological tools which bring together Church and laity through the mediation of the monastic world.

GREGORY'S PLEASANT MEADOW: A VISIONARY BEGINNING

In order to appreciate these developments within the Anglo-Latin visions, we first need to understand why vision literature suddenly flowered in early medieval Europe. It is generally assumed that the *Visio Sancti Pauli* and Gregory's *Dialogi* jointly influenced the birth of the medieval vision, although the formative processes are rarely traced in any detail.[4] I therefore begin by examining Gregory's visionary otherworld as a reaction to the *Visio Sancti Pauli*. As we noted in the second chapter, few patristic authors before Gregory had occupied themselves with the eschatology of the interim. This lack of interest is especially reflected in Augustine's desire to collapse the meanings of paradise, heaven and the bosom of Abraham, so that all three terms indicate an undifferentiated heavenly existence for all good souls before Doomsday. At the same time, a fuller statement on the interim period was provided by the increasingly popular *Visio Sancti Pauli*, with its rich descriptions of the graded punishments and rewards that awaited the ordinary soul after its death.

As early Christianity shaded into Late Antiquity, and the *parousia* appeared less and less imminent, the soul's condition between death and

3 Classic discussions of medieval visions are by Fritzsche, 'Die lateinischen Visionen des Mittelalters', Becker, *Medieval Visions of Heaven and Hell*, and Patch, *Other World*, pp. 80–133, but note my criticisms of this last work as a whole on p. 7. See also Dinzelbacher, *Vision und Visionsliteratur*, and n. 4 below.

4 As attested by the usual sequence of items in anthologies of medieval visions, e. g. Ciccarese's *Visioni dell' aldilà*, or Gardiner's *Visions of Heaven and Hell*, both of which begin with extracts from the *Visio* and from the *Dialogi*. Carozzi, in *Le voyage de l'âme*, p. 98, acknowledges that 'quant au contenue, le modèle [of the medieval vision] combinera la vision du soldat de Grégoire le Grand avec les données de l'*Apocalypse de Paul*', but does not show precisely how this process comes about.

Doomsday must have become the subject of increasing speculation. Towards the end of the sixth century, it appears that the Church could neither evade questions on the interim, nor ignore the particular answer provided by the *Visio Sancti Pauli*. A desire to clarify the 'official' position on interim eschatology and fill this gap in patristic exposition seems to have motivated Gregory's reports of otherworldly visions in Book IV of his *Dialogi*.[5] Gregory's reactionary attitude clearly emerges when we realise that each salient feature of his otherworld is a carefully chosen alternative to a corresponding aspect of the *Visio Sancti Pauli*. Although the *Visio Sancti Pauli* describes the fate of the ordinary righteous as well as that of patriarchs, martyrs and saints, we see everything through the distancing and non-participatory perspective of Paul, the privileged apostle. In contrast, Gregory's visions are presented as the near-death experiences of ordinary individuals who had apparently died but had later returned to life. He thereby provides a rationale behind each visionary's experiences and makes him actively engage with events in the otherworld. Thus, Stephen returns to life because the wrong Stephen had been summoned to death, and the vision granted to the nameless soldier is meant for his own edification and that of others.

The vision of the soldier also contains a highly significant description of the otherworld. The soldier first encounters a bridge spanning a river of pitch and flames. Souls try to cross this bridge, but some fall into the river in the process. This innovative use of the bridge motif, probably through the influence of Zoroastrianism, has been frequently noted in discussions of vision literature.[6] However, it has gone largely unnoticed that the bridge enables Gregory to place his otherworld on a horizontal plane. He thereby eliminates the soul's ascent through a series of heavens as implied in the *Visio Sancti Pauli*. In fact, the bridge as a joint means of linking and trial is simply a horizontal transformation of the ladder hung with instruments of torture, described in the third-century *Passio Perpetuae*.[7] Like the ladder in

[5] An overview of Gregory's interim eschatology is given by McClain, *The Doctrine of Heaven*, pp. 13–26.

[6] For example, by Dinzelbacher, *Vision und Visionsliteratur*, p. 114, Ciccarese, 'Le più antiche rappresentazioni del purgatorio', p. 41, and Carozzi, 'Géographie de l'au-delà', pp. 428–9. The Persian origins of the bridge and river motif are noted by Patch, *Other World*, pp. 8–9, and the motif itself discussed by Morgan, *Dante and the Medieval Other World*, pp. 34–37.

[7] J. A. Robinson, ed., *Passio Sanctarum Perpetuae et Felicitatis*, Texts and Studies 1 (Cambridge, 1891), pp. 66–8.

the *Passio Perpetuae*, Gregory's bridge leads to a shining meadow full of white-robed and rejoicing people, which is another early Christian motif. The white-robed people in the *Passio Perpetuae* signified, at least to Tertullian, the reunification of the martyr's soul and body immediately after death.[8] Although this millenarian interpretation does not seem to have been consciously propagated during the time Gregory wrote the *Dialogi*, the image of rejoicing people clad in white remained a convenient iconographic description of the blessed.

Tertullian had also interpreted the meadow seen by Perpetua as paradise, but to press this identification would have brought Gregory's otherworld a bit too close to the paradise of the third heaven in the *Visio Sancti Pauli*. Instead, we see Gregory striving for the opposite effect by describing golden mansions and houses situated on the meadow. The overall picture is thus that of a river, followed by an image from nature, on which is superimposed architectural imagery. Gregory thereby destroys the sequence of images found in the *Visio Sancti Pauli*, where the *terra repromissionis* is followed by the Acherusian Lake, and, finally, the City of Christ. Moreover, some houses on the meadow are discoloured by fumes from the river. This detail further blurs the boundaries of this otherworld and prevents the formation of discrete regions with particular characteristics. As a result, neither does the sequence of regions correspond explicitly to a gradation of rewards, nor are the regions of punishment clearly demarcated from those of reward.

In fact, Gregory's focus seems to be not so much the descriptive potential of these motifs as their contribution towards the punishment or reward of souls. This interest in what happens to the soul rather than where it happens, along with the desire to distance his accounts from the overly descriptive *Visio Sancti Pauli*, leads Gregory to avoid terms such as heaven, hell, or paradise. At the same time, he encourages a symbolic rather than a literal understanding of these images, as is seen in his answer to Peter's question:

> quid est hoc, quaeso te, quod in amoenis locis cuiusdam domus laterculis aureis aedificari videbatur? Ridiculum est ualde, si credimus quod in illa uita adhuc metallis talibus egeamus.[9]

[8] Waszink, ed., *De anima*, LV, ch. 4, p. 862.

[9] Vogüé, ed., *Dialogues*, IV, ch. 37, p. 134: 'Why is it, I ask you, that in these pleasant places one saw someone's house being built of gold bricks? It seems completely ridiculous to believe that in that life we should still need such metals.'

As Peter usually voices the doubts and queries of an ordinary reader, it is significant that Gregory inserts the phrase *locus amoenus* within a question from him. Gregory could have hardly been unaware of the connotations this phrase had gathered by his time. From the fourth century onwards, Christian Latin poets such as Avitus, Prudentius, Cyprianus and Lactantius frequently evoke the terrestrial paradise of Eden through the classical topos of the *locus amoenus*.[10] The phrase becomes associated not only with nature at its most agreeable, but with Eden and its features as enumerated in Genesis, namely, the four rivers, the tree of knowledge and of life, and the terrestrial location.

Yet, a meadow bordering a sulphurous river and dotted with golden mansions is hardly reminiscent of Eden. Gregory's reply to Peter shows that he deliberately uses this resonant phrase to convey what this meadow is *not*. If the *locus amoenus* is the dwelling-place of righteous souls, the *mansiones* symbolise alms-giving and other deeds of charity by which they earn their place in it (p. 134). Gregory thus indicates that his version of the *locus amoenus*, while depicted through a combination of horticultural and architectural images, is neither the Garden of Eden nor the heavenly Jerusalem, but the symbolic representation of an otherworld from whose actual description he thereby deflects attention.

It is highly probable that visions such as those reported in the *Dialogi* were already in circulation before Gregory decided to present them as alternatives to apocryphal descriptions such as the *Visio Sancti Pauli*.[11] His contemporary, Gregory of Tours, also recounts such visions in his *Historia Francorum*.[12] In one, Sunniulf, Abbot of Randau, sees a river of flames and a bridge leading to a big white house. Another vision describes how the severely ill monk Salvius ascends to heaven during a period of apparent death. The similarities of content and the common monastic environment of these two sets of visions indicate that the world of Christian learning was not unaware of the utility of these visions in shaping popular conceptions of the otherworld.

The spate of visions which emerge in the succeeding centuries from monasteries all over Merovingian and Visigothic Europe, has been used by several cultural historians to illustrate the appropriation of popular elements

[10] See below, p. 142. [11] As argued also by Le Goff, 'Learned and Popular Dimensions'.

[12] B. Krusch and W. Levison, eds., *Gregorii episcopi Turonensis libri Historiarum X*, MGH SRM 1 (Hannover, 1951), IV, ch. 33, p. 166 and VII, ch. 1, pp. 324–6.

by an originally learned tradition.[13] Given that we cannot recover what the visionaries themselves actually saw, the role of monastic redactors in shaping the thoughts of the laity becomes all-important, a process which has also to be viewed in terms of oral, folkloric discourse being transformed through the written word.[14] Whatever dialectical terminology (folkloric vs learned discourse; popular vs elite culture) we may wish to impose on this process, we should not forget that, throughout the Middle Ages, the vision of the otherworld remained a channel for the circulation of ideas *between* the lay and the monastic world. This awareness is particularly illuminating when we survey the modifications of Gregory's otherworld by succeeding authors.

SEVENTH-CENTURY DEVELOPMENTS OF GREGORY'S OTHERWORLD

In the seventh century, vision literature evolves into a self-conscious genre, which formulates its characteristic literary conventions by turning to motifs found in Gregory's vision of a soldier.[15] Features such as the near-death condition of the visionaries, which Gregory had deliberately utilised to rationalise their entry into the otherworld, become fossilised into the necessary topoi of a visionary account. Gregory's accompanying caveats are also increasingly ignored by successive visions. We thus see the reintroduction of older motifs deriving from apocryphal and possibly folkloric sources into the visionary genre, which gradually returns to describing the otherworld more fully.[16]

[13] See Schmitt, 'Les traditions folkloriques', Le Goff, 'Learned and Popular Dimensions', p. 22, and Gurevich, 'Popular and Scholarly Medieval Cultural Traditions', pp. 88–9.

[14] For a defence of these terms, see Schmitt, '"Religion populaire" et culture folklorique', but note also the caveats by Hall, 'Introduction', pp. 9–10. For the irrecoverability of the 'original' visions, see Morgan, *Dante and the Medieval Other World*, pp. 11–13, Sims-Williams, *Religion and Literature*, pp. 248–9, Holdsworth, 'Visions and Visionaries in the Middle Ages', p. 149, Dinzelbacher, *Vision*, p. 231, and Carozzi, 'Géographie de l'au-delà', p. 449.

[15] These topoi are inventoried by Morgan, *Dante and the Medieval Other World*, pp. 11–83. Their occurrence in individual visions may be traced through the synopses provided by Gardiner, in *Visions of Heaven and Hell* and *Sourcebook*.

[16] For a similar argument, although one using the terms 'popular' and 'learned' in a strictly opposed fashion, see Le Goff, 'Learned and Popular Dimensions', p. 34, and Ciccarese, 'La *Visio Baronti*', p. 52. For the elaboration of Gregory's motifs within succeeding visions, see Ciccarese, 'Rappresentazioni del purgatorio', p. 44; the consequent abuse of Gregory's authority is remarked upon by Carozzi, 'Géographie de l'au-delà', pp. 425–6.

The soul of the visionary again ascends through diverse regions of the otherworld, into which the blurred boundaries of Gregory's otherworld become once more differentiated. The more complex sights now seen entail an angelic guide for the soul, another feature of apocryphal accounts, and this further facilitates the description of aerial combat between angels and the demonic denizens of a zone below the otherworld proper.[17] Within the latter, the sequence of regions seen is usually places of darkness and horror followed by places of overpowering light and beauty. The visionary recognises and speaks to eminent people who are now dead, often to provide justification for being granted this sight of the otherworld, the authenticity of which is reiterated through various declarations. All these features are present in the major visions of the seventh and early eighth centuries, whose retrogressive trends bring the genre back to the point where Gregory had begun his process of sanitising the *Visio Sancti Pauli*.

Why was early medieval monasticism so receptive to the vision of the otherworld as to develop it into a recognisable literary form? The answer perhaps lies in the historical circumstances of the world outside the monastery. Barbarian hordes had devastated the world of Late Antiquity and its social structures inherited from the Roman Empire, even as Gregory was composing his *Dialogi*. Out of those ruins a new social system was being created, which sought continuity and stability by including the dead within the activities of the living.[18] This social climate was most conducive to the growth of a genre which not only described the realm of the dead but also illustrated how this realm may be repeatedly penetrated and linked to this world. Early medieval strategies to incorporate the dead into the society of the living regularly devolved around the Church. As Patrick Geary emphasises, this was not a one-way process whereby the Church seized power willy-nilly from the laity.[19] Rather, on viewing the Church as the main institution of social order, the laity more or less willingly

[17] For the aerial combat, see Amat, *Songes et visions*, pp. 376–8, Ntedika, *L'Evocation de l'au-delà*, pp. 259–60, and Stone, 'The Metamorphoses of Ezra', pp. 10–11; for the shaping of a vertically-oriented otherworld through the soul's ascent, see Carozzi, 'Géographie de l'au-delà', p. 477.

[18] As demonstrated, for instance, and in very different ways, by Bullough, 'Burial, Community and Belief in the Early Medieval West', Paxton, *Christianizing Death*, and Geary, *Living with the Dead*, especially pp. 77–92.

[19] For his explicit rejection of such a 'conspiracy theory', see Geary, *Living with the Dead*, p. 90.

transferred to it all powers of arbitration between the living and the dead. In this gradually developing system, the monastic world emerged as a two-tiered space of mediation. As a site for prayer as well as land ownership, it was the visible meeting-place for the interests of the Church and the surrounding lay world, while within its walls, individuals drawn from both worlds mingled and exchanged ideas.[20] Such 'acculturation', as Le Goff terms it, was further encouraged by the interchangeability of monastic and pastoral duties in pre-Reform Anglo-Saxon England, as in much of pre-Carolingian Europe.[21] The boundaries between clerical, monastic and lay worlds often met in the personae of individuals, making attempts to pigeon-hole the respective cultural attitudes of these worlds tricky, if not futile.

A literary index to these social developments may be seen within the increasing liminalities of the visionary genre. The visionary is no longer Gregory's soldier or man of business, but someone on the borderline between the monastic and lay worlds.[22] The visionary experience happens when he is between the states of life and death, and usually at dawn, which is the time between night and day. The changing character of the visionary is an especially interesting pointer to whom the visions claim to speak for. In reporting them, the monastic world articulates the voice not only of the laity, but increasingly, of those who straddle both socio-cultural spheres, be it the saint who reaches out from the monastery, or the lay brother who reaches in. Thus the vision of the otherworld becomes a powerful ideological weapon, and is progressively recognised and wielded as such by the monastic redactors. Fittingly, it is in the Carolingian Empire, with its

[20] See, in this context, B. Rosenwein, *To Be the Neighbor of Saint Peter: the Social Meaning of Cluny's Property, 909–1049* (Ithaca, NY, 1989), and note the comments of Le Goff, 'Learned and Popular Dimensions', p. 29: 'The tavern, and in particular, the public square have been cited as places of social and cultural exchange during the Middle Ages. One should also stress the role played by monasteries. The intercourse between the "educated" monks and the "uneducated" members of the monastic *familia*, including the equally "rustic" guests of the monastery, as well as the relationships between the monastic "elite" who belonged socially and culturally to the dominant strata of society (and exercised authority in the monastic setting), and "simple", semi-literate monks, must have provided an exceptionally favorable breeding-ground for these forms of acculturation.'

[21] See Constable, 'Monasteries, Rural Churches, and the *Cura animarum*', Amos, 'Monks and Pastoral Care in the Early Middle Ages', the various essays in Blair and Sharpe, eds., *Pastoral Care Before the Parish*, and Sims-Williams, *Religion and Literature*, pp. 115–43 and 144–76.

[22] Sims-Williams, *Religion and Literature*, at pp. 244–5.

flaunted partnership of religion and royalty, that the political power of the vision reaches its apogee.[23]

SEVENTH-CENTURY CONVENTIONS, EIGHTH-CENTURY REAPPROPRIATIONS

Poised in fine balance between the Merovingian and Carolingian visions are the two Anglo-Latin visions from the early eighth century. That Bede and Boniface were aware of the visionary genre and situated their reports within it is obvious from their use of the framework that had developed in preceding visions. The souls of both visionaries, the Monk of Wenlock and Dryhthelm, are led out of their bodies by angels during a period of grave illness and apparent death. They enter the otherworld, where they witness, in different regions, the rewards and punishments meted out to other souls. The angelic guides explain the meaning of these sights before the souls return to their bodies. The presence of this framework has led to the assumption that Boniface and Bede were familiar with preceding continental visions, even though actual evidence for the circulation of such visions in early eighth-century England is rather slender.[24]

The only visionary account that is definitely known at this time is that of the Irish monk Furseus in the *Vita Sancti Fursei*, written at Péronne around 657 AD; Bede not only includes excerpts from the Vision of Furseus in the *Historia Ecclesiastica* but also refers to the general availability of the entire *Vita*.[25] It is tempting to speculate that the *Visio Baronti*, a vision from Bourges which dates itself to c. 679 AD, could have also been known to Bede, especially as in several later Anglo-Saxon manuscripts, the *Vita Sancti*

[23] As discussed by Carozzi, *Voyage de l'âme*, pp. 319–68, Dutton, *The Politics of Dreaming*, Geary, *Living with the Dead*, pp. 50–76, and Levison, 'Die Politik in Jenseitsvisionen'. For the political aspects of an earlier, Merovingian vision, see Y. Hen, 'The Structure and Aims of the *Visio Baronti*', *JTS* ns 47 (1996), pp. 477–97.

[24] Cf. the remarks by Carozzi, 'Géographie de l'au-delà', p. 448, and Ciccarese, 'Rappresentazioni del purgatorio', p. 52.

[25] *HE*, III, ch. 19, pp. 271 and 33–5. The *Vita Sancti Fursei* is also used in B. Colgrave, ed., *Felix's Life of Guthlac* (Cambridge, 1956), p. 17 and pp. 179–80. The two visions of Furseus are omitted by B. Krusch, ed., 'Vita Virtutesque Fursei Abbatis Latiniacensis', MGH SRM 4 (Hanover and Leipzig, 1902), pp. 423–49, but Ciccarese edits the relevant portions in *Visioni*, pp. 190–225; see also her 'Le visioni di S. Fursa'.

Fursei travels together with the *Visio Baronti*.[26] However, neither is it certain when exactly the *Visio Baronti* was consigned to its present form, nor do we have clear evidence of its availability in Anglo-Saxon England before the ninth century.[27] There is, of course, the possibility of oral transmission, but this option cannot help us ascertain whether the conventions established by earlier visions reached eighth-century England in any form other than the *Vita Sancti Fursei*, and possibly the *Visio Baronti*. Nevertheless, the *Vita Sancti Fursei* exhibits all the conventions of the otherworldly vision which I have enumerated above. We can therefore turn to it, at least, as a definite source for the familiarity with these conventions which is demonstrated by both Bede and Boniface.

While Bede claims first-hand knowledge of the *Vita Sancti Fursei*, it is Boniface who reproduces these conventions more faithfully in his account of the Wenlock brother's vision. His soul is conducted high above the earth by angels. It first passes through a zone of fire, which recalls the four fires seen by Furseus. He is also confronted by a procession of his vices and virtues personified.[28] In the subsequent tour of the otherworld proper, the brother is first led through its different regions. On the return journey, he sees various contemporary personages, including Ceolred, King of Mercia, just as Furseus and Barontus meet senior monks from their own monasteries. Boniface, however, emphasises that Ceolred, unlike the monks seen by Furseus and Barontus, was alive at the time the vision was experienced.

Bede, in contrast, dispenses with all details that do not pertain to a straightforward tour of the otherworld. After an introductory paragraph on

26 See Levison's description of the manuscripts containing the *Visio Baronti*, in the introduction to his edition, 'Visio Baronti Monachi Longoretensis', pp. 372–5, esp. p. 374; the Vision of Dryhthelm and the Vision of the Monk of Wenlock also often travelled together with these items. In addition, Lapidge points to a late Anglo-Saxon booklist from Peterborough which has as item 51, 'Vita Sancti Fursei et Baronti visio'; see his 'Surviving Booklists', p. 78.

27 In fact, as an eleventh-century booklist from Worcester also includes 'Barontus' alongside Old English translations of various liturgical books, Lapidge suggests that 'an Old English translation of the *Visio Baronti* is [perhaps] in question, though no such translation has come down to us' ('Surviving Booklists', pp. 63–4).

28 The sources of these individual details have been dealt with by Sims-Williams, *Religion and Literature*, pp. 250–9, who concludes at p. 259: 'the first part of the vision shows the influence – probably at various levels and by various stages – of a number of Latin texts describing the experience of death or seeming-death'.

Dryhthelm's background, he launches straightaway into the narrative of the vision itself:

> Narrabat autem hoc modo quod uiderat: 'Lucidus', inquiens, 'aspectu et clarus erat indumento, qui me ducebat. Incedebamus autem tacentes, ut uidebatur mihi, contra ortum solis solstitialem.'[29]

This abrupt beginning glosses over the manner in which the soul exits the body, and enables Bede to omit the element of ascent. Dryhthelm and his guide walk (*incedebamus*, *ambularemus*), not rise, and the only direction mentioned emphasises horizontal movement. Later, continuing motion is signalled through changes in horizontal orientation, as they now move *quasi contra ortum solis brumalem*. This avoiding of ascent is seen even more clearly in Bede's curtailed account of the Vision of Furseus, which omits all details of the original description, except for the four fires seen by Furseus. Once in the otherworld, Dryhthelm, unlike Furseus, Barontus and the Monk of Wenlock, does not meet anyone he knows.

Thus, while both Bede and Boniface subscribe to the framework of a typical vision, Bede eschews most of the features which are post-Gregorian additions. As the truncated yet recognisable framework of Dryhthelm's vision reveals, Bede wishes to weed out the unorthodoxies that had accumulated within the visionary genre and restore to it Gregory's original ideas. But if Bede is an editor, Boniface is a synthesiser of all available conventions. His use of the framework of the vision points to a desire both to clarify Gregory's laconic and unclear description of the otherworld, and to reorganise the untidy elaborations of the Merovingian visions.

INTERNAL SYMMETRIES: THE FOUR-FOLD OTHERWORLDS OF BEDE AND BONIFACE

Although this difference in motivation emerges more sharply in the two descriptions of the otherworld, it has similar consequences for their overall geography. Both Bede and Boniface replace the cluttered otherworlds of earlier visions with a four-part structure, symmetrically organised into two penal and two pleasant regions. According to Boniface, the Monk of

[29] *HE*, V, ch. 12, p. 488: 'He described what he had seen in this way: "I was guided by a man of shining countenance and wearing bright robes. We went in silence in what appeared to be the direction of the rising sun at the summer solstice"' (trans. Colgrave and Mynors).

Wenlock first arrives at a place of darkness and horror.[30] Fiery pits belch forth flames, through which fly lamenting and screaming souls. Below the pits, *quasi in inferno inferiori*, the Wenlock brother hears an even greater lamenting of souls, the intensity of which is impossible to describe. He next enters a place of wonderful pleasantness and fragrance, full of rejoicing people. Beyond it, separated by a fiery river of pitch, he can see shining walls. Souls hurry across a bridge over the river, some falling in, but all emerging to complete the journey. Dryhthelm's itinerary is similar. He enters a broad and vast valley full of darkness and flames, in which souls are undergoing hideous tortures. Through the mouth of a great pit he discerns a lower region of worse horrors. Mysteriously traversing a great wall, he arrives in a shining meadow, where people in white rejoice. Beyond, he perceives an even more marvellous place, but is led back to the meadow before he can enter it.

Both visions emphasise the internal symmetries of the otherworld. The first region of punishment and the first pleasant region are accessible to the visionary, unlike the two other regions, while a spatial symmetry operates in the first two regions each being anterior to the inaccessible region. These symmetries are perpetuated through the functions of the four places, which the Anglo-Latin visions, unlike their predecessors, explicitly discuss. According to the angel accompanying the Monk of Wenlock, the souls dwelling in the region below the pits will suffer forever. However, those in the pits will suffer only till Doomsday, when they shall be granted reprieve and admitted to the eternal rest of heaven. The everlasting torture of the second region of punishment is paralleled by the everlasting joy of the souls who cross the bridge into the region of the shining walls, which is identified as the heavenly Jerusalem. The first pleasant region, however, is simply defined as *famosus Dei paradisus* before the narrative turns to the river and the bridge. The souls crossing the bridge from paradise to the heavenly city are described as venial sinners who need to be cleansed before they can enter the heavenly city.

Thus, Boniface presents a pair of hierarchies, where a provisional and a permanent hell are matched by the interim paradise and the everlasting heavenly city. He also attempts to fit four categories of souls onto this scheme. However, he fails to explain the basis on which these distinctions

[30] The following analysis summarises Tangl, ed., *Bonifatius-Briefe*, Letter 10, pp. 11–12, and *HE*, V, ch. 12, pp. 488–94.

are made, why some souls suffer less than others, and what differentiates their sins from the sins of those retained in the pits until Doomsday. These obscurities are absent from the Vision of Dryhthelm. By separating the description of the regions from the explanation of their functions, Bede lets the regions visited by Dryhthelm unfold in one sequence, which is punctuated by two terse comments only. Dryhthelm wonders, first, whether the dark valley he first enters is hell, and, later, whether the shining meadow is heaven. The angel, reading his thoughts, answers, first, *non enim hic infernus esse est ille quem putas*, (p. 490) and, subsequently, *non hoc est regnum caelorum quod autumas* (p. 492). These stylised definitions are both more evasive than Boniface's, and more effective in communicating the internal symmetries of the otherworld.

Likewise, the function of each region, and the relation of the part to the whole, are better conveyed through the single explanatory monologue delivered by the angel on Dryhthelm's return journey (p. 494). On returning to the meadow, Dryhthelm is told that the dark valley is a place of temporary punishment for the *animae examinandae et castigandae.* As in the Wenlock Vision, these souls too remain here till Doomsday, but Bede clarifies the reasons for their temporary detention: they were venial sinners who had repented and confessed before dying. In contrast, souls can never leave the flaming pit, which is the *os gehennae.* The wonderful place inaccessible to Dryhthelm is the kingdom of heaven, where the souls of those *in omni uerbo et opere et cogitatione perfecti* enter immediately and permanently after their death. The flowery meadow, however, houses those who are nearly perfect:

> ipse est, in quo recipiuntur animae eorum qui in bonis quidem operibus de corpore exeunt; non tamen sunt tantae perfectionis, ut in regnum caelorum statim mereantur introduci; qui tamen omnes in die iudicii ad uisionem Christi et gaudia regni caelestis intrabunt.[31]

Admittance into the meadow serves as their reward, while its inferiority to the heavenly kingdom punishes them for slight imperfections.

[31] *HE*, V, ch. 12, p. 494: '[This] is where the souls are received of those who depart from the body practising good works, but they are not in such a state of perfection that they deserve to be received immediately into the kingdom of heaven; nevertheless all of them at the day of judgement will be received immediately into the presence of Christ and the joys of the heavenly kingdom' (trans. Colgrave and Mynors).

CONCEIVING OF FOUR PLACES: BEDE, BONIFACE AND THE *PROGNOSTICON*

If Boniface is the first author to describe a visionary otherworld comprising four regions, including an interim paradise, Bede first successfully expresses through this structure the interim fate of four categories of souls: the perfect, the not completely perfect, the bad and the not completely bad. Collectively, both writers represent the first use of the visionary genre to regularise a correspondence between four places and the interim fate of four categories of souls. This new development immediately raises a number of questions. Why do both Anglo-Latin visions, but none earlier than them, divide the otherworld into two symmetrical zones, further subdivided into two penal and two pleasant regions? From where do Boniface and Bede derive this structure, and do they derive it independently?

Given the vast body of scholarship on early medieval visions, it is somewhat surprising that these issues have hardly been addressed before.[32] There seem to be two reasons for this oversight. Firstly, most such studies examine these visions as precursors of the concept of purgatory within the tripartite otherworld as most influentially described by Le Goff.[33] Le Goff's insistence on the idea of a tripartite division being a conceptual breakthrough of the twelfth century leads him to posit three-fold otherworlds in twelfth-century vision literature, which actually persist with variations on the four-fold theme.[34] Even while exposing the fallacies of this argument, however, critics have continued to accept the four-fold division of souls which Le Goff imposes on Augustine's statement from *Enchiridion*.[35]

32 See, most recently, Carozzi's otherwise detailed discussion of the Anglo-Latin visions in *Voyage de l'âme*, pp. 194–253. An exception is Sims-Williams, whose suggested relationship between the two visions in *Religion and Literature*, pp. 259–67, is discussed below, pp. 95–7.

33 An attitude best illustrated by Le Goff himself in his *Birth of Purgatory*, pp. 112–16, where the Anglo-Latin visions are treated in a markedly cursory fashion. Gurevich's criticisms in 'Notes in the Margin', especially pp. 80–7, are directed against Le Goff's neglect of visionary material, so that Gurevich's own discussion of vision literature in *Medieval Popular Culture*, pp. 104–52, replicates the focus on the penal regions at the expense of the pleasant.

34 As persuasively argued by Easting, 'Purgatory and the Earthly Paradise', pp. 24–34.

35 Thus, while dismantling Le Goff's interpretations of the *Tractatus de purgatorio Sancti Patricii* as presenting a four-fold otherworld, Easting declares, '[f]ar from being rejected, Augustine's four-fold division survives in the *Tractatus*' ('Purgatory and the Earthly Paradise', p. 31); similarly, Watkins, 'Doctrine, Politics and Purgation', p. 229, declares, '[i]n Ireland the four-fold *post-mortem* division of souls, as conceived by Augustine, had been embraced'.

In chapter 2, I demonstrated that this statement represents merely one of many stances taken by Augustine on this issue.[36] To isolate the views he expresses in one part of the *Enchiridion* and present it as a categorical statement is in itself misleading; but even more so is Le Goff's contention that Augustine divides souls into four categories within this passage.[37] This claim allows him to see Bede and Boniface as passively reproducing Augustine's four-fold division in their otherworlds, which twelfth-century thinkers subsequently contract into three. This monolithic view of a millennium of speculation on the subject undoubtedly enhances his own presentation of the twelfth century as the crucible of purgatorial thought. As we have seen, however, Augustine's words seem not to bear out Le Goff's interpretation. If any division of souls emerges through his characteristic evasiveness, it is a three-fold one of *boni*, *mali* and *non ualde boni*/*non ualde mali*, with no clear separation of the latter two groups.[38] The innovators are, therefore, Bede and Boniface, who expand Augustine's three original categories of *boni*, *mali* and *non ualde boni* into four and map them onto a definite geography of the otherworld.

The second reason why the origin of this four-fold structure has not been given the attention it deserves is the frequent but usually unsubstantiated assumption that the Anglo-Latin visions were influenced by Celtic conceptions of the otherworld.[39] As St John Seymour declared:

> Drithelm [*sic*] was a Northumbrian, living in a kingdom where the Celtic Church was very strongly entrenched. Furthermore, Wenlock was a Celtic foundation. May it not be therefore that in these two visions we have preserved for us specimens of the eschatology of the English Celtic Church at about the end of the seventh century, an eschatology which was now in full agreement with that of the Anglo-Saxon Church . . . [?] If this be so, it would appear that belief in a division of the Other-World into Purgatory, Hell, Paradise and Heaven . . . was first formally put forward by the Celtic Church in England.[40]

It is beyond the scope of this discussion to debate the full implications of this early but still influential point of view. A few general points need,

36 See above, pp. 28–30.

37 *Birth of Purgatory*, p. 115. See, in this connection, the observations of Gurevich, 'Notes in the Margin', p. 87.

38 As I have analysed above, p. 29.

39 For examples of this tendency, see Le Goff himself, *Birth of Purgatory*, pp. 108–10.

40 Seymour, *Irish Visions of the Otherworld*, pp. 58–9; see also his 'Eschatology of the Early Irish Church', p. 195.

however, to be emphasised. Firstly, more recent scholarship has shown that the concept of the 'Celtic otherworld', or even the 'Irish otherworld' is by no means unproblematic, as is the exact reference of both the terms 'Celtic' and 'otherworld'.[41] Secondly, different Celtic writings variously locate this 'otherworld' in, under or across the sea, in a cave or under a mountain.[42] Thirdly, the genres of the *echtrae* (otherworldly journey) and *immram* (voyage-tale) which give expression to these conceptions in Old Irish and Hiberno-Latin literature present their own difficulties of terminology, cross-influence and dating.[43]

Some of the similarities between the Anglo-Latin visions and the pre-tenth-century Irish or Hiberno-Latin material can be explained as independent use of an influential and widely known text. An obvious example here is the *Navigatio Sancti Brendani*, whose author describes the reward awaiting the *successores* of Brendan as the *terra repromissionis sanctorum*,[44] a term which recalls the *Visio Sancti Pauli*.[45] It can also be argued that influences between the cultures worked both ways. Therefore, while the strong spatial element of these voyages may be seen as having influenced the spatialisation of the Anglo-Latin visions, the Anglo-Latin visions may equally well have helped streamline the different loci of the Irish voyages into structures approaching their four-fold otherworlds. The only influential Irish 'vision' proper from before the twelfth century, *Fís Adamnán*, does seem to subscribe to a four-fold division of souls, which, however, coexists alongside various other eschatological schemes, and is far less clear-cut than Seymour would have us believe.[46] Seymour isolated the four-fold scheme through some remarkable surgery that he performed on *Fís Adamnán*, but, just as we can no longer accept those results,[47] so we must reject what seems

41 As most persuasively demonstrated by Sims-Williams, 'Some Celtic Otherworld Terms'.

42 *Ibid.*, and Carey, 'The Otherworld in Irish Tradition'.

43 See Dumville, '*Echtrae* and *Immram*', and 'Two Approaches'.

44 See C. Selmer, ed., *Navigatio Sancti Brendani abbatis: from Early Latin Manuscripts*, University of Notre Dame Publications in Mediaeval Studies 16 (Notre Dame, IN, 1959), pp. 78–81, chs. 27–8. For the identity of these *successores*, see Dumville, 'Two Approaches', pp. 90–2.

45 In this context, see G. Orlandi, ed., *Navigatio Sancti Brendani*, I, pp. 124–9.

46 See Seymour, *Irish Visions*, p. 31 and *passim*.

47 As Dumville has demonstrated in '*Fís Adamnán*'; see also his comments on p. 73 regarding the 'difficulties in the way of accepting Seymour's argument that the text makes a four-fold division of souls'.

to have been one of his underlying premises: the desire to see the Celtic Church as the fountainhead of Insular interim eschatology. It is not impossible that the Irish author had learnt of the four-fold scheme after Bede and Boniface had propagated it, and woven it into his own eclectic eschatology.[48]

The force of these various assertions about the Anglo-Latin visions has, in fact, deflected critical attention from the striking similarity which exists between their four-fold otherworlds and a late patristic work which contains precisely these four divisions: the *Prognosticon* of Julian of Toledo. In an earlier chapter,[49] I noted that Julian of Toledo opens the second book of his *Prognosticon* by citing Isidore's belief in two paradises, the earthly Garden of Eden, and a celestial interim paradise which is equated to the paradise of the Good Thief (ch. 1). Referring to a lost work by Julianus Pomerius, Julian then clarifies that the interim paradise is reserved for those souls who are not completely perfect and must therefore wait until Doomsday to enter the kingdom of heaven (chs. 2, 10). He thus uses Isidore's two paradises to introduce an additional contrast between paradise and heaven: the first, an interim location for the righteous, and the second, a permanent abode for the completely perfect. He further states that the bosom of Abraham is sometimes interpreted as paradise, but then cites Augustine's arguments for it being an upper region of hell before the Harrowing (chs. 3, 4). Julian asserts thereby that there are two hells as well, with the second, more infernal one situated below the first. In support of these ideas, he looks towards Augustine's rather vague statement in the *Enchiridion* that, during the interim, souls are housed in receptacles according to their actions (ch. 9).

In *Prognosticon* II we see how stray comments culled from preceding centuries of patristic exposition can be assembled into a seemingly complete statement on the interim state. Nevertheless, these ideas are still held in solution here, and it is in the Anglo-Latin visions that they first crystallise into a coherent visionary landscape. This, then, is one of the main contributions of Boniface and Bede. Through the visionary genre, they give a single, cohesive form to contemporary, late-patristic ideas on the interim state, and make these ideas more accessible to monastic and lay audiences alike. Yet, how necessary is it to postulate this intervening step of the

[48] See below, p. 180. [49] See above, p. 44.

Prognosticon? While there is no manuscript evidence for its presence in early eighth-century England, Augustine and Isidore *were* widely known.[50] Bede and Boniface could have independently put together their respective comments on two paradises and two hells in exactly the same manner as did Julian,[51] qualifying independently the nature of the righteous in the interim paradise. The *Prognosticon* could simply have been a parallel reaction to the same stimuli that triggered the structure of each Anglo-Latin vision.

This train of reasoning, while perfectly safe and satisfactory, nevertheless ignores the remarkable correspondence between the otherworld of the Anglo-Latin visions and the delicate balance of ideas in the *Prognosticon*, and the possibilities this opens up for early knowledge of the *Prognosticon* in Anglo-Saxon England. Cultural links between Spain and Ireland, both on the Western periphery of the medieval world, have long provided a topic for scholarly speculation.[52] While many earlier assertions made thereby have since been abandoned,[53] it is nevertheless generally accepted that between Spain and Insular centres there did exist a channel of rapid transmission of manuscripts and ideas. Indeed, commentators on the dissemination of Julian's works have relied on this assumption.[54] Thus, Hillgarth sees the numerous ninth-century copies of the *Prognosticon* in continental monasteries such as Reichenau and Bobbio as indications of the important Insular role in its early transmission, and attributes the absence of early manuscripts from Anglo-Saxon England to its status as a well-used and constantly recopied work.[55]

As the *Prognosticon* was written c. 688 AD, the rapid movement of manuscripts from Spain to Insular centres could have ensured its arrival in England in thirty years' time, only a few decades before Alcuin refers, sig-

[50] See Hillgarth, ed., *Iuliani opera*, pp. xxv–xxxvi.

[51] As observed more generally by Hillgarth, 'St Julian in the Middle Ages', p. 21.

[52] See, for instance, Bishop, 'Liturgical Note', pp. 277–8, De Bruyne, 'Fragments retrouvés', 318–35, and Dumville, 'Biblical Apocrypha and the Early Irish'.

[53] Cf. Wright's recent comments in *Irish Tradition*, p. 22, n. 84, and pp. 64–5; earlier objections to De Bruyne's 'series of over-ambitious proposals' were voiced by H. Chadwick, *Priscillian of Avila* (Oxford, 1976), p. 190.

[54] See Beeson, '*Ars Grammatica*', pp. 50 and 70, and Hillgarth, 'St Julian in the Middle Ages', pp. 18–19.

[55] Hillgarth, ed., *Iuliani opera*, pp. xlii–iii: 'Here, as so often, it would seem that the losses sustained by Norman or Muslim destruction of monastic libraries are less grave than those we have suffered from the excellent intentions of the Carolingian librarians.'

nificantly enough, to its citation of Julianus Pomerius.[56] Both Bede and Aldhelm knew Julian's *Ars Grammatica*.[57] It is not unimaginable that the *Prognosticon*, too, should have made its way to both southwest England and Northumbria. If we consider the four-fold structure as deriving from the *Prognosticon*, then its earliest appearance in the Anglo-Latin visions is also explained. Earlier visions did not have access to the *Prognosticon*, either because it was not yet written or because it had not yet been transmitted to Merovingian centres. From the ninth century onwards, both the *Prognosticon* and the Anglo-Latin visions were widely disseminated in continental monasteries. There, their simultaneous presence could have only validated further the four-fold otherworld.

Did Boniface and Bede know and use the *Prognosticon* perhaps almost simultaneously but independently, or did Boniface, as author of the earlier version, learn of it first? The historical circumstances would support either possibility. Boniface knew Aldhelm, who would have made as good use of the *Prognosticon* as the *Ars Grammatica*.[58] In Northumbria, the libraries of Monkwearmouth and Jarrow, as well as the contact with Irish monks and travellers, would have provided an equally receptive context for its transmission.[59] Yet, it seems somewhat improbable that Bede and Boniface should have independently turned to the *Prognosticon* to deviate so strikingly and similarly from earlier versions, and within a few years of each other. One approach to this problem is that of Sims-Williams's. Taking up Bede's statement that a monk named Hæmgisl had elicited information about Dryhthelm's out-of-body experiences, he suggests that Hæmgisl's version circulated in the south and influenced the Monk of Wenlock some years before Bede reported it in the *Historia Ecclesiastica*.[60]

Nevertheless, apart from Bede's statement, we have no other information about an earlier version of the Vision of Dryhthelm. Moreover, this

[56] Hillgarth, ed., *Iuliani opera*, p. xlii, n. 7. For the date of the *Prognosticon*, see Hillgarth, 'St Julian in the Middle Ages', p. 9.

[57] See Beeson, '*Ars Grammatica*', pp. 56–67, and also pp. 67–9 for his argument that the Insular tradition of the *Ars Grammatica* started in Britain rather than Ireland.

[58] According to Beeson, '*Ars Grammatica*', p. 69, Boniface could have personally carried the *Ars Grammatica* to Fulda.

[59] For the contacts between the Irish and the Anglo-Saxons, see Chadwick, *Celt and Saxon*, and Hughes, 'Evidence for Contacts'; for a summary of the scholarship on this subject, see Wright, *Irish Tradition*, pp. 1–2.

[60] Sims-Williams, *Religion and Literature*, p. 264; see *HE*, V, ch. 12, p. 496.

statement itself can be read as a literary topos – the standard link with external reality that the typical vision provides to vouchsafe its truth-value and legitimise its dissemination. Boniface, too, includes such links; angels instruct the Wenlock brother to relate the vision to an ascetic named Begga, and Boniface says that he received reports of the vision both from the Abbess Hildelith of Barking, and from the visionary himself. However, Boniface fails to connect logically the supposed versions of Begga, Hildelith and the Wenlock brother, while Bede presents a single, clean line of transmission from Dryhthelm to Hæmgisl, still alive at the time of writing, and then to himself.

Even if we do consider Bede's words to be stamped with his historiographic authority, and accept, with Sims-Williams, that an earlier version of Hæmgisl's account had influenced the Monk of Wenlock, this relationship remains on what Sims-Williams himself calls the 'irrecoverable' level of what the visionaries saw.[61] It is more fruitful, perhaps, to consider the shape gained by these experiences through being consigned to writing, which, in this case, is the four-fold structure recalling the *Prognosticon*. As the *Historia Ecclesiastica* was completed in 733 AD, well over a decade after Boniface reported the Wenlock Vision, on the written level at least the most logical direction of influence seems to be from Boniface to Bede. In fact, Boniface's personal acquaintance with Bede's works dates from only after 746–7 AD, when he wrote to Ecgberht of York and to Monkwearmouth and Jarrow, asking to be sent some of Bede's writings.[62]

Other historical circumstances would favour the suggestion that Bede knew of the Wenlock Vision. Bede's major informant for West-Saxon and Mercian material was Pehthelm, Bishop of Whithorn.[63] Pehthelm and Boniface both belonged to Aldhelm's circle, and a letter from Boniface to Pehthelm, dated 735 AD, demonstrates the cordial relations that existed between the two.[64] In the *Historia Ecclesiastica*, moreover, two miracle stories are ascribed to Pehthelm, both in Book V (chs. 13 and 18). The first

[61] Sims-Williams, *Religion and Literature*, p. 248. For Bede's historiographic methods, see Levison, 'Bede as Historian', Colgrave, 'Bede's Miracle Stories', Ward, 'Miracles and History', Barnard, 'Bede and Eusebius', and Ray, 'Bede, the Exegete'.

[62] Tangl, ed., *Bonifatius-Briefe*, Letters 75 and 76, pp. 156–9.

[63] See Whitelock, 'Bede and his Teachers and Friends', p. 31.

[64] See Tangl, ed., *Bonifatius-Briefe*, Letter 32, pp. 55–6, where Boniface asks Pehthelm's legal advice, and reports that he is sending him 'a fleecy and colourfully-spotted towel to wipe his feet with'.

is an account of a vision seen by Coenred, King of Mercia, in which angels and devils reveal to him the record of his good and bad deeds. It is not improbable that Pehthelm could have also related to Bede the vision of the Monk of Wenlock, which contains an account of the fate of another Mercian king, Ceolred, Coenred's successor. Significantly, the vision of Coenred immediately follows that of Dryhthelm.

In light of these assorted facts and trends, the following hypothesis seems not unattractive: Pehthelm related to Bede a version of the Wenlock Vision, which Boniface, influenced by ideas from Julian, had recorded. Bede recognised in it the underlying structure inspired by the *Prognosticon*, which he had meanwhile also learnt of, possibly through Irish intermediaries. He cast in a similar mould the locally known visionary experience of Dryhthelm. Among the changes he made was the clarification of the categories of souls, for which he turned to Augustine's division of souls in the *Enchiridion*. This sequence of events would also explain the rather puzzling omission of Boniface's name from the *Historia Ecclesiastica*, which nevertheless speaks of the missionary activities of his close associates Willibrord and Wilfrid.[65] Bede perhaps did not wish to damage his own credibility by laying open to view an obvious influence, and one which, as we shall soon discover, contained elements that he seems not to have quite approved of.

This hypothesis accounts for the differences as well as the similarities between the two visions, which cumulatively suggest that Bede not only knew but also consciously improved on Boniface's version of the otherworld. An analysis of their descriptive techniques confirms both this dependence and their divergent approaches towards the ideas conveyed in the *Prognosticon* – a divergence already seen in their respective uses of the visionary framework.

VISUALISING FOUR PLACES: BEDE, BONIFACE AND GREGORY'S MEADOW

Both Boniface and Bede needed a suitable descriptive form for the two pairs of locations in the *Prognosticon*. As we have seen, the narrative movement of the visions proved highly useful for this purpose. The visionary's progress through the zone of punishment and through that of reward presents them as coexisting in one spatio-temporal continuum, while setting

[65] See Wormald, 'Bede and Benedict Biscop', p. 146.

out the spatial relationship between the two regions comprising each zone. The unfolding narrative also confers a temporal distinction between each first and second region, as the visionaries have to cross first the interim regions before being able to discern the permanent ones. Their movement enacts that of the souls which belong to one of the provisional categories and who have to wait in the interim regions until the final decisions of Doomsday. In the act of articulation, the vision binds the still-separate ideas of the *Prognosticon* into a single narrative space and converts the abstract into the physical and visual, becoming thereby the earliest literary witnesses to the spatio-temporal distinctions between the four regions.

To express the qualitative hierarchies between the two pairs of regions, both authors turn to the descriptive repertoire which the visionary genre had developed over the past two centuries.[66] In their choice of motif and descriptive style, however, they diverge. Boniface employs phrases and definitions with immediate visual impact and strong semantic content, employing what could be termed an 'iconographic' style. Bede, in contrast, is more of an 'impressionist', concentrating on sensuous elements to convey an illusion of verisimilitude. He spells out the meaning of what he presents, but leaves the reader to put together the definition.

This difference is marked in their respective evocations of the pleasant regions. The Monk of Wenlock sees a 'mire amoenitatis locum, in quo pulcherrimorum hominum gloriosa multitudo miro laetabatur gaudio'.[67] This description recalls Gregory's 'prata, atque uirentia odoriferis herbarum floribus exornata, in quibus albatorum hominum conuenticula esse uidebantur'.[68] However, Boniface omits the details of the flowers, the light, and the white robes of the blessed, focusing instead on the emotional dimensions of the meadow's beauty. By thus deleting the sensory elements found in Gregory's description, he orients the Wenlock Vision towards the blessedness of the souls rather than the appearance of the meadow. For instance, the lone sensory detail of the fragrance permeating the meadow derives

[66] For these motifs, see Morgan, *Dante and the Medieval Other World*, pp. 11–50.

[67] Tangl, ed., *Bonifatius-Briefe*, Letter 10, p. 11: 'a place of wonderful pleasantness in which a glorious multitude of the most beautiful men rejoiced with exceeding joy'.

[68] Vogüé, ed., *Dialogues*, IV, ch. 37, p. 130: 'flourishing meadows adorned with fragrant flowers of herbs, in which could be seen companies of white-robed men'.

from the blessed, while for Gregory, the souls are delighted *by* the fragrance.[69]

Boniface conveys the natural beauty of the meadow by introducing it as a *mire locus amoenitatis*. In this echo of the *locus amoenus* topos, he consciously places this region within a long tradition of literary landscapes. We have seen how Gregory had used the phrase *locus amoenus* to explain the symbolic meaning of the meadow and the mansions. Later visions routinely incorporate this phrase within their otherworlds, where, losing the symbolic value Gregory had preferred, it becomes instead a descriptive cliché for natural imagery. As a celestial paradise populated in the present by rejoicing souls, Boniface's *locus amoenitatis* is no more reminiscent of the paradise of Eden than is Gregory's meadow. Unlike Gregory, however, Boniface actually defines the *locus amoenitatis* as the paradise of God. Before the Wenlock Vision, the noun *paradisus* appears only twice in a visionary context, in the *Visio Baronti* and the Vision of Valerius, Abbot of Bierzo in Spain.[70] Only in the latter is it also called a *locus amoenissimus*. Here, the elaborate catalogue of flowers recalls the descriptions of Eden in Christian Latin poetry, as, for instance, that given in the *Cathemerinon* of Prudentius. On the other hand, the four gates of the *paradisus* seen by Barontus are descriptively reminiscent of the heavenly Jerusalem of Revelation.[71]

The images used by Boniface give his *paradisus* a significance somewhat different from these visions. The otherworld of the *Visio Baronti* uses only architectural images, while that of the Vision of Valerius uses natural imagery only. But beyond paradise in the Wenlock Vision, and inaccessible to the visionary, lie the shining walls, an iconographic image of the heavenly Jerusalem. Gregory's superimposition of architectural images on the meadow is separated out into two regions, conceptually and descriptively separate. By shifting the *mansiones* and *habitacula* beyond the *locus amoenitatis*, Boniface disambiguates Gregory's description. The meadow emerges as the interim paradise, hierarchically subordinated to heaven through the sequential use of natural and architectural images.

Boniface further expresses this hierarchy through the river and bridge, for which he again reinterprets Gregory's use of these motifs. Unlike

[69] Cf. Tangl, ed., *Bonifatius-Briefe*, Letter 10, p. 11, and Vogüé, ed., *Dialogues*, IV, ch. 37, p. 130. [70] Ciccarese, *Visioni*, p. 282.

[71] Levison, ed., *Visio Baronti*, chs. 8–11, pp. 383–5.

Gregory, who contrasts the river with its farther bank, Boniface places the river in between two regions to heighten their difference. He thereby changes its function from a punitive mechanism, as in Gregory's otherworld, to a necessary preamble to life in the heavenly city. Souls who fall into the river are immersed in the flames in varying degrees before they can climb back, more radiant than before, to continue their crossing. Thus the river and the bridge enable good souls to become even better, by endowing them with splendour appropriate to inhabitants of the heavenly Jerusalem, which in turn signals its qualitative difference from paradise.

While the graded immersion in a flaming river clearly recalls the *Visio Sancti Pauli*,[72] there are larger correspondences of imagery between the latter and the Wenlock Vision. To communicate the hierarchy between the interim paradise and heaven, and the merits of the souls within them, Boniface uses an image from nature, followed by a river, and finally an architectural image. Now, a very similar arrangement is seen in the *Visio Sancti Pauli* with its sequence of the *terra repromissionis*, the Acherusian Lake and the City of Christ, which conveys the gradation of delights for different categories of the righteous.

The pervasive influence exercised by the *Visio Sancti Pauli* on the medieval imagination thus finds early illustration within the Wenlock Vision. It appears that Boniface has internalised the imagery of the *Visio Sancti Pauli* to such an extent that he cannot help recalling it in his own description of the otherworld. Perhaps this is an unavoidable consequence of his particular approach to the visionary form, and his place within the history of its development. For his account of the interim state, Gregory chose images his readers could relate to. This necessitated a broad similarity between the descriptive constituents of his otherworld and those of the *Visio Sancti Pauli*, which Gregory then distorted through a different arrangement and interpretation of these images. Two centuries of visionary elaborations of Gregory's otherworld reach their logical end in Boniface's account, which freshly reappropriates those elements from the *Visio Sancti Pauli* that Gregory had reacted against.[73]

[72] Sims-Williams, *Religion and Literature*, pp. 260–1.

[73] These similarities of sequence and images between the *Visio Sancti Pauli* and the Wenlock Vision on the one hand, and between the latter and Gregory's description on the other, are noted by Carozzi, *Voyage de l'âme*, p. 214: 'On retrouvait donc le même type de succession: Paradis ou Terre des Promesses – fleuve ou lac Acherusa – Jérusalem céleste. Le lac y avait la même fonction purificatrice que le fleuve de feu, et les âmes des justes

In thereby laying bare the apocryphal alignments of the interim paradise, Boniface betrays elements of the same sensibility that we had detected in anonymous vernacular prose writers. Bede's version of the interim paradise is, in contrast, carefully steered away from any verbal or visual correspondences with the *Visio Sancti Pauli*, as evident in his avoiding of the term *paradisus* itself through paraphrasing it as 'not heaven'. Bede also follows very closely Gregory's account of the flowery meadow, thus continuing the 'back-to basics' attitude noted in his version of the framework enclosing the four-fold otherworld.

Bede not only replicates almost verbatim many details of Gregory's description but also systematically heightens its sensuous elements, specifying the breadth of the meadow, the exact appearance of the flowers, and the intensity of the fragrance:

> Et ecce ibi campus erat latissimus ac laetissimus, tantaque flagrantia uernantium flosculorum plenus, ut omnem mox fetorem tenebrosi fornacis, qui me peruaserat, effugaret admirandi huius suauitas odoris. Tanta autem lux cuncta ea loca perfuderat, ut omni splendore diei siue solis meridiani radiis uideretur esse praeclarior. Erantque in hoc campo innumera hominum albatorum conuenticula sedesque plurimae agminum laetantium.[74]

The brilliance of the light suffusing the meadow is communicated through its comparison with an apprehensible phenomenon, the radiance of the noonday sun. Again, this detail recalls and elaborates upon Gregory's reference to 'mansiones diversorum singulae magnitudine lucis plenae' (p. 130). Other details from Gregory are transformed in keeping with more recent developments in interim eschatology, such as the *mansiones*, which reappear twice to describe the groups of souls seen by Dryhthelm. While Gregory's use of *habitacula* as a variation on *mansiones* reinforces the architectural

résidaient "interim" dans la Terre des Promesses. Il n'est donc pas impossible que "l'Apocalypse de Paul" ait servi de source pour ci passage.' As this comment indicates, however, Carozzi appears not to detect the pattern of subversion and reappropriation underlying their relationship, placing them instead in a straight line of descent.

[74] *HE*, V, ch. 12, p. 492: 'There was a very broad and pleasant plain, full of such a fragrance of growing flowers that the marvellous sweetness of the scent quickly dispelled the foul stench of the gloomy furnace which had hung around me. So great was the light that flooded all this place that it seemed to be clearer than the brightness of daylight or the rays of the noontide sun. In this meadow there were innumerable bands of men in white robes, and many companies of happy people sat around' (trans. Colgrave and Mynors).

imagery superimposed on the meadow, Bede's use of *mansiones* is more ambivalent. Dryhthelm apparently sees assemblies of figures clad in white sitting together on the meadow, rather than housed in dwellings. Thus, both *mansiones* and the earlier *sedes* could be interpreted as either metaphorical abodes or actual structures. The former interpretation would remove the architectural element which prevents the identification of Gregory's meadow as the interim paradise, while the latter interpretation would have the opposite effect. Bede's descriptive equivocation at this point is similar to his evasive definition of the interim paradise.

Bede's description of the meadow manages, on the whole, to be both 'theologically correct' and descriptively rich. By relying solely on sense-impressions, he conveys the hierarchy between the two pleasant regions without the revealing image sequence adopted by Boniface. If the fragrance and light of the meadow surpasses known phenomena, that which proceeds from the region beyond it make the meadow pale into insignificance. The greater desirability of the region beyond the meadow is conveyed by intensifying the same sensuous qualities that constitute the meadow's appeal. A further sensuous element of sweet singing is added. The emphasis on the synaesthetic perception enables him to avoid the sequence of natural and architectural imagery, the outright use of definitions, and the actual description of heaven, which, strictly speaking, only the blessed can know about. Unlike the Monk of Wenlock, who can at least see the walls of the heavenly city, Dryhthelm apprehends its joys through sense-impressions which cloak its specific appearance.

Furthermore, Dryhthelm refers to the region that lies beyond the meadow as a *locus amoenitatis*, a phrase which, as we have observed, also appears in the Wenlock Vision. Bede's application of this phrase to the heavenly city again indicates a direct response to Boniface's explicit separation of paradise and heaven through contrasting imagery. To call the kingdom of heaven a *locus amoenitatis* is a verbal manoeuvre similar to inserting *mansiones* into the interim paradise. It also implies Dryhthelm's complete ignorance of what lies beyond. This underscoring of Bede's theological consistency reinforces the overall illusion of verisimilitude produced through the use of direct reporting and his descriptive technique.

The respective techniques applied by Boniface and Bede to the pleasant regions reappear in their description of the two regions of punishment. Boniface's evocation of the interim paradise through one image, the *locus amoenitatis*, is paralleled by his use of the single, resonant image of the flaming pits for the provisional hell. Just as he conveys the qualitative superiority of heaven through the greater splendour of its souls, he describes the greater suffering of those below the pits to impress upon us the unimaginable intensity of that region's horrors. Similarly, Bede matches the fragrance, light and sweet music characterising the pleasant regions with contrasting sense impressions of stench, darkness and the clamour of the damned in the regions of punishment. Those very senses which are pandered to in paradise and heaven are thus subjected to unbearable assaults in their infernal counterparts. Interestingly, even as the *locus amoenitatis* of the Wenlock Vision is applied to heaven in the Vision of Dryhthelm, so do the pits of the former vision's provisional hell reappear as the latter's permanent hell. This pattern of shifts is in keeping with our suggested relationship between the two visions, which also finds confirmation in Bede's more conscious chiselling of the four-fold otherworld through his descriptive technique.

The two Anglo-Latin visions testify to the dynamic and fluid interaction between different attitudes towards similar concerns – in this case, the nature of the interim condition, the spatialisation of the otherworld, and the relationship between this world and the next – that characterises the production and consumption of texts in medieval culture. Bede's Vision of Dryhthelm can be read as a 'learned' *re*-appropriation of a literary form whose character had itself transformed from 'learned' to 'popular', even as this history is more effectively captured, perhaps, in the Wenlock Vision. In Boniface's account, contradictory and complex legacies of the interim paradise coexist undisturbed within the structure and the imagery of the otherworld. Bede, who has read enough of Augustine, Gregory, Julian *and*, probably, the *Visio Sancti Pauli* to recognise each stratum of this legacy, struggles to balance the necessary and the useful against what he sees as the gratuitous and the unorthodox.[75]

BEDE'S SOLUTION: ARTICULATIONS, EVASIONS AND COMPROMISES

Although Bede succeeds to a remarkable degree in achieving this balance, some compromises are inevitable. In fact, as noted in connection with the narrative implications of the visionary form, in articulation itself there is

[75] See Laistner, 'The Library of the Venerable Bede', pp. 248–9.

compromise. Through descriptive technique, Bede distances himself from the *Visio Sancti Pauli*, but the idea of a hierarchy of reward for good souls in the interim period remains as strong in Bede as in Boniface. Likewise, despite the absence of the term paradise, the interim state remains associated with the image of a pleasant meadow, distinct from a qualitatively superior heaven. Rhetoric constantly undercuts argument to expose those weak spots most vulnerable to later reinterpretation.

One such response is Ælfric's fresh incorporation of architectural elements into the image of the meadow. Not content with translating Bede's ambivalent *mansiones* as *wununga*, Ælfric further encloses the meadow within a *burg*, so that Bede's undefined antechamber to heaven is now literally subsumed into heaven. The new sequence of imagery reinforces the complete subordination of an interim condition in paradise to one in the heavenly kingdom. However, the Vision of Dryhthelm was also available to vernacular readers through the Old English translation of the *Historia Ecclesiastica,* which, as we saw in the second chapter, did not share Ælfric's fastidiousness.[76] The Wenlock Vision, too, was translated into Old English, as of course, was the *Dialogi*.[77] The continued currency of these visions through the Anglo-Saxon period and their frequent juxtaposition with Gregory's reports within the same manuscript, means that they were constantly reappropriated and understood in terms of each other in many different ways.

Bede could not have been unaware of all these compromises and future possibilities. Why, then, does he describe a pleasant interim state at all, instead of simply presenting a tripartite otherworld of heaven, hell and a provisional region which housed Augustine's third category of souls? We return to the question raised by Ælfric's writings, which display a constant tension between the necessity to retain an interim paradise and the desire to do away with it. Thus, two of the most self-conscious and authoritative writers in Anglo-Saxon England appear similarly disposed

[76] See above, p. 46.

[77] In fact, the translation of Boniface's letter to Eadburg is found in the manuscript Cotton Otho C. i, the principal text in which is Bishop Wærferth's unfinished translation of Gregory's *Dialogi*. For an edition of the Old English version of Boniface's letter, and a discussion of the manuscript context, see Sisam, 'An Old English Translation of a Letter from Wynfrith to Eadburga'. The Old English version of the *Dialogi* is edited by H. Hecht, *Bischof Waerferths von Worcester Übersetzung der Dialoge Gregors des Grossen*, BaP 5 (Leipzig, 1900, repr. Darmstadt, 1965).

towards the interim paradise. To understand their motivations, we need to review the mechanisms of movement within the four regions of the otherworld.

In the Wenlock Vision, souls wait in the provisional hell until Doomsday; but the situation is more complex in paradise. While some groups of rejoicing souls wait in a leisurely fashion, others hurry frantically over the bridge. Is paradise merely a clearing-house for some souls, then, and a waiting-room for others? Boniface himself appears at a loss here as 'the famous paradise of God' is the only region in his otherworld whose function remains unexplicated. The Vision of Dryhthelm refines considerably this confused picture. Its provisional hell houses the souls of those who have delayed to confess and amend their sins, but who nonetheless repented on their deathbeds. Because they have confessed, they will be received into the kingdom of heaven after death. But Bede also specifies that many of these souls can be aided before Doomsday by the prayers, alms, fasting of the living, and especially through masses:

> Vallis illa, quam aspexisti flammis feruentibus et frigoribus horrenda rigidis, ipse est locus in quo examinandae et castigandae sunt animae illorum, qui differentes confiteri et emendare scelera quae fecerunt, in ipso tandem mortis articulo ad paenitentiam confugiunt, et sic de corpore exeunt; qui tamen, quia confessionem et paenitentiam uel in morte habuerunt, omnes in die iudicii ad regnum caelorum perueniunt. Multos autem preces uiuentium et elimosynae et ieiunia et maxime celebratio missarum, ut etiam ante diem iudicii liberentur, adiuuant.[78]

Similar injunctions are made by Ælfric in his *Sermo ad populum in octavis pentecosten dicendus* (Pope XI).[79] Both writers emphasise the importance of penitence and deathbed confession, also adjuncts to personal salvation which depended on the interdependence of Church and lay person, and which emerged as crucial in the early Middle Ages.[80]

[78] *HE*, V, ch. 12, p. 494: 'The valley that you saw, with its awful flaming fire and freezing cold, is the place in which those souls have to be tried and chastened who delayed to confess and make restitution for the sins they have committed until they were on the point of death; and so they died. But because they did repent and confess, even though on their deathbed, they will all come to the kingdom of heaven on judgement day; and the prayers of those who are still alive, their alms and fastings and specially the celebration of masses, help many of them to get free even before the day of judgement' (trans. Colgrave and Mynors). [79] See above, p. 43.

[80] As demonstrated by Paxton, *Christianizing Death*; on the subject of penitence, see also A. J. Frantzen, *The Literature of Penance in Anglo-Saxon England* (New Brunswick, NJ, 1983).

However, these souls in the provisional hell cannot move directly to heaven, bypassing the not absolutely perfect souls who continue waiting in paradise until Doomsday. The use of distinguishing between two intermediate categories of souls, and assigning them to two interim locations, now becomes apparent. Paradise provides a waiting-room, not only for those who are not absolutely perfect, but also for those who can be removed from the tortures of the provisional hell through the intervention of the living, and housed thenceforth in the interim paradise. In other words, it enables the smooth functioning of rites and rituals which benefit the Church by furthering its social role as intermediary between the living and the dead. In Bede's hands, therefore, the vision achieves its full ideological potential as a genre which simultaneously serves the causes of different social groups.

Bede's attitude to the interim condition and paradise varies within his writings, however. The spatialisation and hierarchisation of the interim paradise appear only in the Vision of Dryhthelm; his exegesis reveals a more Augustinian approach which seeks to collapse all differences in the scriptural references to *paradisus*. *In Genesim*, for instance, contains a forceful assertion that paradise is where Adam and Eve first dwelt (hence the Garden of Eden), and that it represents a type of the Church as well as of our future fatherland (in heaven). This equation between the terrestrial paradise of Eden and the kingdom of heaven is tightened through references to the tree of life from Revelation (Apc II. 7) and the paradise promised to the Good Thief and the saints.[81] He concludes the argument by using the image of the flaming sword to bring together these different paradises:

> Quae etiam custodia bene uersatilis esse adseueratur pro eo quod quandoque ueniret tempus, ut etiam remoueri potuisset. Remota est namque Enoch a peccatoribus translato; remota Elia in curru igneo rapto; remota omnibus electis cum, Domino baptizato, aperti sunt ei caeli; remota item singulis electis cum baptismi fonte lauantur; remota iisdem perfectius cum soluti a uinculis ad celestis paradisi gloriam suo quique tempore conscendunt.[82]

[81] Jones, ed., *Libri quatuor in principium Genesis*, I, ch 2. 8, pp. 45–6.

[82] *Ibid.*, ch. 3. 24, p. 71: 'This safeguard is declared, in fact, to be fairly moveable, according to what and when occasion should arise, so that it could actually be removed. For it was withdrawn when Enoch was translated from sinners; it was withdrawn when Elias was caught up in the chariot of fire; it was removed for all the elect when, at the Lord's baptism, the heavens were opened; likewise, it is removed for individual elect when they are washed in the baptismal font; it is withdrawn for the same men more completely when they are released from chains and ascend to the glory of the heavenly paradise, each in their own time.'

Through sustained application of typology, therefore, Bede brings together several paradises: the Garden of Eden, the paradise of those assumed in the body, the paradise of the Good Thief and the kingdom of heaven. This exegetical context offers neither room nor need to entertain the possibilities of an interim paradise, separate from heaven.

Conversely, in his homily *In aduentu*, Bede freely refers to souls being released from the provisional hell into paradise before Doomsday through the beneficial effect of alms, prayers, intercession and penitence:

Ceterum sunt plures in ecclesia iusti qui post carnis solutionem continuo beata paradisi requie suscipiuntur expectantes in magno gaudio in magnis congaudentium choris quando recepto corpore ueniant et appareant ante faciem Dei. At uero non nulli propter bona quidem opera ad electorum sortem praeordinati sed propter mala aliqua quibus polluti de corpore exierunt post mortem severe castigandi excipiuntur flammis ignis purgatorii et uel usque ad diem iudicii longa huius examinatione a uitiorum sorde mundantur uel certe prius amicorum fidelium precibus elemosinis ieiuniis fletibus et hostiae salutaris oblationibus absoluti a poenis et ipsi ad beatorum perueniunt requiem.[83]

Visualising this paradise, and thereby engaging in its differentiation from heaven, does not seem essential to Bede's homiletic purpose. Accordingly, he appears less concerned here about the use of the term *paradisus* than he is in the Vision of Dryhthelm, even though the functions of the interim paradise remain exactly the same in both instances: a waiting-room to heaven, where those released from being tried and chastened – exactly as in the Vision of Dryhthelm – can join the nearly perfect and the blessed in their interim state of joy and repose.

[83] Hurst, ed., *Opera homiletica*, I. 2, pp. 12–13: 'But more numerous are the righteous men in the Church who, after release from the flesh, are immediately received in the blessed peace of paradise, waiting in a state of great exultation, and in rejoicing crowds for the time when they may come with their body restored and appear before the countenance of God. However, quite a few men who, on account of their good works, at any rate, have already been marked out for the assignment of the elect, but who, because of certain evil deeds, polluted by which they have departed from the body, and for which after death they have to be harshly castigated, are consumed by the flames of the purging fire and are cleansed from the stain of sins by means of lengthy scrutiny of it – either continually until the day of Judgement or certainly after first being freed from punishments – through the prayers, offerings, fastings and lamentations of their faithful friends and by the sacrifices of a beneficial volunteer even they can reach the peace of the blessed.'

We now realise why those authorities concerned about the unorthodox affiliations of the interim paradise cannot escape describing it. The connection between intercession and the interim state, present even in the writings of Augustine, received a new fillip in Gregory's descriptions of the otherworld in the *Dialogi*.[84] From Gregory onwards, the desire to link Church and laity through intercession increases in step with the specificity granted to the interim paradise. The Anglo-Latin visions make patristic attitudes towards this specificity accessible to a larger audience, but through pressures of literary form, the interim paradise is spatialised and strongly associated with natural imagery that reinforces its separation from the heavenly kingdom. These compromises in turn enable a greater emphasis on the importance of intercession, alms-giving and mass, and are thus accepted by first Bede and later, Ælfric. While the Vision of Dryhthelm better reflects Gregory's aims, the Wenlock Vision reiterates how easily these aims were superseded by the desire simply to describe the interim state more fully. Together, they indicate that the interim paradise had become an intrinsic part of the popular Anglo-Saxon world-view and, in their articulation of it, contribute to its future shape.

THE DISSEMINATION OF THE FOUR-FOLD OTHERWORLD

The four-fold structure appears in vernacular homiletic prose from the ninth century onwards, where, within the 'Three Utterances' and the 'Theban Legend' exempla, it is used to restate popular cosmology in both penitential and hortatory contexts. Since the transmission history of many of these texts reveals links with Insular centres on the Continent, it appears that the four-fold otherworld was disseminated to Insular foundations by Anglo-Saxon missionaries, such as Boniface himself. The Latin 'Three Utterances' texts and *Transitus W* suggest that the millenarian hierarchy between an interim abode and paradise was current on the Continent during the eighth and ninth centuries.[85] The four-fold otherworld must have assisted in the redefinition of this hierarchy as one between paradise and heaven. In the following centuries, the direction of borrowing would have been reversed, as the newly redefined hierarchies between paradise and heaven re-entered the world of Anglo-Saxon vernacular texts. This

[84] See, in this connection, Vogel, 'Deux conséquences de l'eschatologie grégorienne'.

[85] This suggestion is confirmed by the analysis below, pp. 116–17.

explanation would also account for the Hiberno-Latin connections of many of these witnesses to the four-fold structure: Redaction XI, the 'Theban Legend' as seen within Vercelli IX and the abbreviated 'Three Utterances' tradition.[86] It seems not improbable that, at these Continental Insular centres to which the Anglo-Latin visions were disseminated, their descriptions dovetailed with Irish interest in apocryphal traditions to produce texts attesting to both 'Irish symptoms' and the four-fold otherworld. It is in the context of this cross-pollination, perhaps, that we should view the composite eschatology of a text such as the *Fís Adamnán*. At the other end of the scale of descriptive expansiveness is the Old English *Vision of Leofric* from the eleventh century.[87] This work, actually a collection of different 'mini-visions' purportedly seen by the eponymous Leofric, Earl of Mercia, opens with a glimpse of a flowering meadow populated by groups of rejoicing people, and includes a bridge of trial which the visionary has to cross over. It is difficult to decide whether this relatively brief image derives from the otherworlds of Boniface or Gregory, with or without a passing nod at the Vision of Dryhthelm, as it appears to evoke simultaneously all three visions and their Old English translations. Thus the Anglo-Latin visions propagated a whole iconographic vocabulary for the expression of beliefs regarding the otherworld and interim eschatology, which was in turn validated by their continuing transmission alongside newer examples of vision literature in the later Anglo-Saxon period.

This investigation into the Anglo-Latin visions has shed light on the use of the interim paradise in both Ælfric and the anonymous prose writers, even as it has illuminated the importance of the concept in the working out of what would later become known as purgatory. The complex relationship between the two visions on the one hand, and between visionary and homiletic literature on the other, belies the usual characterisation of Anglo-Saxon writers as generally uninterested in questions of the interim state, or offering little innovation in purgatorial ideas. The visions reveal that in Anglo-Saxon England, as in later periods of European culture, learned engagement with what I described earlier as 'the common cultural stock'[88]

[86] These connections have been best investigated by Wright, 'Apocryphal Lore and Insular Tradition', and *Irish Tradition*, pp. 175–273; see also Wack and Wright, 'A New Source'.

[87] Napier, ed., 'An Old English "Vision of Leofric"'. See also Silverstein, 'The "Vision of Leofric"', Pulsiano, 'Hortatory Purpose', and Gatch, 'Poetry and Liturgy'.

[88] See above, p. 75.

inevitably leads to compromise and innovation,[89] but they also remind us of the influence of the literary form on the successive phases of reappropriation that determine the evolution of an idea. In the next chapter, the reappearance of these compromises and reappropriations within Anglo-Saxon supplicatory texts will enable us to pursue further their implications and extend our understanding of monastic attitudes towards the interim paradise.

[89] See N. Z. Davis, *Society and Culture in Early Modern France: Eight Essays* (Stanford, CA, 1975) and C. Ginzburg, 'The Witches' Sabbat: Popular Cult or Inquisitorial Stereotype?', in *Understanding Popular Culture*, ed. Kaplan, pp. 39–51, at p. 48. For the role of mediators in these processes of compromise, see the descriptively rich analysis of superstition among the lower clergy by M. R. O' Neil, '*Sacerdote ovvero strione*: Ecclesiastical and Superstitious Remedies in 16th Century Italy', in *Understanding Popular Culture*, ed. Kaplan, pp. 53–83.

5

Private hopes, public claims? *Paradisus* and *sinus Abrahae* in prayer and liturgy

> Suscipiat te christus qui creavit te et in sinum abrahae angeli deducant te.[1]

> Dirigas angelum pacis qui custodiat animam meam et perducat eam in locum refrigerii, et pertransire faciat intrepidam principatus et potestates tenebrarum.[2]

> Obsecro te domine praesta mihi post obitum meum prosperum iter ad perennis paradisi peruenire suauitatem. Ibique cum sanctis animabus mihi requiescere liceat usque ad tempus resurrectionis.[3]

Three separate terms for the soul's post-mortem destination are seen in these supplications for the soul's safety after death. An antiphon from the funeral mass refers to the soul's journey to the *sinus Abrahae*, while the terms *locus refrigerii* and *paradisus* appear in two Anglo-Latin prayers preserved in the Royal Prayerbook (London, British Library, Royal 2. A. xx) and the Book of Cerne (Cambridge University Library, Ll. 1. 10) respectively. This chapter charts the shifting fortunes of the definitions *sinus Abrahae*, *locus refrigerii* and *paradisus* in the larger literary groups represented by these texts – the early medieval funeral liturgy, and Anglo-Latin prayers from the eighth and ninth centuries. By analysing the contrasting use of these terms within private prayer and public worship, I explore further that monastic ambivalence towards the concept of the interim paradise, which we have already discerned in the writings of Bede and Ælfric.

1 Sicard, *Liturgie de la mort*, p. 67: 'Let Christ who created you receive you, and into the bosom of Abraham let angels lead you.'

2 Kuypers, ed., *Cerne*, fol. 34r, p. 215: 'May you send an angel of peace who will take custody of my soul and will lead it to the place of refreshment, and make it cross over unshaken the dominions and the powers of darkness.'

3 *Ibid.*, p. 84: 'I beg you, Lord, grant to me after my passing away that a prosperous journey arrives at the sweetness of perpetual paradise. And there may it be allowed me to rest with holy souls until the time of resurrection.'

Four prayerbooks, codicologically similar and with several textual links, were compiled for private devotion in Southumbrian monasteries between the latter half of the eighth century and the beginning of the ninth.[4] The earliest is the Royal Prayerbook, usually dated to the second half of the eighth century.[5] The latest is the Book of Cerne, compiled in early ninth-century Mercia.[6] Chronologically in between are the Book of Nunnaminster (London, British Library, Harley 2965) and the Harley Fragment (London, British Library, Harley 7653), both generally assigned to the late eighth century or the beginning of the ninth.[7] These collections give voice to the deepest hopes and fears of individual Anglo-Saxon monks and nuns. The authors of the prayers supplicate not for salvation after Doomsday, but for the safety of the soul when at its most vulnerable: the moment of death, when, exiting from the body, it may be either beset by demons or escorted by angelic choirs to a haven of peace and rest.

The changing terminology used within the prayerbooks for this dwelling-place reflects the progressive incorporation of the interim paradise into the monastic world-view, and the development of the concept itself

4 For the most recent discussion of these prayerbooks as a group, see Brown, *Book of Cerne*, especially pp. 41–3 and 173–8. See also Sims-Williams, *Religion and Literature*, pp. 273–327. For their dates, see Sims-Williams, *Religion and Literature*, p. 275, Gneuss, 'Liturgical Books', p. 138, and Morrish, 'Dated and Datable Manuscripts', pp. 518–19.

5 Printed as an appendix by Kuypers, ed., *Cerne*, pp. 200–25. Sims-Williams, *Religion and Literature*, p. 298, n. 103, refutes the argument made by Morrish, 'Dated and Datable Manuscripts', p. 519, for an early ninth-century origin for the Royal Prayerbook.

6 Kuypers, ed., *Cerne*; prayers are cited according to his numbering. An early ninth-century date is proposed by Sims-Williams, *Religion and Literature*, p. 276. For its compilation in a Mercian centre, see H. Sweet, ed., *The Oldest English Texts*, EETS os 83 (London, 1885), p. vii, and Brown, *Book of Cerne*, pp. 21–4. Arguments for an earlier date and Northumbrian affiliations have been made on the basis of seventh-century Irish elements within individual prayers, by Kuypers, ed., *Cerne*, pp. xiv–xxx, Hughes, 'Irish Influence', and Dumville, 'Liturgical Drama and Panegyric Responsory', 374–406. The contested identity of the 'aedeluald episcopus', mentioned twice in the manuscript (in the headletters of an acrostic on fol. 21r and in the breviary), has added to the debate over the origin and date of the Book of Cerne; see in this context, the exchange between S. Kuhn, 'From Canterbury to Lichfield', *Speculum* 23 (1948), 619–27, and K. Sisam, 'Canterbury, Lichfield and the Vespasian Psalter', *RES* ns 7 (1956), 1–10, and *RES* ns 8 (1957), 372–3. The issue remains controversial; for a summary of its history, see Brown, *Book of Cerne*, pp. 132–6 and 155–6.

7 Birch, ed., *An Ancient Manuscript*. The Harley fragment is printed as an appendix by F. E. Warren in *The Antiphonary of Bangor: an Early Irish Manuscript in the Ambrosian Library at Milan*, HBS 10 (London, 1893), II.

through its use within supplicatory texts. A contrapuntal perspective to the same concerns is provided by the early medieval funeral mass, which seems to consistently reject the idea of the interim paradise while praying for the dead person's soul. This divergence between liturgy and prayer helps us reinterpret the interface between 'popular' and 'learned' sensibilities in the Anglo-Saxon monastic world as the difference between its personal and public faces. At the same time, changes in the liturgical language after the tenth century and the transmission history of the prayers together suggest growing ecclesiastical disapproval of the interim paradise in later Anglo-Saxon England.

THE EARLY MEDIEVAL FUNERAL RITE AND THE ANTIPHON *IN PARADISUM*

Before embarking on a comparison between Anglo-Latin prayers and the funeral mass, however, we need to place the latter within its larger liturgical context. Early medieval Europe has been characterised by 'liturgical anarchy and ritual chaos'.[8] Different rites evolved in particular regions, competing, coexisting and influencing each other. A dearth of manuscript evidence from England and favourable circumstances for transmission means that any or all of these forms could have been known in Anglo-Saxon England between the seventh and ninth centuries.[9]

Fortunately, the funeral rite itself remains relatively stable amidst this liturgical flux.[10] A core of antiphons and orations identifiable as the original Roman rite is retained, virtually unchanged, throughout the seventh- and eighth-century liturgical revisions that resulted in the Old and Frankish Gelasian sacramentaries.[11] This core is fully preserved as *Ordo*

[8] The phrases are Vogel's, *Medieval Liturgy*, p. 4.

[9] For some caveats concerning the 'literary' analysis of Anglo-Saxon liturgy, see Gatch, 'Old English Literature and the Liturgy'.

[10] The most comprehensive comparative study of the Western funeral rite is by Sicard, *Liturgie de la mort*. For an anthropologically inspired approach to the early medieval funeral rite and its standardisation during the Carolingian period, see now Paxton, *Christianizing Death*.

[11] See Sicard, *Liturgie de la mort*, pp. 1–27 and 54–102. The Old Gelasian is discussed in detail by A. Chavasse, *Le Sacramentaire Gélasien (Vaticanus Reginensis 316): sacramentaire presbytéral en usage dans les titres Romains au VIIe siècle*, Bibliothèque de théologie 4 (Paris and Tournai, 1958); see also Vogel, *Medieval Liturgy*, pp. 64–76.

49 of the *Ordines Romani*, contained in the manuscript Vatican, Biblioteca Apostolica, Ottobonianus 312.[12] A set of instructions for the Roman funeral rite is provided here under the rubric *Ordo qualiter agatur in obsequium defunctorum*. These antiphons and orations could have been introduced early into Anglo-Saxon England as part of the Roman rite brought over by Augustine's mission.[13] Equally, they could have been later disseminated either through the Old Gelasian, the only surviving copy of which (Vatican, Biblioteca Apostolica, Reginensis latinus 316) was produced in Chelles, a Frankish monastery with strong Anglo-Saxon connections, or through those Frankish Gelasians known to the eighth-century Anglo-Saxon Church.[14] Significantly for our argument, this otherwise stable funeral rite contains one element which undergoes considerable change: the antiphon *In paradisum*. The vicissitudes it undergoes serve to highlight the impact made by ideas about the interim paradise on the funeral rite itself.

Ordo 49 opens with the antiphon *Suscipiat te*, cited at the beginning of this chapter. Its hope for the soul's safe passage to the bosom of Abraham is echoed by the antiphon *Chorus angelorum* which immediately follows:

> Chorus angelorum te suscipiat et in sinu abrahae te collocet, ut cum lazaro quondam paupere aeternam habeas requiem.[15]

It would appear that these two antiphons refer to the millenarian hierarchy between the fate of the ordinary faithful, placed in the bosom of Abraham before the Second Coming, and that of the martyrs and the corporally assumed, who are in paradise. Such preservations of millenarian terminology within medieval liturgy are far from uncommon.[16] The next step of the rite, the oration *Deus apud quem*, clarifies that the bosom of Abraham repre-

[12] Andrieu, ed., *Ordines Romani*, pp. 523–30. For a description of *Ordo* 49, see H. Frank, 'Die älteste *Ordo defunctorum* der römischen Liturgie und sein Fortleben in Totenagenden des frühen Mittelalters', *ALW* 7 (1962), 360–415, and, for a general account of the *Ordines*, Vogel, *Medieval Liturgy*, pp. 135–54.

[13] A suggestion made by Sims-Williams in *Religion and Literature*, p. 274.

[14] *Ibid.*, p. 274. For the possibility that the Old Gelasian was compiled for English use, see Hohler, 'Service-Books', p. 61. Eighth-century Anglo-Saxon use of Frankish Gelasian sacramentaries is established by Bullough, 'Alcuin and the Kingdom of Heaven', p. 11, especially n. 26. A detailed account of the Frankish Gelasians may be found in B. Moreton's *The Eighth-Century Gelasian Sacramentary: a Study in Tradition* (Oxford, 1976).

[15] Sicard, *Liturgie de la mort*, p. 70: 'May a choir of angels receive you and place you in the bosom of Abraham, so that with Lazarus, formerly the poor man, you may have eternal rest.'

[16] As demonstrated, for example, by Botte, '*Prima resurrectio*'.

sents a temporary state for the soul, and looks further to its resurrection *in die nouissimo magni iudicii*.[17] The juxtaposition of the antiphons *Suscipiat te* and *Chorus angelorum* with *Deus apud quem* suggests that, whatever the original signification of the reference to *sinus Abrahae* within the antiphons, in *Ordo* 49, at least, they are identified with an interim place for the good soul until the Last Judgement. This reinterpretation of the millenarian hierarchy in terms of the distinction between the interim paradise and heaven is in keeping with the developments we traced in the previous chapter. The use of *sinus Abrahae* in the liturgy to signify what elsewhere is increasingly defined as paradise thus recalls the reference to *Abrahames fæðm* in Napier XLVI.[18]

This reading is supported by what seems to be a clear reference to the interim paradise within the antiphon prescribed by *Ordo* 49 before the commencement of the funeral procession:

In paradiso Dei ducant te angeli [in tuo] aduentu suscipiant te martyres, perducant te in ciuitatem sanctam Hierusalem.[19]

Bernard Capelle first collated the variants of this antiphon to conclude that its original form, still preserved today in some tenth-century Ambrosian sacramentaries, was as follows:

In paradisum deducant te angeli, et cum gloria [cum gaudio] suscipiant te sancti martyres Dei.[20]

This statement, representing therefore the earliest phase of the antiphon, also appears to articulate millenarian beliefs, but those concerning the fate of the privileged martyr rather than the ordinary faithful. It hopes for the deceased soul's passage to paradise, escorted by angels, and its reception in

17 Although *Ordo* 49 does not specify which oration is required at this point, Sicard deduces it to be the *Deus apud quem*, found earliest in the sole copy of the Old Gelasian; for the arguments, text and variants, see Sicard, *Liturgie de la mort*, pp. 88–90.

18 See above, p. 58.

19 Andrieu, ed., *Ordines Romani*, IV, p. 529: 'Let angels lead you to the paradise of God, may the holy martyrs receive you on your arrival, may they lead you through into the holy city, Jerusalem.' See also Sicard, *Liturgie de la mort*, p. 4.

20 Capelle, 'L'antienne *In Paradisum*', p. 263: 'Let angels bring you into the paradise of God, and in glory [in exultation] let the holy martyrs receive you on your arrival.' However, as the *Ordines* had not yet been discovered and edited, Capelle could not utilise the version in *Ordo* 49. This omission is made good by Ntedika's updated comparison of the versions in *L'Evocation de l'au-delà*, pp. 163–4.

paradise by the martyrs. The phrase *et cum gloria* and its variation *cum gaudio* consolidate this interpretation, as, within the millenarian scheme, only those of the highest perfection would be allowed to enter the company of the martyrs. For the rest of the ordinary faithful, interred in the underground vaults of the bosom of Abraham, *gaudia* or *gloria* would hardly seem appropriate until the First Resurrection and their subsequent release into the paradise of martyrs.

From this point of view, it seems reasonable to conclude that the addition of the second part to the antiphon, *perducant te in ciuitatem sanctam Hierusalem*, brings the old millenarian belief more in line with the newer hierarchy between paradise and heaven. However, Capelle was reluctant to consider the possibility that paradise could in fact refer to an interim location within the liturgy. His difficulties in acknowledging the interim paradise as a viable concept during the early Middle Ages are graphically illustrated by his attempts to marginalise the obvious conclusions to be drawn from his own investigations. Within his main argument, he insists:

> l'histoire de l'antienne attestant clairement que le mot *Paradisus* y avait le sens de *Ciel* . . . A Milan comme en Espagne, à Rome, en Gaule, partout enfin, *Paradisus* a toujours eu, en liturgie, le sens de *Ciel*.[21]

Nevertheless, running almost parallel to these assertions is a voluminous footnote, in which he admits that several problems of translation and interpretation could be solved by the adoption of a different perspective:

> On n'évite ces difficultés qu'en admettant que le voyage comporte, en fait, deux étapes: les anges conduisent l'âme au 'paradis', là les martyrs viennent la chercher pour l'introduire dans la céleste Jérusalem; 'paradisus' devient ainsi un lieu intermédiaire.[22]

Joseph Ntedika, who continued Capelle's investigations into *In paradisum* by incorporating into them the evidence of the subsequently discovered *Ordo* 49, also found it hard to accept that *In paradisum* could, in fact, refer to an 'intermediate place':

> Rien ne perce d'une distinction entre un ciel d'attente et un ciel définitif. Il se peut que nous ayons tantôt l'un, tantôt l'autre; il est même possible qu'on ne se préoccupe d'aucune distinction de ce genre.[23]

[21] Capelle, 'L'antienne *In Paradisum*', p. 266. [22] See *ibid.*, p. 265, n. 30.

[23] Ntedika, *L'Evocation de l'au-delà*, p. 169; see also his preceding arguments, pp. 163–9. But for a different conclusion, see Sims-Williams, *Religion and Literature*, p. 264.

We have already noted the ideological barriers which prevent theologians such as Capelle and Ntedika from taking this deductive step in their otherwise salutary and extremely detailed investigations.[24] However, accepting that the antiphon does indeed refer to the interim paradise can allow us to read rather differently the meaning of the antiphon as well as the successive changes in its development.

Not only does the second phase of the antiphon's development consist of a thorough overhauling of the old, millenarian beliefs but also this process itself seems to have taken place in at least three stages. Each stage appears to be represented by surviving variations in the two-part *In paradisum.* In the version preserved in the tenth-century Sacramentary of Fulda, the following scenario is imagined:

In paradysum deducant te angeli et cum gaudio suscipiant te martyres perducant te in ciuitatem sanctam Hierusalem.[25]

Here, angels first escort the soul to paradise, where martyrs receive it *cum gaudio.* The antiphon hopes that subsequently the soul shall be led through (*perducere*) to the holy city of Jerusalem. We see here a clear correspondence between the two parts of the soul's journey, and the two pleasant regions described in the Anglo-Latin visions: the martyrs dwell in the interim paradise until the arrival of Doomsday, and in the heavenly Jerusalem after that event. The movement of the soul enhances this distinction between paradise and heaven, and the addition of the prefix *per* to *ducere* might be seen as providing further emphasis on the movement *through* the first location to the second.

In the Hartker Antiphonary, which dates from the end of the tenth century and is preserved in St Gallen, 390–391, we see some further developments in the mutual relationship of these two stages:

In paradysum deducant te angeli in tuo aduentu suscipiant te martyres et perducant te in ciuitatem sanctam Hierusalem.[26]

Here, the soul is ushered into paradise neither *cum gaudio* nor *cum gloria*, but *in aduentu*. Also, the statements 'may angels lead you to paradise' and 'may

[24] See above, p. 4.

[25] Ntedika, *L'Evocation de l'au-delà*, p. 164: 'Let angels bring you into paradise and in exultation let the martyrs receive you; let them lead you through to the holy city, Jerusalem.'

[26] *Ibid.*, p. 164: 'Let angels bring you into paradise; on your arrival let the martyrs receive you and let them lead you through to the holy city, Jerusalem.'

martyrs receive you' are no longer joined together by the copula *et*; this now links the martyrs to the next stage of the journey: 'and may they lead you to the holy city of Jerusalem'. These adjustments, albeit small, could be read as representing a conscious decrease in the element of joy associated with the sojourn in the interim paradise, and a corresponding increase in the efficacy of the martyrs in ensuring the soul's movement from paradise to heaven. Later in this chapter, even more unambiguous evidence from the Book of Cerne will support this claim and clarify its implications.

It is by no means completely clear, however, where the sphere of the martyrs' influence is to be located. Are the martyrs in paradise or in heaven, or in both places? Again, the compiler of the Book of Cerne also faces this question, as we shall see later; here, let us focus instead on the solution which seems to have been adopted within *Ordo* 49. Its form of *In paradisum* differs from the St Gallen and Fulda versions of the antiphon in imagining the soul as arriving at *paradisus Dei* rather than *paradisus*; the verb *ducere*, not *deducere* is reserved for the action of the angels, with *perducere* remaining the verb used for the martyrs, and there is no use at all of *et*. The significance of these points emerges when we turn to the two antiphons which *Ordo* 49 prescribes at the end of the ceremony, once the body has been placed in the grave:

> In regnum Dei deducant te angeli cum gloria, suscipiant te martyres in regnum tuum; domine, de terra formasti eum et carnem induisti eum, redemptor meus, domine, resuscita eum in nouissimo die.[27]

The first, *In regnum Dei*, is a variation of *In paradisum* which focuses exclusively on its second stage – the moment of the Last Judgement, as indicated by its two references to the kingdom of heaven, an unambiguous mention of resurrection and the phrase *cum gloria*. The two antiphons, sung one after the other, would have brought out the parallels between paradise and heaven as well as their differences. The phrase *in paradiso Dei* anticipates *in regnum Dei* better than *in paradisum* does; the verb *deducere* joins *perducere* and *ducere* in order to delineate the different escorts for the soul on its two journeys, here described three times; the reservation of *cum gloria* for the second antiphon suggests that the greater joy is in the movement from the para-

[27] Andrieu, ed., *Ordines Romani*, IV, p. 530, and Sicard, *Liturgie de la mort*, p. 4: 'Into the kingdom of God let the angels lead you with glory, let the martyrs receive you into your kingdom; Lord, you created him out of earth and you clothed him in flesh, my redeemer, Lord, bring him back to life on the very last day.'

dise of God to the kingdom of God. At the same time, the repetition of *suscipiant te martyres* in both antiphons allows for the possibility that the martyrs dwell in both paradise and the kingdom of heaven.

This technique of lexical evasion is encountered time and again in the language of the liturgy and prayer, as we shall see later in this chapter. In the case of *Ordo* 49, the addition of *In regnum Dei* simultaneously preserves and undercuts the two-stage journey of the soul which is captured within the two parts of *In paradisum*. *In regnum Dei*, together with the final antiphon, *De terra formasti*, have been seen as injecting the hope of resurrection into the funeral rite.[28] Such a consequence might well have been intentional, as it assists a reinterpretation of *paradisus* within the antiphon as the eschatological rather than the interim paradise.[29] In this context, it is intriguing that two variations of the full form of *In paradisum* are preserved in two tenth-century manuscripts from centres of strong Anglo-Saxon influence, Fulda and St Gallen, with the latter also being connected with Redaction XI and the abbreviated tradition of the 'Three Utterances' exemplum. If the fourfold otherworld of the Anglo-Latin visions contributed to belief in the interim paradise within Insular centres on the Continent, as was suggested in the previous chapter,[30] did this influence stretch to the liturgy?

We can only speculate about this set of coincidences, but they seem supported by the fact that the two-part version of *In paradisum* was otherwise rejected by the formulators of the Old and Frankish Gelasian sacramentaries. A lone, truncated reference to the antiphon appears in one Frankish Gelasian, Zurich, Zentralbibliothek, Codex Rheinau 30, which leaves unclear whether both its parts were intended.[31] *In paradisum* is also absent from Benedict of Aniane's Gregorian Supplement to the 'new' Roman or Gregorian liturgy, which could have reached England either through Benedict's connections with Alcuin, or in the course of its general diffusion throughout Carolingian Europe.[32] In fact, Capelle suggests that the

[28] Ntedika, *L'Evocation de l'au-delà*, p. 165. *De terra formasti* also occurs once earlier in the rite, between *Chorus angelorum* and *In paradisum* and as the body is being placed in the coffin; see Andrieu, ed., *Ordines Romani*, IV, p. 529, and Sicard, *Liturgie de la mort*, p. 4.

[29] As the manuscript of the *Ordines Romani* is from the eleventh century, but the *Ordines* themselves, according to Andrieu, probably from the sixth, such reinterpretation could theoretically have taken place any time within this period.

[30] See above, p. 109.

[31] Capelle, 'L'antienne *In Paradisum*', pp. 254–5.

[32] See, in this connection, Bishop, *Liturgica Historica*, pp. 62–76, and Vogel, *Medieval Liturgy*, pp. 79–97; for Alcuin's role in the production of the Gregorian sacramentary, see

antiphon had been deliberately avoided in the Gregorian Supplement, although he does not discuss the possible reasons behind this exclusion.[33]

The gradual elimination of *In paradisum* in successive revisions of the funeral rite is accompanied by the retention of all references to the bosom of Abraham and the accumulation of references to the eschatological sense of *paradisus*. The following reference to *paradisus* occurs in the oration *Suscipe domine*, first seen in the Old Gelasian sacramentary, and retained in Frankish Gelasians such as the Phillips Sacramentary:

> Suscipe domine animam servi tui illius . . . inter paradysi rutulos lapides gaudium possideat . . . et inter pulsantes pulsans portas caelestis hierusalem apertas reppereat et inter videntes deum facie ad fatiem videat et inter audientes auditu caelesti caelestem sonum exaudiat.[34]

Here, unlike *In paradisum*, the precious stones equate paradise with the heavenly Jerusalem, where, moreover, one can see God face to face as in the heaven of the four-part otherworld. *Suscipe domine* thus appears to incorporate *paradisus* into a hope for the soul's reunification with the body after Doomsday in the bejewelled, architectural paradise of Revelation, rather than its safe-keeping in the interim paradise until then. Apart from *In paradisum*, *Suscipe domine* provides the only occurrence of *paradisus* in the Roman, Gelasian and Gregorian funeral liturgies. Was *paradisus* then retained in the funeral rite only when it bore an eschatological implication? This possibility is strengthened by the variation of *In paradisum* as *In regnum Dei* at the conclusion of *Ordo* 49.

Thus, the funeral rites likely to have been known in Anglo-Saxon England from the seventh to the early ninth centuries prefer *sinus Abrahae* to *paradisus* in describing the soul's immediate post-mortem fate, and tend to emphasise the synonymy of *paradisus* and *regnum Dei*. These preferences are in keeping with Augustine's equation of paradise, heaven and the bosom

footnote 32 (*cont.*)
Vogel, *Medieval Liturgy*, pp. 100–2. The author of the Supplement was thought to be Alcuin himself before J. Deshusses established otherwise in 'Le "Supplément" au sacramentaire grégorien: Alcuin ou Saint Benoît d'Aniane?', *ALW* 24 (1982), 19–46.

33 Capelle, 'L'antienne *In Paradisum*', pp. 258–9.

34 Sicard, *Liturgie de la mort*, pp. 314–15: 'Receive, lord, the soul of that servant of yours . . . let him possess joy amongst the glowing gems of paradise . . . and knocking, amongst those knocking, may he discover open the doors of the heavenly Jerusalem, and amongst those seeing, may he see God face to face, and amongst those hearing, may he hear the heavenly sound with heavenly hearing.'

of Abraham, later adopted by Ælfric in his homiletic exegesis. Yet, this was the same period during which Julian's *Prognosticon* and the otherworldly visions interacted to separate the interim paradise from heaven within the four-fold otherworld. We have also noted that the bosom of Abraham is hardly mentioned in Old English texts, and that newer versions of texts such as the *Transitus Mariae* and the 'Three Utterances' homilies regularly substitute paradise for the bosom of Abraham in their descriptions of the soul's fate after death.

Placed against this wider background, the formulators and revisers of liturgy seem decidedly conservative, even old-fashioned, in refusing to acknowledge the interim paradise within the language of public ritual. However, an attempt at compromise may be seen in the additional use of the phrase *locus refrigerii* within the funeral rite. This phrase appears to originate not in Roman usage, but in the various Gallican liturgies practised north of the Alps. Thus, it is not in *Ordo* 49 where *locus refrigerii* is first encountered, but in the oration *Te domine*, found with variants in Gallican rites such as the *Regula sanctarum uirginum* of Caesarius of Arles and the Gallican Bobbio Missal, and also seen in the Old Gelasian sacramentary.[35] The Old Gelasian sacramentary also contains the oration *Opus misericordiae*, which hopes for the soul's transfer to the *locus refrigerii et quietis in sinu abrahae*.[36] Here, we see a clear equation of the two terms, probably in an effort to explicate the meaning of the bosom of Abraham.[37] It is interesting that this liturgical use of *locus refrigerii* echoes its original application: the phrase is an expansion of *refrigerium interim*, 'interim refreshment', a description often applied by the millenarians to the state of the faithful in the bosom of Abraham.[38]

As the Old Gelasian sacramentary resulted from the intertwining of Roman and Gallican practices,[39] it could be argued that one of its direct consequences was the importation of *locus refrigerii* from Gallican orations like the *Te domine*. It was possibly felt that the opaque and rather old-fashioned

35 See Sicard, *Liturgie de la mort*, pp. 265–7. The Gallican liturgy is discussed by Vogel, *Medieval Liturgy*, pp. 1–4.

36 Sicard, *Liturgie de la mort*, p. 325: 'The place of refreshment and quiet in the bosom of Abraham'.

37 An identification noted also by Ntedika, *L'Evocation de l'au-delà*, p. 197, n. 258.

38 For the use of the phrase by Tertullian and Cyprian, see Stuiber, *Refrigerium interim*, pp. 52–5 and 68–9 respectively; and pp. 105–17 for its use in funerary inscriptions.

39 See Vogel, *Medieval Liturgy*, pp. 64–9.

sinus Abrahae could be enhanced by the greater descriptive force of *locus refrigerii*, usually qualified further by the evocative terms *lux*, *pax* and *quies*.[40] Thus, while the Gallican liturgy appears to have used only *locus refrigerii*, and the Roman liturgy *sinus Abrahae*, the Gelasian compromise results in the simultaneous use of both terms. This suggestion is strengthened by references to *Opus misericordiae* in Frankish Gelasians such as the Phillips Sacramentary which, it should be recalled, were also characterised by the weeding out of references to the interim paradise.

SUBSTITUTES FOR *SINUS ABRAHAE*: CHANGING PREFERENCES WITHIN THE PRAYERBOOKS

How are these liturgical definitions of the soul's post-mortem fate reflected in the language of the Anglo-Latin prayerbooks? The production of four prayerbooks within the same region and in quick chronological succession, before their Carolingian counterparts appeared on the Continent, suggests that they answered a specific Anglo-Saxon demand for extra-liturgical supplicatory material. Their function as private supplements to public worship is further confirmed by their physical characteristics as well as their regular alteration of liturgical formulae, which were probably perceived as being too stylised and ossified for the expression of personal pleas.[41] This attitude is reflected in the complete reversal of liturgical practice concerning the term *sinus Abrahae*, which is alluded to only once in the four prayerbooks. The prayer *Erraui in montibus* from the Royal Prayerbook concludes as follows:

> Domine ihesu suscipe spiritum meum quia anima mea turbata est ualde. In manus tuas commendo spiritum meum suapte ne dormiam in morte ut non timeam a timore nocturno neque a demonio meridiano. Recipe me in requiem abrahae ubi patrum requiescunt animae.[42]

[40] For a full investigation of the terms *lux*, *pax* and *quies* in the liturgy, see Bishop, 'Liturgical Note', pp. 266–75.

[41] This use of liturgical material by the authors of the prayers in the Book of Cerne is obvious from even a quick glance at Bishop's 'Liturgical Note'; for liturgical influences on the Royal Prayerbook and the Harley Fragment, see Sims-Williams, *Religion and Literature*, pp. 310–17; for connections between the liturgy and the Book of Nunnaminster see Birch, ed., *Nunnaminster*, pp. 20–2.

[42] Kuypers, ed., *Cerne*, fol. 44v, p. 220: 'Lord Jesus, receive my spirit since my soul is very troubled. Into your hands themselves I commend my spirit lest in death I sleep, so that

This metaphoric interpretation of *sinus Abrahae* indicates the desire to elucidate a phrase whose denotative force is no longer explicable. That this reference occurs only in the earliest prayerbook suggests an increasing unwillingness to incorporate *sinus Abrahae* into prayers for the soul's safety. Despite Augustine's argument that the bosom of Abraham had shifted from hell to heaven after the Harrowing, there was perhaps a general belief that the phrase simply referred to an upper region of hell, as suggested by Julian in Book II of the *Prognosticon*.[43] In any case, the reaction to the phrase *sinus Abrahae* seen within the prayerbooks is more representative of the larger Anglo-Saxon response to the concept.

In contrast, *locus refrigerii* recurs relatively often in the prayerbooks. The origin of the phrase within Gallican liturgy means that it could have circulated in Anglo-Saxon England even before the first Gelasian sacramentaries arrived in England.[44] However, within the prayerbooks as a whole, its use is gradually superseded by that of *paradisus*, a development most marked in the Book of Cerne. Its seventy-four prayers and hymns contain several supplications for the soul's entry to *paradisus* after death, one reference to *locus refrigerii*, and none at all to *sinus Abrahae*. In the Royal Prayerbook, *locus refrigerii* appears once and *paradisus* twice. The somewhat later Book of Nunnaminster contains two references to *locus refrigerii*, but none at all to *paradisus*. Conversely, its probable contemporary, the Harley Fragment, uses *paradisus* twice but not *locus refrigerii*, although its seven remaining leaves give too incomplete an indication of what it might have originally contained.[45] In other words, the Book of

I am not afraid of nocturnal fears nor the noonday demon. Receive me in the repose of Abraham where the souls of the fathers rest.' [43] See above, p. 93.

[44] See, in this context, Cabrol, 'Le *Book of Cerne*', Hughes, 'Irish Influence', and Sims-Williams, *Religion and Literature*, p. 274.

[45] This distribution of the terms *locus refrigerii* and *paradisus* across the prayerbooks is in keeping with the increasing complexity of content and presentation in those prayerbooks which survive intact; see Brown, *Book of Cerne*, pp. 151–5, for a fuller description of their contents, and pp. 141–2 for her interpretation of this comparative evidence: 'There remains little reason to believe that Cerne was substantially a copy of an earlier compilation. The earlier materials which it employed may have circulated in pamphlet form (the final section of Harley 2965 may preserve one of these) or in association with other materials . . . But there is no real evidence to suggest that the structural complicatons found in the ninth-century Mercian prayerbooks did not mark a new development in the devotional tradition.' For the alternative view of the Book of Cerne as being substantially a copy of an earlier Northumbrian core, see Dumville, 'Liturgical Drama', pp. 395–7, and Bestul, 'Continental

Cerne clearly prefers *paradisus* to *locus refrigerii*, the Book of Nunnaminster displays the opposite preference, and the Royal Prayerbook uses both terms as well as the bosom of Abraham. Are these choices random or dictated by a functional difference between *paradisus* and *locus refrigerii*? Moreover, how do the authors of the prayers distinguish between the eschatological and interim senses of *paradisus*? To answer these questions, as well as fully appreciate the prayerbooks' divergence from the liturgical norm, we need to turn to the actual prayers themselves.

In the earliest of the four collections, the Royal Prayerbook, *paradisus* and *locus refrigerii* appear to be used synonymously. In *Te fortissime*, the following supplication is made for the soul's post-mortem journey:

> Ut per aetherias potestates prospero cursu sospitalique itinere ad portas paradisi uiam arctam ualeam transuolando ascendere et ad sedes amoenitatis sanctas ac desiderandas semperque perfruendas.[46]

This wish is repeated in *O unigenitus*, cited at the beginning of this chapter, where the term *locus refrigerii* appears. Identical concerns are expressed in the prayer *Erraui in montibus*, which contains the sole reference to the *requies Abrahae* discussed above. Notwithstanding this lack of agreement on its destination, the soul's ascent through perilous regions remains the common focus of the prayers. The emphasis on the dangers of this journey reverberates throughout the collection. In several of the prayers the soul's destination remains nameless, with the supplication merely being for its unimpeded journey through the air.[47] Significantly, similar fears are sounded in Gallican orations such as the *Te domine*:

> Digneris domine dare ei locum lucidum et locum refrigerii et quietis. Liceat ei transire portas infernorum et vias tenebrarum maneatque in mansionibus sanctorum et in luce sancta quam olim abrahae promisisti et semini eius. Nullam laesionem susteneat anima eius sed cum magnus dies ille resurrectionis ac

footnote 45 (*cont.*)
Sources', pp. 104–5. It should be noted that none of the Cerne prayers which refer to an interim paradise have been proposed as belonging to this core.

46 Kuypers, ed., *Cerne*, fols. 36r–36v, p. 216: 'That I may have the strength crossing in flight to ascend the narrow way to the gates of paradise through the aerial powers on a prosperous course and safe journey and to the holy seats of pleasantness which are to be longed for and ever enjoyed.'

47 See, for instance, *Uerus largitor* and *Ymnorum solus dignus*, Kuypers, ed., *Cerne*, fols. 36v and 37v, pp. 216–17.

remunerationis advenerit. Resuscitare eum digneris domine una cum sanctis et electis tuis.[48]

The gates of hell and dark pathways which lie *en route* to the mansions of the saints are not specified in any part of the original Roman rite, and so appear to be particular concerns of the Gallican liturgy. It should be recalled that seventh-century visionaries like Furseus and Barontus also ascend through zones of various aerial dangers before they can enter more pleasant regions, as does the Monk of Wenlock, although Dryhthelm's horizontal journey is free from these aerial struggles.[49]

In fact, the Wenlock Vision shares some interesting verbal parallels with the prayers in the Royal collection. The phrase *locus amoenitatis*, used by Boniface to describe the post-mortem abode of the good soul, is reminiscent of both *locus refrigerii* and *sedes amoenitatis*. Another prayer in the Royal collection contains the phrase *locus tartarus*, which reappears in Boniface's description of the purgatorial region in the Wenlock Vision.[50] These verbal and conceptual correspondences fit in neatly with the Worcester provenance Sims-Williams suggests for the Royal Prayerbook,[51] and raise the tempting possibility that the authors of the prayers knew the Vision of the Monk of Wenlock. It is even possible, conversely, that Boniface was directly acquainted with some of these prayers, although this would push their date to before 717 AD.[52] Whatever their actual connection, it is important to note that the authors of the prayers and the visions obviously share the same world-view, in which nocturnal worries of impending death, demonic tortures and the safe-keeping of the soul preoccupied the imagination.

[48] Sicard, *Liturgie de la mort*, pp. 266–7: 'Deign, Lord, to grant him a place of light and a place of refreshment and quiet. Allow him to cross the portals of hell and the ways of darkness, and remain in the mansions of the saints and in the blessed light, which you once promised to Abraham and his descendants. May his soul sustain no lesion, but, when that great day of Resurrection and remuneration arrives, deign to raise him up, Lord, together with your saints and elect.' I cite the version from the Old Gelasian; Sicard also prints parallel texts of the versions of the *Te domine* found in the *Regula sanctarum uirginum* and the Bobbio Missal. [49] See above, p. 87.

[50] *Uerus largitor*, London, Kuypers, ed., *Cerne*, 36v, p. 216.

[51] Sims-Williams, *Religion and Literature*, pp. 279–82.

[52] In his 'Liturgical Note', p. 283, Bishop makes this claim even for the prayers in the Book of Cerne: 'I conclude that the prayers in this collection may be safely taken by the historian as representing the type of devotional feeling prevalent in England in the youth of men like Willibrord, Boniface or Willibald.'

Despite these similarities, there is an important difference between the visions and the prayers, related to their respective functions. The prayers do not contain the spatial, temporal, qualitative *and* terminological distinctions between paradise and heaven which the visions, as holistic descriptions of the otherworld, set out so exhaustively. It is not unexpected, however, that supplications for the soul's well-being should dwell upon the dangers of its journey after death rather than the differences between its immediate destination and heaven. There is another reason why these distinctions remain implicit in the prayers. In the Vision of Dryhthelm and the homily *In aduentu*, Bede had specified that the intercession of saints and the mercy of God were required for the soul's arrival at the interim paradise, either immediately after death, or after having spent some time in the provisional hell.[53] In the Wenlock Vision, similarly, those in the meadow automatically cross over the bridge to the heavenly Jerusalem, even though some are cleansed once again in the flaming river. If the authors of the prayers similarly considered the soul's promotion to heaven as being assured once it reached the interim paradise, further supplication for its entry into heaven would have seemed unnecessary to them.

These ideas are echoed in the *Oratio ad Sanctum Michaelem* in the Book of Nunnaminster, whose author calls upon Michael to take custody of the supplicant's soul after death:

> Ut in nouissimo die benigne suscipias animam meam in sinu tuo sanctissimo, et perducas eam in locum refrigerii pacis et lucis et quietis, ubi sanctorum animae cum laetitia et innumerabile gaudio futurum iudicium et gloriam beatae resurrectionis expectant.[54]

The phrase, *in nouissimo die*, which refers to Doomsday in *Deus apud quem* and *De terra formasti*, is here used for the moment of death. This transfer of eschatological terminology to personal or interim eschatology shows the freedom with which the authors of the prayers used their liturgical sources, even while indicating that, for the supplicant, the soul's fate after death was as important a consideration as its condition after Doomsday. The reference to the *animae sanctorum* waiting for Doomsday in the *locus refrigerii*, makes

[53] See above, p. 107.

[54] Birch, ed., *Nunnaminster*, fol. 36r, p. 87: 'On the last day, may you benignly receive my soul into your most holy bosom, and lead it to the place of refreshment, of peace and light and quiet, where the souls of the saints await the future judgement and the glory of the blessed resurrection with happiness and unmeasurable exultation.'

clear the difference between the state of waiting in the interim and that of ultimate heavenly joys. As in the Royal Prayerbook, there is no further request for intercession to ensure the soul's participation in the post-Doomsday rejoicing.

PARADISUS AND TWO-PART SUPPLICATIONS IN THE BOOK OF CERNE

A very different picture emerges when we turn to the prayers collected at the beginning of the ninth century in the Book of Cerne. In its third prayer, cited at the beginning of this chapter, the soul's stay in *paradisus* is stated as being *usque ad tempus resurrectionis*. Cerne 3, unlike several other prayers in the Book of Cerne, does not appear in the three earlier prayerbooks. It thus represents, together with two other prayers in the Book of Cerne, the first time that the prayerbooks define unambiguously the soul's abode after death as the interim paradise. That the soul remains in paradise only until Doomsday is further emphasised by a second supplication for the soul's fate *after* this event:

> Et post ea permitte me piissime pater aliquam partem aeternae beatitudinis habere cum sanctis et electis, et tuam gloriosissimam faciem uidere sine fine cum beatis et perfectis in saecula saeculorum.[55]

While the intensification of the soul's joy after the Resurrection is an expected outcome of its reunification with the body, the author of this prayer makes more than a merely quantitative distinction between the soul's condition before and after Doomsday. Cerne 3 speaks of seeing God face to face in the presence of the saints and the elect (*sancti et electi*) after the Resurrection – a considerable change from the state of rest alongside other blessed or holy souls (*sanctae animae*) that is expected in paradise. As in the oration *Suscipe domine* and the Anglo-Latin visions, therefore, the ability to see God is reserved for the company of heaven, which will include the ordinary good soul only after Doomsday.

A further development is signalled by the two supplications in Cerne 3. As stated above, the authors of prayers from the Royal Prayerbook and the

[55] Kuypers, ed., *Cerne*, p. 84: 'And after these things allow me, most holy father, to have some part of the eternal beatitude with the saints and the elect, and to see your most glorious countenance without end, with the blessed and the perfect, world without end.'

Book of Nunnaminster reiterate the belief that intercession helps souls escape from the provisional hell, but is not needed by those souls already waiting in paradise. In contrast, the double supplication in Cerne 3 suggests a new belief in the need for two stages of intercession: first, for the soul's safe arrival in paradise, and second, for its later transfer to heaven. The two supplications now highlight the distinction between the two locations, and change the function of the interim paradise from a waiting-room to a courtroom, as it were. No longer guaranteed a place in heaven, its inhabitants now require further intercession, and possibly further alms-giving and masses made on their behalf,[56] to ensure a favourable fate after Doomsday.

We have already seen how the genre of vision literature was catalysed by the early medieval need to bring together the different groups of the living and the dead, and how the monastic world responded to this need by taking on a mediatory role between the living and the dead on the one hand, and the Church and the laity on the other. In voicing the links that were thereby developed between intercession and the interim period, the prayers examined thus far resonate with this mood of the early Middle Ages. But the author of Cerne 3 strengthens this link by pointing to the greater influence of intercession upon the fate of the good soul, which renders the separation of paradise and heaven even more effective from the point of view of the Church. The funeral rite's apparent resistance to the interim paradise contrasts again with the prayerbooks, which, in the course of the eighth century, actually sharpen the relationship between the four-fold otherworld and the soul's interim fate.

Other prayers from the Book of Cerne also register these changes. The litany-like Cerne 29 opens with a short invocation to the Trinity and subsequently asks the nine angelic orders to intercede for the forgiveness of the supplicant's sins. The author then calls upon Michael and the other angels to take custody of the soul:

> Ut suscipiant animam meam in nouissimo die et perducant eam ad amoenitatem paradisi.[57]

This entire statement is almost identical to that quoted above[58] from the Nunnaminster *Oratio*, except for the appearance of the phrase *amoenitas par-*

56 A development which is seen in twelfth-century texts, discussed below, pp. 184–6.

57 Kuypers, ed., *Cerne*, p. 126: 'That you may receive my soul on the last day and lead it to the pleasantness of paradise.'

58 See above, n. 54.

adisi where the other prayer has *locus refrigerii*. Cerne 29 then invokes the apostles to ensure that

> in die iudicii . . . anima mea laeta aspiciat deum patrem omnipotentem et dominum nostrum iesum christum.[59]

It thereby alludes to the temporal difference between paradise and heaven by specifying Doomsday as the moment when the possibility of seeing God face to face can be realised.

Another litany-like prayer, Cerne 1, is comparatively less explicit in differentiating between paradise and heaven, but nevertheless seems to allude to the distinction through descriptive means. Its opening invocation to the Trinity is followed by a deprecation to the archangel Michael in his role as psychopomp:

> Rogo mihahelem archangelum sanctum et gloriosum qui ad animas custodiendas potestatem accepit, ut animam meam suscipere dignetur a corpore meo exituram, atque in amoenitatem paradisi perducere ac ibi conlocare in requiem beatorum spiritum.[60]

The supplicant next asks Gabriel and the angelic orders for intercession, presumably to ensure that Michael carries out his task. Then begin extensive invocations to the patriarchs, prophets, apostles, Mary, all virgins, Christ, and John the Baptist. Further intercession is requested from all saints and martyrs, and more specifically, Gregory and Stephen, before ending with a general plea for eternal life. Two descriptive pauses punctuate this rather rambling series of deprecations. Firstly, the nine angelic orders are briefly described:

> Intercedite pro me qui cotidiae ante thronum gloriae laudes aeterno deo sine fine concinnant.[61]

Later, a similar statement is made regarding the saints and martyrs, who are also asked to intercede for the soul:

[59] *Ibid.*, p. 127: 'On Judgement Day . . . let my joyful soul see God, the omnipotent father and our lord Jesus Christ.'

[60] *Ibid.*, p. 80: 'I ask Michael the holy and glorious archangel, who accepts authority towards the guarding of souls, that he should think it worth taking up my soul from its body, when it is about to leave [it], and lead it into the pleasantness of paradise and place it there in the repose of blessed spirits.'

[61] *Ibid.*, p. 8: 'Intercede on my behalf, those [of you] who daily before the throne of glory clamour with praises to eternal God without end.'

Una simul cum omnibus sanctis martyribus . . . qui semper adstant in conspectu agni amicti stolis albis et palmę in manibus eorum, et clamant voce magna dicentes: salus deo nostro qui sedis super thronum et agno.[62]

Both statements convey that the two sets of intercessors are permanently positioned close to members of the Trinity: the angels stand *cotidiae* before the throne of God, and the white-robed saints and martyrs are *semper* in the sight of the lamb of Christ. As in Cerne 3, these privileges are not claimed for the supplicant's soul.

These descriptions structure the supplications in Cerne 1 into two parts, corresponding to the two stages of intercession noted in Cerne 3 and 29. In the first part, angels intercede in heaven for the soul's journey to paradise, while in the second, the saints and martyrs, also in heaven, intercede for the soul's future transfer to heaven.[63] The image of the white-robed martyrs in heaven contrasts with the Vision of Dryhthelm, where the white-robed blessed were seen in the flowery meadow, and the Nunnaminster *Oratio*, where the *sanctorum animae* wait in the *locus refrigerii* until Doomsday. By being assigned to heaven rather than the heavenly antechamber, the saints can be imagined as continually interceding with God on behalf of the merely 'saintly', whose post-Doomsday fate now hangs in balance as they wait in the interim paradise. Cerne 1 thus presents a descriptive equivalent to the verbal distinction between the *sancti et electi* and *sanctae animae* we noted in Cerne 3, although, unlike both Cerne 3 and Cerne 29, its author does not make explicit the causal link between the intercession of the apostles, saints and martyrs and the ability to see God in heaven. In this respect, it recalls the two-part version of *In paradisum*, which hopes that martyrs will usher the soul into the heavenly Jerusalem, without specifying exactly how they would do so.

These three prayers in the Book of Cerne demonstrate what was already discernible in our discussion of *In paradisum*: the supplicatory function of the prayers and the increasing importance of intercession together developed and refined the qualitative distinction between the interim paradise

[62] *Ibid.*, p. 82: 'Likewise together with all the saints and martyrs . . . who always stand in the sight of the lamb, clothed in white robes and palms are in their hands, and they cry with a great voice, saying, "Hail to our God, who sits upon the throne, and to the lamb."'

[63] As this sequence of invocations is predetermined by the hierarchic order used in litanies, this could be one reason behind the author's choice of it over the alternative historic order, which is followed in other litany-like prayers in the Book of Cerne.

and heaven. This hierarchy is deepened through the new dependence of the good souls in paradise upon the superior merit of those in heaven, and the state of rest enjoyed by those in paradise is contrasted by the more active joys of the heavenly host. These implications are progressively well-defined in Cerne 1, 29 and 3 respectively, a sequence which coincides nicely with the fact that both Cerne 1 and 29 appear in earlier prayerbooks: the former in the Royal Prayerbook,[64] and the latter in the Harley Fragment,[65] which is placed chronologically between the Royal Prayerbook and the Book of Cerne. In fact, despite the textual overlap between all four prayerbooks, Cerne 1 is the only prayer which refers to the soul's post-mortem destination *and* is shared by the Royal Prayerbook and the Book of Cerne. Perhaps the other prayers in the Royal Prayerbook, with their accent on the dangers of the soul's post-mortem journey, were considered somewhat passé by a compiler half a century later, more interested in the new hierarchy between paradise and heaven.

The few but significant differences between Cerne 29 and its Harley counterpart also point towards a conscious tinkering with an earlier prayer to suit a later set of beliefs. The version in the Harley Fragment calls upon the scriptural angels Michael, Gabriel, Raphael and Uriel as well as Raguel, Heremiel and Azael, who are named only in apocryphal works such as *I Enoch*. This list, while providing a fascinating glimpse into the persistence of extra-canonical information in the medieval West, is nevertheless shorn of its more dubious members in Cerne 29. Secondly, Cerne 29 contains the following invocation before calling upon the apostles:

> Similiter et obsecro per deum patrem caeli et terrae omnes patriarchas prophetas apostolos martyres confessores uirgines uiduas innocentes et omnes sanctos dei, ut intercedant pro me in omni tempore.[66]

This addition fills some gaps in the list of those invoked by the Harley prayer, and sums up the different types of intercessors with the phrase *omnes sancti*. Unlike the Harley prayer, it also introduces the verb 'to intercede' before the description of the beatific vision, thereby emphasising the nexus between all saints, intercession and the sight of God.

64 Kuypers, ed., *Cerne*, fols. 18r–19v, p. 208.

65 As *Pater et Filius*, Warren, ed., *Antiphonary*, II, fol. 4r, p. 85.

66 Kuypers, ed., *Cerne*, pp. 126–7: 'And likewise, through God, the father of heaven and earth, I appeal to all the patriarchs, prophets, apostles, martyrs, confessors, virgins, widows, innocents and all saints of God, that they intercede for me at all times.'

The circulation of Cerne 1 and 29 in earlier prayerbooks indicates that the process of double supplication did not emerge suddenly in the early ninth century. Different beliefs about intercession and paradise must have coexisted from the mid-eighth century onwards, as attested by the existence of Cerne 1 in the Royal Prayerbook alongside other prayers which focus on the soul's post-mortem journey rather than its destination. By the time the Book of Cerne was compiled, or alternatively, for the compiler, the idea of two stages of intercession corresponding to two different locations perhaps seemed more attractive than the other, older view endorsed by the Anglo-Latin visions, and also found in prayers from the Royal Prayerbook and the Book of Nunnaminster.

PARADISUS AND *LOCUS REFRIGERII*: TWO OPTIONS FOR THE INTERIM

The presence of two competing mechanisms for personal salvation in the prayerbooks now explains their fluctuation between *locus refrigerii* and *paradisus*. *Locus refrigerii* appears in those prayers, such as the Royal *O Unigenitus* and the Nunnaminster *Oratio ad Sanctum Michaelem*, which adhere to the scheme of intercession set out by Bede and Boniface. In contrast, in those prayers which refer to *paradisus*, a greater importance is granted to intercession and the saints placed accordingly in heaven. This correspondence is most striking in the latest prayerbook, the Book of Cerne.

It thus appears that *locus refrigerii* and *paradisus* respectively connote the older and the more recent supplicatory processes evident in the prayers. The apparent synonymy of these terms in the Royal Prayerbook can then be explained by its thematic preoccupations as well as its early date. At the same time, the Book of Nunnaminster's exclusive use of *locus refrigerii* suggests either a preference for the earlier view or a rejection of the later, based perhaps on a reluctance to use the term *paradisus*. This deliberate conservatism could underlie the use of all available qualifiers in the other appearance of *locus refrigerii* in this collection, within the prayer *De sepulchro*:

> Praesta mihi quaeso quietis sedem et requiem purae beatitudinis locumque refrigerii lucis et pacis.[67]

[67] Birch, ed., *Nunnaminster*, pp. 77–8: 'Grant me, I beg you, a quiet abode and a repose of pure beatitude and a place of refreshment, light and peace.'

This attitude would have precedence in the absence of *paradisus* within both the Vision of Dryhthelm and the funeral mass practised in England. The individual prayerbooks thus exhibit that same diversity of response towards the interim paradise seen in the different versions of the 'Theban Legend' exemplum in later vernacular homilies, or in the fluctuations between paradise and the kingdom of heaven in the two Old English versions of the *Life of Margaret*.[68]

A further dimension to the weighted use of *paradisus* in the prayerbooks emerges when we realise that its application to the soul's post-mortem destination is always accompanied by the terms *amoenitas* or *suauitas*. Conversely, whenever these qualifiers are absent, a more general, eschatological meaning of *paradisus* appears. For instance, the phrase *requies paradisi deliciarum* is used in an eschatological description of the heavenly city in the Harley Fragment and in Cerne 50.[69] Likewise, Cerne 18 uses the phrase *portas paradisi* in an eschatological context.[70] Interestingly, a prior reference to the soul's post-mortem journey in the same prayer calls upon Michael to save it from various dangers, but makes no reference to its arrival at *paradisus*. The authors of the prayers thus use lexis to differentiate between the old and new schemes of intercession, *and* the eschatological and interim meanings of *paradisus*: the eschatological sense is conveyed through phrases like *portas paradisi* and *paradisus deliciarum*, while *amoenitas paradisi*, *sedes amoenitatis* and *suauitas paradisi* remain reserved for that interim paradise whose inhabitants require further intercession to enter heaven.

Intriguingly, while *paradisus deliciarum* and *portas paradisi* are exegetical and homiletic commonplaces, *amoenitas paradisi* and *suauitas paradisi* are frequent only in Mozarabic liturgy.[71] In the absence of firm evidence, however, the possible dependence of the prayers on Mozarabic sources remains in the realm of conjecture; a more plausible influence is perhaps Boniface's use of *locus amoenitatis*, itself unprecedented in vision literature. Whatever their source, it is clear that the authors of the prayers deliberately apply a relatively unusual turn of phrase to highlight a specific meaning of

[68] See above, pp. 64–9.

[69] See Warren, ed., *Antiphonary*, II, fol. 7r, p. 86, and Kuypers, ed., *Cerne*, pp. 149–50.

[70] Kuypers, ed., *Cerne*, p. 114.

[71] See Bishop, 'Liturgical Note', pp. 240–3, where he lists these and other parallels between Mozarabic liturgy and the Anglo-Latin prayers and Cabrol, 'Le *Book of Cerne*', p. 214, but note the reservations expressed by Sims-Williams, *Religion and Literature*, p. 313.

paradisus. This fastidious approach to terminology, most evident in the Book of Cerne, is probably prompted by the same anxiety towards meaningful supplication that leads to the general rejection of the term *sinus Abrahae* within the prayerbooks.

It is perhaps this anxiety which persuades the compiler of the Book of Cerne to include a solitary reference to *locus refrigerii* among all its prayers referring to *paradisi amoenitas/suauitas*. The Nunnaminster *Oratio ad Sanctum Michaelem* reappears as Cerne 53, which, moreover, immediately follows a repetition of Cerne 3.[72] Among all the prayers analysed here, Cerne 3 contains the clearest statement of the correspondence between *paradisus* and the two-stage supplicatory process. Its repetition as Cerne 52, often considered evidence for the compiler's use of two separate exemplars, thus becomes more meaningful if seen as a deliberate attempt to juxtapose the two views about the good soul's fate after death.

Cerne 53 is perhaps included as a precautionary measure against the possibility that the older view was the right one after all, or in case an inappropriate term was being used in prayer. Similar lip service to reservations about the interim paradise is paid through the ambiguous use of *portas paradisi* in Cerne 30, repeated as Cerne 69:

> Domine deus aperi mihi portas paradisi post obitum meum, ut in electorum tuorum numero mihi requiescere liceat, coram te Christe et coram angelis tuis.[73]

Does this supplication refer to the moment after death, or after Doomsday? While the phrase *post obitum meum* indicates the former, the references to the elect, Christ and the angels evoke associations with heaven. It seems that the polysemantic capacity of *paradisus*, whereby it shifts into different meanings according to its collocates, is here exploited to blur the lines between the interim paradise and the heavenly city. Once again, we note the sense of caution which undercuts the Book of Cerne's policy of incorporating prayers that term the post-mortem abode *paradisus*, in spite of the rejection of this meaning of paradise within funeral liturgy.

72 Kuypers, ed., *Cerne*, pp. 152–3.

73 *Ibid.*, p. 130: 'Lord God, open to me the gates of paradise after my death, that I be allowed to rest with the number of your elect, in the presence of you, O Christ, and in the presence of your angels.'

THE TENTH CENTURY AND BEYOND: A REFORMED ATTITUDE TOWARDS *PARADISUS*?

The transmission history of these various prayers through the Anglo-Saxon period shows that the compiler of the Book of Cerne was perhaps right to err on the side of caution. Though the Anglo-Saxon prayerbooks were extensively quarried later by Carolingian compilers of similar anthologies, none of the prayers which refer to *amoenitas paradisi* and *suauitas paradisi* are thus reused.[74] Neither do these particular prayers reappear in the late Anglo-Saxon devotional anthologies of the tenth and the eleventh centuries. In contrast, Cerne 53, with its reference to *locus refrigerii*, reappears in two eleventh-century prayerbooks contained in the manuscripts London, British Library, Arundel 155 and Arundel 60 respectively. Cerne 18, whose author uses *portas paradisi* in an eschatological context, is also found in Arundel 155, as well as a pseudo-Alcuinian Carolingian prayerbook, *De Psalmorum usu liber*. The ambiguous reference to *portas paradisi* in Cerne 30 reappears in a prayer to Christ and the Apostles in the mid-eleventh century collection preserved in London, British Library, Cotton Galba A xiv.[75]

These observations are in keeping with the tendencies visible in pontificals and other liturgical documents from tenth-century Anglo-Saxon England.[76] *Paradisus* is employed in some benedictions found in early Anglo-Saxon pontificals, but these occurrences communicate either a very general meaning of reward for a good Christian life, or firmly eschatological connotations which are brought out through simultaneous references to the tree of life and the heavenly Jerusalem.[77] They also often connect by a copula references to the heavenly kingdom and the celestial paradise, as in the following benediction for the Ninth Sunday after Pentecost:

[74] I summarise details from *ibid.*, pp. xxxii–xxxiii, and Brown, *Book of Cerne*, pp. 141–3.

[75] See Muir, ed., *A Pre-Conquest English Prayerbook*, pp. 50–1.

[76] Some early Anglo-Saxon pontificals are edited by Banting, ed., *Anglo-Saxon Pontificals*, and Turner, *Claudius Pontificals*; Turner also provides an introductory summary of the Anglo-Saxon witnesses to the pontifical tradition. The general development of pontificals is summarised by Vogel, *Medieval Liturgy*, pp. 225–39.

[77] See, for instance, the benediction for the Wednesday after Easter in the Egbert Pontifical (Paris, Bibliothèque Nationale, lat. 10575), in Banting, ed., *Anglo-Saxon Pontificals*, p. 71, and in the pontifical termed Claudius I (London, British Library, Cotton Claudius A. iii), Turner, ed., *Claudius Pontificals*, p. 13.

Confirmet uos in spe regni caelestis . . . et uos ad caelestis paradysi hereditatem perducat.[78]

The eschatological meaning of *caelestis paradisi hereditas* in these pontificals is further confirmed by the simultaneous appearance of references within benedictions to the eternal joys of heaven, or the eternal inheritance of the heavenly fatherland.[79] There are, however, no references to *paradisus* as a post-mortem destination for the soul in these pontificals. Even more telling is the evidence from an early tenth-century funeral rite included in the complex liturgical compilation known as the Leofric Missal (Oxford, Bodleian Library, Bodley 579).[80] According to Capelle, this rite is based on the Gregorian Supplement.[81] It includes, therefore, the antiphon *Suscipiat te* and the orations *Opus misericordiae* and *Deus apud quem*, all of which utilise the term *sinus Abrahae*. Also included is the oration *Suscipe domine*, which uses *paradisus* in an eschatological sense. Not unexpectedly, the antiphon *In paradisum* does not find a place here.[82] Other tenth-century material in the Leofric Missal echoes this attitude: as in the pontificals, *paradisus* refers to the Garden of Eden or is anchored to the phrase *caelestis patriae hereditas*.[83]

The language of tenth-century Anglo-Saxon liturgy thus indicates a continuation of the same orthodoxy towards vocabulary and its attendant concepts that was noted in funeral rites from nearly two centuries previously. Given this more or less unchanging backdrop, do the prayerbooks, especially the Book of Cerne, represent a fleeting rebellion against ecclesiastic conservatism, a momentary lapse from 'learned monasticism' into what may be seen as 'popular taste'? The answer to this question is complicated

[78] Banting, ed., *Anglo-Saxon Pontificals*, p. 79; Turner, ed., *Claudius Pontificals*, p. 19: 'Let him [God] strengthen you in the hope of the kingdom of heaven . . . and let him lead you to the inheritance of the celestial paradise.'

[79] As, for instance, in a benediction for the Tenth Sunday after Pentecost, in Turner, ed., *Claudius Pontificals*, p. 20, and for the birth of an apostle, in Banting, ed., *Anglo-Saxon Pontificals*, p. 100.

[80] See Warren, ed., *Leofric Missal*, pp. 198–203. The rite is part of what Warren terms 'Leofric A' and describes as a Gregorian sacramentary produced in early tenth-century Lotharingia. However Hohler, 'Service-Books', p. 78, maintains that Leofric A is 'patently English'. For the debate over the differing origins of the components first distinguished by Warren as Leofric A, B and C, see Banting, ed., *Anglo-Saxon Pontificals*, pp. xxiii–xxiv.

[81] Capelle, 'L'antienne *In paradisum*', p. 257.

[82] This antiphon is absent from all funeral rites based on the Gregorian Supplement, as Capelle points out in 'L'antienne *In paradisum*', pp. 257–9.

[83] Warren, ed., *Leofric Missal,* p. 20, for instance.

by several factors, not least of all the monastic milieu of the production and use of the prayerbooks. Though the prayers themselves were not always recopied, continuous annotation attests that the prayerbooks themselves were in constant use till the eleventh century. More importantly, their increasing references to the interim paradise indicate that those sensibilities we may term 'learned' and 'popular' are as difficult to separate in the prayerbooks as in the Anglo-Latin visions.

The visions of the otherworld had presented a complex interface between elements which scholarship would tend to dichotomise as 'popular' and 'learned' elements within early medieval monasticism. While the visionaries were liminally situated between the monastic and lay worlds, their original reporters, subsequent scribes and immediate audience belonged to the former environment. Elucidation, correction and fascination jostled within the same narrative and cultural space, which perpetrated both the problem of speculations on the afterlife and its intended prophylactics in the form of the visions described by Gregory and Bede. The function of the prayerbooks as materials for private devotion makes this circularity even more evident. There was no audience consciously intended for the prayerbooks, in a way that there was one even for the liturgical antiphons and orations; their compilers were almost certainly themselves the sole users.[84] Furthermore, the circumstances of the production and preservation of the prayerbooks means that these user-compilers were as much part of the monastic world as were the implementers and transmitters of liturgy.[85] Thus while the funeral liturgy, representing the official stance of the Church, propagated the terms *sinus Abrahae* and *locus refrigerii* to the laity, the monastic world, at least in early Anglo-Saxon England, increasingly prayed to be sent to *paradisus* after death.

[84] Brown, *Book of Cerne*, p. 183: 'Whoever originally owned the Book of Cerne is likely to have been involved in its production, whether in a supervisory/advisory capacity or perhaps even as the Artist-scribe.'

[85] *Ibid.*, p. 183: 'What can be said of the circumstances of the book's physical production is that it was made in a scriptorium whose scribes were used to writing literary and diplomatic materials in Latin and the vernacular, in a highly proficient cursive Minuscule script.' This identification would have been further encouraged by the nature of pre-reform Anglo-Saxon monasticism, which frequently blurred the distinctions between monasticism proper and the secular clergy, especially with regard to pastoral duties; in this connection, see Sims-Williams, *Religion and Literature*, pp. 115–43, Knowles, *Monastic Order in England*, especially pp. 3–56 and 592–606, and Blair and Sharpe, eds., *Pastoral Care Before the Parish*.

This private rejection of doctrinal orthodoxy by those involved in its public celebration brings us to Bishop's remark that 'the study of liturgy . . . must also be a study of religious psychology', and Sims-Williams's extension of this viewpoint to the study of private prayerbooks.[86] The prayers are, furthermore, indices to religious psychology, expressed through the written word. As literary artefacts, they reveal a conscious element of choice in the use of the most resonant and expressive phrase to articulate specific concerns. In the context of the soul's post-mortem fate, this appears to be either *amoenitas paradisi* or *paradisus amoenitatis*, with their simultaneous evocations of the delights of the classical and early Christian *locus amoenus*, the four-part otherworld of the visions, and the imagery of nature used for the paradise of the third heaven in the *Visio Sancti Pauli*.

Despite this apparent deviation from theological strictness, however, the allegiance to the Church remains fundamentally uncompromised within the prayerbooks. It is the use of *paradisus*, not *locus refrigerii*, which signals their development of the interim paradise to give more importance to the intercession of saints and martyrs and the resultant joys of heaven. In thus pressing the interim paradise into the service of the ecclesiastic establishment, the prayers take the ambivalence of the Anglo-Latin visions a step further. Ultimately, if the prayerbooks deviate from what liturgy promotes, they do so in order to search for the best possible way personally to supplicate for a suitable afterlife within the parameters of what is ultimately beneficial to the Church.

Yet, we have also noted that these forms of supplication seem unacceptable or, at the very least, unfashionable in tenth-century Anglo-Saxon England. Indeed, the new language of liturgy aggressively promotes not merely the bosom of Abraham as an alternative to the interim paradise, but the alternative, eschatological meaning of *paradisus* itself, a strategy highly reminiscent of Ælfric's insistence on the synonymy of *neorxnawang*, *heofon* and *Abrahames wunung*. It is therefore significant that the tenth-century liturgical documents examined here and Ælfric's anxieties over doctrine and orthodoxy share a common historical context – that of the Benedictine Reform.[87] It is possible that one of the effects of the Reform is a renewed orthodoxy in the use of liturgical and devotional terminology specifically with regard to the concept of the interim paradise. Especially significant in

[86] Bishop, *Liturgica Historica*, p. 123; Sims-Williams, *Religion and Literature*, p. 327.

[87] For which see now Gretsch, *Intellectual Foundations*.

this context is the language employed by Æthelwold within the New Minster Refoundation Charter of 966 AD:

Qui paradisiacae uoluptatis amenitate locatus nullius rei patiebatur dispendium sed ei totius mundi ad uotum subpeditabat facultas [88]

This description of pre-lapsarian life echoes the scriptural *paradisus uoluptatis*, but, in its simultaneous echo of *locus amoenitatis*, we may detect the realignment of this phrase, highly evocative of the interim paradise, with the Garden of Eden. Does Æthelwold's clarion call to a reformed way of life embed within its ornate style an example of how *paradisus amoenitatis* should henceforth be interpreted? These suspicions are confirmed by his later equation of the *limites paradisi* and the *sublimia regni celorum sedilia* (ch. 9), the point of which is to draw attention to the inaccessibility of both places after the Fall. These assertions bring us back to the typological equation of the Garden of Eden and the heavenly Jerusalem, advocated from Augustine onwards, but which – as we have seen repeatedly in the course of this book, and encounter again in the following chapter – always leaves open possibilities for the reintroduction of the interim paradise.

The Anglo-Latin prayerbooks have allowed us to trace the development of the interim paradise during the period between the Anglo-Latin visions and the appearance of vernacular prose and to see how the concept developed within different literary environments and over a span of three centuries. They also illuminate the changes in Anglo-Saxon monastic responses to the interim paradise. Pre-Reform monasticism tacitly accepted the interim paradise while overtly rejecting it in public worship, but this compromise was evidently seen as unsatisfactory in later centuries, when the Anglo-Saxon ecclesiastical establishment set about its task of reorganising monastic and clerical life. It is this stricter, more self-conscious attitude, then, which seems to have led some learned authors towards deliberate 'self-

88 No. 745 in P. H. Sawyer, *Anglo-Saxon Charters: an Annotated List and Bibliography*, Royal Historical Society Guides and Handbooks 8 (London, 1968), cited here from *Charters of the New Minster, Winchester*, ed. S. M. Miller, Anglo-Saxon Charters 8 (London, forthcoming), no. 23, ch. 2: 'Man, having been placed in the pleasantness of paradisiac delight, endured the lack of nothing, but the abundance of the whole world supplied everything he required' (trans. Miller, ed., *Charters*). For Æthelwold as the author of this charter, and for its style, iconography, authorship and historical implications, see Gretsch, *Intellectual Foundations*, pp. 129 and n. 98, 236–7 and n. 30, and 309–10.

fashioning',[89] which is manifested in their declared distance from the unwitting heresies and follies of the 'unlearned'.[90] It is this distance which, in turn, emerges as a divide between popular and learned sensibilities. As we have seen, this divide is neither unbreachable nor sits neatly upon the opposition between 'named author' and 'unnamed compiler/scribe/homilist'. Nevertheless, it cannot be denied that it does allow us to align an untroubled acceptance of the interim paradise within certain types of writing, and its attempted occlusion, through the synonymy of paradise and heaven, within others. What were the wider effects of these continuing and even heightened tensions surrounding the concept in Anglo-Saxon England? These questions are taken up in the two remaining chapters, which examine the evidence from poetry and late Old English prose.

[89] For the coining and implications of this phrase, see S. Greenblatt, *Renaissance Self-fashioning: From More to Shakespeare* (Chicago, IL, 1980).

[90] For its manifestations within Ælfric's writings, see Hill, 'Reform and Resistance'; also useful in this context are Gretsch's comments on Æthelwold and Ælfric in *Intellectual Foundations*, pp. 10–11, and the citations from Ælfric's 'Preface to Genesis' therein.

6

Doctrinal work, descriptive play: the interim paradise and Old English poetry

> Geseh he geblowene bearwas standan
> blædum gehrodene, swa he ær his blod aget.[1]

This picture of blossoming trees that spring up wherever Andreas's blood falls on the paved streets and rocky ground of Mermedonia seems to confirm the view that 'in Old English literature, heaven is often confused with paradise'.[2] The image brings to mind not only the regenerative powers of nature, but nature at its most ideal: the Garden of Eden. At the same time, the immediate context suggests that it offers us a glimpse of the post-mortem reward that awaits the martyr. Is this reward the kingdom of heaven, or does the imagery of nature suggest, instead, the flowering, fragrance-filled meadow of the interim paradise?

In this chapter, I analyse the apparent confusion between images of paradise and those of heaven in Old English poetry as a response to two, contradictory pressures: the typological equation of paradise and heaven and the belief in an interim paradise, separate from heaven. In the previous chapter, we noted that the synonymy of paradise and heaven was part of the 'learned self-fashioning' of certain authors throughout the Anglo-Saxon period, and seemed to have been encouraged particularly within the intellectual climate of the Benedictine Reform. However, we have also seen that the very same authors who advocate this synonymy often resort to evasion and compromise to accommodate the idea of the interim paradise. Through such compromises, furthermore, as in the Vision of Dryhthelm, the descriptive and conceptual differences between the interim paradise and heaven are further accentuated. I now demonstrate that similar compromises also shape poetic descriptions of the Garden of Eden, the heavenly kingdom and the interim paradise, although here we may restate the dialectic as one between orthodoxy and poetic craft.

[1] *Andreas*, lines 1448–9: 'There he saw blossoming groves stand, laden with leaves, wherever he had earlier spilt his blood.' Unless noted otherwise, citations of Old English poetry are taken from the relevant volume of *ASPR*.

[2] Tristram, 'Stock Descriptions', p. 106.

Old English poets wishing to describe heaven and the Garden of Eden had before them two options: visual imagery, and what may be termed aural abstractions. Within the former option, paradise is described as a green meadow, and heaven as a treasure-filled hall or stronghold. There is little possibility of confusing the two ideal spaces; but there appears little scope for their descriptive conflation. Poets wishing to equate paradise and heaven through descriptive means appear to have resorted fairly regularly to the latter option: aureate diction, syntactic patterning and sub-lexical ornamentation on the one hand, and a focus on abstract joys on the other, all features equally appropriate to paradise and heaven. What might seem, on first sight, a confused transfer of stylistic methods associated with heavenly joys to the description of paradise thus may represent instead a deliberate use of aural abstractions to further the synonymy of paradise and heaven, and to prevent the interpretation of *neorxnawang* as the interim paradise. However, this coexistence of visual and abstract resources could also be brought together within a single poem to create richly suggestive ambiguities, and to subvert doctrinal work through descriptive play.

VISUALISING PARADISE: *NEORXNAWANG* AS THE GREEN MEADOW

Within the imaginative vocabulary of Christianity, the term paradise has always connoted ideal natural beauty. The visualisation of this beauty is conditioned by the specific aesthetic expectations of different cultures at different times. In Genesis (Gen. II. 8–10), the Garden of Eden is described as *paradisus uoluptatis*, the paradise of delights, full of shady and fruit-bearing trees, and watered by four rivers. As was observed in the first chapter, various apocryphal works elaborate on this rather laconic description; for instance, the numerous versions of the *Vita Adae et Evae* add long lists of spice-trees and fruit-trees to their accounts of Eden.[3] Christian Latin poetry on the Creation and Fall presents the beauty of pre-lapsarian Eden in stylised set-pieces modelled on the classical topos of the *locus amoenus*.[4] For poets such as Avitus, Cyprianus Gallus and Dracontius, *paradisus* is Eden, a garden characterised by the synaesthetic appeal of flowers, fountains, gentle breezes and temperate weather.[5]

[3] See above, p. 18, n. 14. [4] See above, pp. 71 and 81.

[5] See Nodes, ed., *Avitus: the Fall of Man*, pp. 25–30, Peiper, ed., *Cyprianus Gallus: Heptateuchos*, pp. 2–3, Moussy and Camus, eds., *Les Louanges de Dieu: Dracontius*, pp.

In Old English poetry, such manneristic presentations of Eden are relatively rare. One example is that provided in *Genesis A*:

þa sceawode   scyppend ure
his weorca wlite   and his wæstma blæd,
niwra gesceafta.   neorxnawang stod
god and gastlic,   gifena gefylled
fremum forðweardum.   fægere leohte
þæt liðe land   lago yrnende,
wylleburne.   nalles wolcnu ða giet
ofer rumne grund   regnas bæron,
wann mid winde   hwæðre wæstmum stod
folde gefrætwod.   heoldon forðryne
eastreamas heora   æðele feower
of þam niwan   neorxnawonge.[6]

While Scripture provides the descriptive outline of this passage, the vocabulary employed to evoke the beauty of Eden relies on neither apocryphal nor Christian Latin descriptive traditions, even though both traditions were probably available to the poet.[7] Nonetheless, he hardly paints a blurred or indistinct landscape. Visually specific formulaic phrases, centring on the adjectives *wlite*, *fæger*, *rume* and *gefrætwod* emphasise details of brightness, spaciousness and vegetation. The verb *leohte* from *leccan* 'to water' also seems chosen to pun on the adjective *leoht*. In this lexical environment, even the semantically opaque term *neorxnawang* gains resonance through the synonymy of its second element *wang* with *grund* and *folde*, all three being words denoting open spaces capable of supporting vegetation.[8] The positive connotations of these images are magnified through emotive adjectives such as *god*, *gastlic* and *liðe*.

I have demonstrated elsewhere that these visual and emotive elements invariably recur in descriptions of desirable landscapes in Old English

159–61 and 217–22. For the influence of Christian Latin verse on medieval conceptions of paradise, see Evans, '*Paradise Lost*', pp. 107–42, and Patch, *Other World*, pp. 134–41.

6 Doane, ed., *Genesis A*, lines 206–17: 'Then our creator examined the beauty of his works and the glory of his fruits, of fresh creations. Paradise stood, good and spiritual, full of gifts through everlasting benefits. Running water, a welling spring, pleasantly watered the gentle landscape. No clouds as yet bore rain over the spacious area, dark with wind, yet the earth stood ornamented with fruits. Four noble rivers held their onward course out of the new paradise.'

7 See Evans, '*Paradise Lost*', p. 142, and Doane, ed., *The Saxon Genesis*, pp. 93–107.

8 The term *neorxnawang* is discussed more fully below, pp. 145–6.

poetry, which are evoked through a particular cluster of nouns and adjectives.[9] The nouns denote either green open spaces, such as *wang* and its compounds, *folde*, *land*, *grund*, *eorðe*, or areas supporting vegetation, such as *wudu*, *weald*, *holt*, *bearo* and their compounds, or units of vegetation, such as *treo*, *beam*, *blæd*, *wæstm*. Their shared visual qualities are emphasised by the adjectives which regularly accompany them: *grene*, spatial markers such as *rume*, *wide* and *side*, the participles or preterites of verbs of growth, such as *weaxende*, *þeaht*, *geblowen*, and adjectives of brightness such as *beorht*, *torht*, *leoht*, *wlitig* and *fæger*, which are used to idealise a wide range of referents in Germanic poetry.[10] As this combination of adjectives valorises the regenerative and expansive powers of nature, the overall connotative force of the nexus is highly positive.

Although this group of nouns and adjectives often appears in highly complicated lexical forms, all ideal landscapes in Old English poetry utilise at least one phrase consisting of an adjective of greenness, light or space and a noun denoting an open area of vegetation. The most frequent version of this phrase is *grene wang* although variations such as *grene eorð*, *grene land* or *wynsum wang* are also very common.[11] Formulaic equivalents of *grene wang* are also used to idealise landscapes both in the *Heliand* and in Old Norse poetry.[12] It seems that while the phrase *grene wang* derives from Germanic poetic tradition, in Old English poetry it forms the core of a distinct verbal cluster, both functional and ornamental, exhibiting observable rules of composition and expansion.

The landscape described by this formulaic system represents a vernacu-

9 A detailed analysis of the formulaic composition of ideal landscapes in Old English poetry may be found in my M. Phil dissertation, *'Grene' in Old English Poetry: an Investigation into Connotative Meaning and Descriptive Technique* (Unpubl. M.Phil dissertation, Oxford University, 1994). The following discussion summarises the analyses and conclusions made therein. Similar observations are made by Magennis, *Images of Community*, pp. 144–53.

10 See, in this connection, P. Beekman Taylor, 'The Old English Poetic Vocabulary of Beauty', in *New Readings on Women in Old English Poetry*, ed. H. Damico and A. Hennessy Olsen (Bloomington and Indianapolis, IN, 1990), pp. 211–21.

11 *Grene wang/wangas* is found in *Guthlac A*, lines 474–7, lines 742–6; *Menologium*, lines 206–7; *Riddle 12*, line 2; *Riddle 40*, line 83; *Riddle 66*, line 5.

12 See O. Behaghel and B. Taeger, eds., *Heliand und Genesis*, 9th edn., Altdeutsche Textbibliothek 4 (Tübingen, 1984), lines 757, 3080–2, 3135–6 and 4285; for similar examples in Old Norse, see *Atlakviða* 13, *Hárbarðsljóð* 16, *Vǫluspá* 59, in *Edda: die Lieder des Codex Regius nebst verwandten Denkmälern*, ed. G. Neckel (Heidelberg, 1983).

lar equivalent of the *locus amoenus*. Its focus is on natural expanse rather than cultivated garden, and the attributes that make it appealing have a predominantly visual force. For instance, the rejuvenated dwelling-place of Guthlac is described as a blossoming plain (*folde geblowen*) and the description is bracketed off by the statements *smolt wæs se sigewong* and *stod se grene wong*.[13] The same declaration *smylte is se sigewong* occurs in the landscape description which opens *The Phoenix*, and which also involves details of brightness, greenness and open space.[14] In *Genesis A*, the green landscape is evoked fourteen times, in order to describe outdoor spaces as diverse as the earth emerging from primeval chaos, the dry land sighted from Noah's Ark, and the land promised to Abraham and his descendants.[15] Noah re-establishes himself after the Flood in a similar landscape, evoked through the phrases *wlitebeorhte wæstmas*, *geartorhte gife* and *grene folde*,[16] and God's benevolence towards Old Testament patriarchs is always conveyed through a formulaic system which includes adjectives of greenness, brightness and spaciousness and nouns denoting either vegetation or topography.[17]

It is no surprise, then, that the same formulaic system should be utilised by the *Genesis A*-poet to evoke the most ideal landscape of all, the Garden of Eden. However, this description, which otherwise fulfils the lexical and conceptual expectations of the vernacular *locus amoenus*, lacks the adjective *grene*. Recent hypotheses regarding the etymology of *neorxnawang* can help explain this somewhat puzzling absence of greenness in this description. Although its final element *wang* is hardly problematic, the preceding elements of *neorxnawang* remain etymologically obscure. Earlier attempts to analyse the word's etymology often favoured solutions that pointed to the heathen Germanic past, and resulted in interpretations such as 'field of corpses' or 'courts of the dead', while other solutions, involving, for instance, the Old Irish form *n-erc* 'heaven', reflect growing critical acknowledgement of the Celtic influence on Anglo-Saxon culture.[18]

A different set of lexical and cultural data is used in Alan Brown's attempt to solve this etymological crux.[19] He reads *neorxna* as a back-to-front rendering of *groena*, an acceptable early West Saxon or Anglian spelling for *grene*. The reversal is signalled by *x* representing the *gyfu* rune,

[13] *Guthlac A*, lines 742–8. [14] Discussed below, pp. 160–4.

[15] Doane, ed., *Genesis A*, lines 112–23, 1449–54, 1468–74, 1476–80 and 1748–52.

[16] *Ibid.*, lines 1555–6. [17] *Ibid.*, lines 196–8, 1513–17, 1748–52 and 1787–90.

[18] For a summary of scholarship on the etymology of *neorxnawang*, see Brown, '*Neorxnawang*', pp. 610–12. [19] See n. 18 above.

such wordplay presumably being inspired by the habits of eighth-century Insular Latin writers. The whole compound would thus be equivalent to the phrase *grene wang*, which, he notes, is often applied to paradise in Germanic poetry, and which, as we have seen, forms the core of Old English formulaic descriptions of the ideal landscape. While Brown's claim for a 'penumbra of greenness' attached to *neorxnawang* is accepted by Jane Roberts, she rejects his 'complex elucidation', suggesting instead that an embedded plant name within the term could have well satisfied this sense.[20] Her own analysis of *neorxnawang* as *ne* (corpse), *rixa* (rushes) and *wang* forgoes the neat parallel with *grene wang* that Brown's analysis involves, but it does not negate the suggestion that greenness would have been inherent in the very term *neorxnawang*.

Whatever might be the correct etymology of *neorxnawang*, both Brown and Roberts admit that the question of its continuing transparency to the Anglo-Saxons themselves can never be satisfactorily resolved. What is important for the present discussion is the fact that even modern readers can detect in the word a 'penumbra of greenness'. Even though the first part of the term remains obscure and might well have been so to the poet of *Genesis A*, the high frequency with which *wang* collocates with *grene* in Old English poetry ensures that *neorxnawang* generates connotations, if not denotations, of greenness and open space.

The *Genesis A*-poet's later comparison between the green plains surrounding Sodom and Gomorrah and the paradise of God confirms his visualisation of the Garden of Eden in terms of what we may term the vernacular *locus amoenus*:

> him þa Loth gewat land sceawigan
> be iordane, grene eorðan.
> seo wæs wætrum weaht and wæstmum þeaht,
> lagostreamum leoht, and gelic godes
> neorxnawange.[21]

[20] Roberts, 'A Preliminary Heaven Index', p. 215. See also J. Roberts and C. Kay, with L. Grundy, eds., *A Thesaurus of Old English*, I, King's College London Medieval Studies 11 (London, 1995), entries 16. 01. 01. 01, 'heavenly dwelling-place', and 16. 01. 02. 04, 'Earthly Paradise', pp. 653 and 654 respectively.

[21] Doane, ed., *Genesis A*, lines 1920–4: 'Then Lot departed to examine the land beside the Jordan, the green earth. It was moistened by waters and covered with fruits, watered by rivers, and just like God's paradise.'

Furthermore, the few visual details that the *Genesis B*-poet invokes while referring to Eden also involve these descriptive features:

> 'Ac wit þus baru ne magon   bu tu ætsomne
> wesan to wuhte.   Uton gan on þysne weald innan
> on þisses holtes hleo.'   Hwurfon hie ba twa,
> togengdon gnorngende   on þone grenan weald.[22]

We see here the nouns *weald* and *holt*, denoting vegetation and topography, along with the adjective *grene*. Once again, therefore, the Garden of Eden is described through the formulaic system for the ideal landscape.

VISUALISING HEAVEN: *HEOFON* AS THE TREASURE-FILLED HALL

Just as Old English poetry can visualise *neorxnawang* as the ideal outdoors, so are descriptions of ideal indoor surroundings applied to heaven, which is often evoked as a hall or stronghold.[23] The primary inspiration for these descriptions derives from apocalyptic traditions of the heavenly Jerusalem, best seen in Revelation (Apc XXI. 11–21). Here, architectural components of the fortified city, such as towers, walls and gates, are embellished with images of flashing light, emanating from fire, gold and gems, with the catalogues of precious stones forming a descriptive parallel to the catalogues of spices found in apocryphal accounts of Eden. However, even as the constituents of the ideal landscape change in keeping with vernacular compositional traditions, so do the features of the Apocalyptic heavenly city undergo certain transformations in Old English poetry.

Some idea of these transformations may be obtained through the descriptions of heaven in *Christ II* (*Ascension*), such as that provided by the angels witnessing the ascent of Christ:

> We mid þyslice   þreate willað
> ofer heofona gehlidu   hlaford fergan
> to þære beorhtan byrg   mid þas bliðan gedryht,

[22] *Genesis B*, lines 838–41: '"But by no means can we two now remain naked thus, both of us together. Let us go into this forest, into the shelter of this wood." They both turned away, sorrowing together, into the green forest.'

[23] Hume, in 'The Concept of the Hall', discusses mainly the negative portrayal of architecture in Old English poetry, thus considerably simplifying the issue, but see Magennis, *Images of Community*, especially pp. 35–81.

ealra sigebearna þæt seleste
ond æþeleste, þe ge her on stariað
ond in frofre geseoð frætwum blican.[24]

The poet then reiterates that there was *blis in burgum* as Christ rose *ofer hrofas upp* (lines 528–30).

While the basic conception of heaven remains one of architectural splendour, the visual perspective is somewhat different from the walls, gates and towers of Revelation. Instead, *burg* draws attention to the whole structure and its connotations of strength and security, while *gehlidu* and *hrofas*, along with the particle *upp*, emphasise height and majesty.[25] *Frætwe* provides the Anglo-Saxon equivalent of precious gems, while *blican* and *beorht* foreground the visual and emotional appeal of the scene. These particular details may have derived originally from residual conceptions of Valhalla-like Germanic abodes of heroes, but in Old English poetry we see them assembled into a descriptive topos for the ideal indoors. Other features of this ideal Anglo-Saxon indoors can be found elsewhere in *Christ II*, as when the poet relates the consequences of the Harrowing of Hell (lines 570–85). After releasing the souls of the patriarchs from the *feonda burg*, Christ, *cyning on ceastre*, takes them to the *gæsta giefstol* through the *geatu* of heaven, where they shall enjoy happiness, joy and light.

The highly visual quality of these descriptions of heaven has been noted already by Peter Clemoes.[26] Their lexical constituents may now be enumerated. The reference always centres on a phrase comprising an adjective, or noun in the genitive, and a noun which signifies a large architectural unit such as *burg*, *ceaster* or, as we shall see later, *heall*. This phrase is augmented by at least one structural detail, often in the plural, such as *hrofas*, *gehlidu*, *geatu*, *weallas*, *setl* and *stol*. Visual appeal is communicated through nouns denoting treasure and adjectives or verbs expressing brightness. These descriptive details also heighten the emotional desirability of the location,

[24] *Christ II*, lines 518–22: 'With a similar troop we will carry the Lord, the best and noblest of all victorious sons, over the vaults of heaven and to that bright city, with this happy company which you look upon here and see in joy, resplendent with adornments.'

[25] Clemoes, 'Image of the Ascension', pp. 298, n. 1, and 303, n. 3, interprets *gehlidu* as the thin clouds separating the *caelum aereum* from the *caelum aetherium*. I prefer to read a more specific meaning of *gehlidu* as 'covering of a building, i. e. roof', as this accords better with the architectural terminology it collocates with both here and elsewhere in the poetry.

[26] In 'Image of the Ascension'. However, he is more interested in analysing the overall visual impact of the poem than in noting the architectural features within its images of heaven.

which is further emphasised through abstract nouns such as *blis* or *dream*, or through terms signifying *comitatus*-relationships, such as *weorud*, *gedryht* and *þegnas* on the one hand, and *þeoden*, *cyning* and *hlaford* on the other.[27]

The use of architectural imagery to describe the joys of heaven is particularly well illustrated in *Christ I* (*The Advent Lyrics*), especially wherever the poet expands upon the architectural metaphors he found in his source, the 'O' Antiphons.[28] The *lapis angularis* of the antiphon *O Rex gentium* is fashioned into the well-known simile of Christ as the *weallstan*. He is the head of the great hall (*heall mære*, line 4), the unbroken flint (*flint unbræcene*, line 6) that will enable the support of wall against wall (*weall wið wealle*, line 11) and the reconstruction of the house under the roof (*hus under hrofe*, line 14). Similarly, a single reference to Jerusalem, *ciuitatis Dei* in the antiphon *O Hierusalem* is elaborated into a description of *Cristes burglond*, with Christ's throne also mentioned twice as *cynestola cyst* and *engla eþelstol* (lines 50–2). Above the stronghold rises the bright and extensive roof of the heavens (*rodores hrof*, line 60) and within are the souls of the righteous, exultant in glory (line 54).

In a later image in *Christ I*, the ideal qualities of the stronghold and hall are metonymically transferred to the image of an *aþelic ingong* leading into the eternal home (line 308). The gold and surface ornamentation of this door is emphasised in anticipation of the splendour of the stronghold within:

> Eal wæs gebunden
> deoran since duru ormæte,
> wundurclommum bewriþen.[29]

The security, strength and majesty of the heavenly city are further conveyed by mention of the secure bars and the lock of the city gate (*fæstlice forescyttelsas*, line 312 and *ceasterhlides clustor*, line 314). This gate will be unlocked by Christ, who is himself described earlier as a *wealldor* (line 54).

[27] *Ibid.*, pp. 294–5, discusses the application of 'heroic literary tradition' to the 'cult of Christ as king'. For a more general exploration of the fusion of heroic and Christian concepts in Old English poetry, see A. A. Lee, *The Guest-Hall of Eden: Four Essays on the Design of Old English Poetry* (New Haven, CT, and London, 1972).

[28] For details on the sources of *Christ I* and its relationship to the 'O' Antiphons, see Campbell, ed., *Advent Lyrics*, pp. 11–35, and Rankin, 'Liturgical Background of the Old English Advent Lyrics'.

[29] *Christ I*, lines 308–10: 'The huge door was completely bound with precious treasure, wrapped with wonderful fastenings.'

In *Christ I*, we see how architectural terminology for heaven is deployed to highlight the interdependence of the part and the whole. The frequent references to cornerstones, roofs, vaults, gates and walls are accompanied by compounds such as *ceasterhlidu*, *wealldor* and *weallstan*, in which the morphological relationship of the separate elements reaffirms the position of the structural components within larger architectural units. The descriptive resources for the ideal indoors are thus used to convey dynamically the intimate and organic relationship between Christ, heaven and the faithful.

DESCRIPTIVE CONFLATION: THE 'GREEN STREET' TO HEAVEN IN *CHRIST AND SATAN*

Old English poetry thus possesses parallel traditions of idealising indoor and outdoor space through visual description. Having analysed how these traditions are used to describe heaven and paradise respectively, we now turn to their conflation in *Christ and Satan*. Here, heaven has all the trappings of the treasure-filled hall:

> þær is geat gylden   gimmum gefrætewod,
> wynnum bewunden,   þæm þe in wuldres leoht
> gongan moten   to godes rice,
> and ymb þa weallas   wlitige scinað
> engla gastas   and eadige sawla,
> þa ðe heonon ferað.
> þær martiras   meotode cwemað,
> and herigað hehfæder   halgum stefnum,
> cyning in cestre.[30]

This highly visualised description of heaven contains several nouns and adjectives denoting architectural units, treasure and brightness. Abstract concepts are rendered concrete through syntactic association with terms that can be easily visualised, as in the phrase *wynnum bewunden* in variation with *gimmum gefrætewod*, and the image of souls shimmering on the walls of the heavenly city. Such techniques recur throughout the poem, as when the

[30] *Christ and Satan*, lines 647–55: 'There is the golden gate, adorned with gems, wound about with joys, of those who can enter God's kingdom in the light of glory, and around the walls brightly shimmer spirits of angels and the blessed souls of those who depart hence. There martyrs please the lord, and praise the high Father, the king in the city, with holy voices.'

poet renders the noun *ham* more specific through variation with *beorhte burhweallas*, or describes the souls shining brightly as they dwell amidst the *cester* and *cynestol* (lines 293–7).

At the same time, the poet embeds within these descriptions terminology characteristic of ideal landscapes:

> is þær wlitig and wynsum, wæstmas scinað,
> beorhte ofer burgum. Þær is brade lond,
> hyhtlicra ham in heofonrice,
> Criste gecwemra.[31]

As we have seen, the collocation of the adjectives *fæger* and *brad*, *wlitig* and *wynsum*, with nouns denoting topography and vegetation, such as *land*, *folde* and *wæstmas*, is typical of Old English descriptions of ideal landscapes, which here feature within the strongholds of heaven. This penchant for yoking together nouns from separate descriptive traditions is exemplified by the 'green street', which the poet describes as leading to heaven:

> gearwian us togenes grene stræte
> up to englum, þær is se ælmihtiga god.[32]

The lack of literal sense in the phrase *grene stræt* has often been attributed to abstraction, while others have attempted to place the 'green street' within biblical paradigms.[33] However, a more convincing solution to the crux may lie in our reading of it as an attempt to conflate two traditions of visualising ideal space. *Stræt* denotes a highway or a paved Roman road – in other words, an artificial construction. In the phrase *grene stræt*, therefore,

[31] *Ibid.*, lines 213–16: 'It is bright and pleasant there, the fruits shine brightly over the fortresses. There it is a spacious land, the home of the hopeful in the kingdom of heaven, of those obedient to Christ.'

[32] *Christ and Satan*, lines 286–7: '[Let us] prepare ourselves together for the green street up to the angels, where the almighty God is.'

[33] Thus M. D. Clubb, ed., *Christ and Satan* (New Haven, CT, 1925), p. 87, cites Schücking to the effect that '*grene* here has more the meaning of "schön" rather than that of the sensuous "green".' H. T. Keenan, '*Exodus 312*: The Green Street of Paradise', *NM* 71 (1970), 455–60, attributes green to biblical associations of greenness with charity, while A. N. Doane, 'The Green Street of Paradise: A Note on Lexis and Meaning in Old English Poetry', *NM* 74 (1973), 456–65, sees the green street as a formulaic variation on *grene wangas*, but does not find any qualitative difference between the two phrases. See also H. T. Keenan, '*Exodus* 312a: Further Notes on the Eschatological "Green Ground"', *NM* 74 (1973), 217–19.

the poet of *Christ and Satan* brings together a noun connoting architectural imagery, with an adjective associated with ideal landscapes. This results in an image fairly incongruous on the literal level.

Why does the poet of *Christ and Satan* conflate, in this somewhat unsatisfactory manner, elements from the ideal landscape and the ideal indoors? The answer may lie in his composite presentation of heaven, which is visualised as a radiant city, complete with throne, walls and treasure, but also including within its compass shining fruits, broad expanses and greenness. In other words, images of *neorxnawang* are subsumed into the larger picture of *heofon*, even as Ælfric achieves the same effect by enclosing the *grennys* of Dryhthelm's meadow within a *burg*.[34] In both texts, the conceptual equivalent of this iconographic representation is the Augustinian identification of paradise and heaven.

It thus seems that the poet of *Christ and Satan* manipulates traditional poetic diction to underscore a doctrinal point. This contention is in keeping with the poet's overall conservatism in the treatment of other doctrinally sensitive issues. His account of the Harrowing of Hell, for instance, resembles the more orthodox *Latin B* version of the *Gospel of Nicodemus*, which mentions neither Enoch and Elijah nor paradise, and in which all those saved by Christ enter directly into heaven.[35] Similarly, his description of Doomsday lacks the account of the Six Signs before Judgement, which is frequently included in anonymous homilies, but which ultimately derives from the apocryphal *Apocalypse of Thomas*. In general, the poet deviates from Scripture only to follow mainstream patristic tradition as represented by Augustine, Gregory and Bede.[36] Rather ironically, the vocabulary of brightness and fecundity that the poet is committed to use draws his picture of heaven closer to the paradise of the third heaven in the *Visio*, though this describes a glittering city within a fertile landscape rather than the other way around.

NO SPACE FOR THE INTERIM? HEAVEN, PARADISE AND DESCRIPTIVE TYPOLOGY

The visual conflation of paradise and heaven seen in *Christ and Satan* does not appear in any other Old English poem. Far more common is another

[34] See above, p. 46. [35] See further, p. 176 below.

[36] For the sources of *Christ and Satan*, see R. E. Finnegan, ed., *Christ and Satan: a Critical Edition* (Waterloo, Ontario, 1977), pp. 37–55, and Sleeth, *Studies in 'Christ and Satan'*, pp. 50–67.

method of descriptively conflating paradise and heaven, which can be observed in a brief introductory passage from *Guthlac B*, describing Adam's existence in *neorxnawang*:[37]

> Fæder wæs acenned
> Adam ærest þurh est godes
> on neorxnawong, þær him nænges wæs
> willan onsyn, ne welan brosnung,
> ne lifes lyre ne lices hryre,
> ne dreames dryre ne deaðes cyme,
> ac he on þam lande lifgan moste
> ealra leahtra leas, longe neotan
> niwra gefeana. þær he no þorfte
> lifes ne lissa in þam leohtan ham
> þurh ælda tid ende gebidan,
> ac æfter fyrste to þam færestan
> heofonrices gefean hweorfan mostan [.][38]

The joys of life in Eden are evoked through a variation on what Hildegard Tristram terms the *þær is* syntagm.[39] The initial *þær him* is followed by four *ne* phrases, linked by internal rhyme and assonance, as for example in *lyre*, *hryre* and *dryre*, while an *ac* clause sums up the implications of the preceding catalogue. As Tristram has analysed, the same syntactic patterns are commonly used in homiletic and poetic descriptions of heaven. Thus, despite the poetic resources for visualising ideal landscapes, the poet turns to phrases associated with descriptions of heavenly joys in order to evoke the Garden of Eden.[40] Neither is heaven evoked through architectural terminology: the poet uses, instead, the phrase *heofonrices gefea*, while, a few

[37] This passage deviates from the rest of the poem in being largely independent of the account of Guthlac's death given by Felix in the fiftieth chapter of his *Vita Guthlaci*; see, in this context, Roberts, ed., *The Guthlac Poems*, pp. 36–42.

[38] *Guthlac B*, lines 827–37: 'First, through the grace of God, Adam the father was born in paradise, where there was for him the lack of nothing desirable, no withering of prosperity, neither loss of life nor decay of body, neither lessening of happiness nor arrival of death, but he could have lived in that land free of all faults, to enjoy for a long time new joys; there in that radiant home he did not need to expect the end of life and of pleasures through the passing of the world's ages, but, after a while, they would have moved into the fairest of the heavenly kingdom's joys.'

[39] Tristram, 'Stock Descriptions', pp. 102–7.

[40] In *ibid.*, p. 106, Tristram notes this particular instance to support her comment, cited above, that 'in Old English literature heaven is often confused with paradise'.

lines above, *gefean* is used for the joys of pre-lapsarian life in paradise.[41] It thus appears that the poet has deliberately switched diction between the two locations of Eden and heaven, possibly to conform to the typological equation of *neorxnawang* and *heofon*. However, this lexical conflation runs counter to the narrative content of the passage. The poet speculates that had Adam and Eve not sinned, they would have passed on in a little while from Eden into heaven. Thus, while his underlying assumption is that *neorxnawang* and *heofon* are two separate places, his diction reveals a simultaneous anxiety to deny this possibility.

Despite this fundamental ambivalence, the poet of *Guthlac B* achieves the desired identification of the two locations through descriptive strategies, which appear more successful than those employed by the poet of *Christ and Satan*. Unlike the latter, he avoids altogether visual details, and instead uses for each location, abstract ideas couched in diction traditionally associated with the other. While the corresponding visual details cannot be interchanged or amalgamated without conceptual confusion, the abstract diction can be transferred from heaven to paradise without any change in the basic ideas. The successful lexical interchange confirms the validity of the conceptual equation, even as the concentration on abstract ideas means that neither landscapes nor strongholds emerge from the descriptions.

The tendency to equate *neorxnawang* and *heofon* by focusing on their abstract rather than visual characteristics is also seen in *Christ III*. There is a large degree of lexical overlap between its evocation of heavenly joys and its two, comparatively brief references to the Garden of Eden (lines 1389–93 and 1403–7), both of which occur within Christ's speech to mankind on Doomsday.[42] The words and phrases common to these passages and an earlier account of heaven (lines 1344–8) include *lifwelan* (line 1347) and *blædwelan* (line 1391), *beorht eðles wlite* (line 1346), which parallels *neorxnawanges wlite* (line 1405), and the noun *eþel* (lines 1342, 1346 and

[41] *Gefea* recurs through *Guthlac B* as a reference to heavenly joys, as for instance in *ece gefea*, line 1079, *long gefea*, line 1091, *fæger gefea*, line 1181.

[42] The source for this speech is the *Ego te, O homo* speech composed by Caesarius of Arles within his Sermon LVII, as was first established by R. Willard, 'Vercelli Homily VIII and *The Christ*', *PMLA* 42 (1927), 314–30, and explored further by E. B. Irving, Jr, in 'Latin Prose Sources for Old English Verse', *JEGP* 57 (1958), 588–95; see also P. E. Szarmach, 'Cesarius of Arles and the Vercelli Homilies', *Traditio* 26 (1970), 315–23. For Sermon LVII, see Morin, ed., *Caesarii Arelatensis sermones*, pp. 251–4.

1406) which also introduces the poem's penultimate catalogue of heavenly joys (lines 1639–64).[43] At the same time, the nouns *blæd*, *eþel*, *duguþ* and *dream*, which contain a metaphorical level of meaning, and a number of adjectives of brightness are employed across the poem's range of descriptive passages, to further encourage the process of conceptual identification. In the absence of concrete details, moreover, the onus of idealisation falls on sub-lexical ornamentation, such as alliteration, cross-alliteration and assonance, as seen in the extravagant account of heaven which closes the poem. The aural beauty of the description itself communicates the superlative character of what is being described.

The typological function of these aural effects is well illustrated within *Andreas*. Early on in the poem, God promises Matthew that *neorxnawang* awaits him after eight days:

> þe is neorxnawang,
> blæda beorhtost, boldwela fægrost,
> hama hyhtlicost, halegum mihtum
> torht ontyned. þær ðu tyres most,
> to widan feore willan brucan.[44]

Unlike *Guthlac B*, *neorxnawang* in *Andreas* seems to refer not to the Garden of Eden, but to the reward which awaits saints and martyrs after death. As we have noted in the previous chapters, this is the context in which the term paradise was most vulnerable to interpretation as an interim abode. The terminology employed by the *Andreas*-poet indicates that he was highly aware that his description could be thus interpreted. Firstly, only those words are used which are capable of bearing both a literal and a metaphorical significance, such as the noun *blæd*, which is frequently used in landscape descriptions to mean 'leaf', but which also means 'reward, prosperity'. Even though its literal meaning is capable of informing this particular context, *blæd* gains a greater degree of metaphoricity in collocation with the abstract noun *boldwela*. In addition, the three verses in compound variation lead to the syntactic equality of *blæd*, *boldwela* and *ham*, and further encourage an abstract rather than literal and specific reading of *blæd*. Similarly, the syntax

43 Sleeth, *Studies*, pp. 100–4, provides a thorough analysis of the various senses of *eðel* in Old English poetry.

44 *Andreas*, lines 102–6: 'To you is paradise, the brightest of prosperity, the fairest of splendid dwellings, the most hopeful of homes, revealed bright through divine power. There you shall be able to enjoy forever the pleasures of glory.'

influences our understanding of *beorhtost* as an abstract rather than visual quality, in keeping with the ideas expressed by the other superlatives *hyhtlicost* and *fægrost*.

This description of *neorxnawang* is carefully aligned to the heavenly joys described by the disciples as they recount their dream to Andreas:

> Þa comon earnas ofer yða wylm
> faran on flyhte feðerum hremige,
> us ofslæpendum sawle abrugdon,
> mid gefean feredon flyhte on lyfte,
> brehtmum bliðe, beorhte ond liðe.
> Lissum lufodon ond in lofe wunodon,
> þær wæs singal sang ond swegles gong,
> wlitig weoroda heap ond wuldres þreat.
> Utan ymbe æðelne englas stodon,
> þegnas ymb þeoden, þusendmælum,
> heredon on hehðo halgan stefne
> dryhtna dryhten. Dream wæs on hyhte.[45]

This passage is an excellent example of how dense aural ornamentation, achieved through variations of rhythm, alliteration, rhyme and assonance, conveys the transcendent beauty of heaven, rather than visual description of the sort seen in the *Christ I* or in *Christ II*. The predominant sounds are *y* as medial vowel, liquids such as *l* and *r* and fricatives such as *f*, which together communicate the joyous flight of the eagles. The only line lacking these sounds is *us ofslæpendum sawle abrugdon*, which corresponds to the pause in the birds' flight as they pluck out the souls. The *-yht* consonant cluster, repeated through the description of the flight, recurs again in the last line cited, sealing off this passage as a discrete segment. This distribution of the *-yht* words also links the concept of upward flight with joy and hope, as the *dr-* of *dream* and *-yht* of *hyht* represent, through tmesis, the meaning of *dryhten*.

[45] *Andreas*, lines 863–74: 'Then eagles came over the surging of the waves, to travel in flight, exultant in their wings; they plucked out the souls from us as we slept, bore them with joy in flight through the air, happy in revelry, bright and gentle, they lovingly adored, and dwelt in praise, there where was unceasing song and ethereal progress, a shining throng of hosts and a troop of glory. Encircling the noble one, angels stood, thanes in groups of thousands; around the prince with holy voices they praised to the heights the Lord of lords. Joy was in exultation.'

This *-yht* sound was anticipated in the earlier account of *neorxnawang*, in the phrase *hama hyhtlicost*. Also, the phrase *blæda beorhtost* in that description finds lexical echoes here in the adjectives *beorht* and *wlitig*. The disciples next describe the inhabitants of heaven, with two lines of internal rhyme marking the end of the description:

> þær wæs wuldres wynn,   wigendra þrym,
> æðelic onginn,   næs þær ænigum gewinn.[46]

Here, the predominant sounds are again *i* or *y*, though combined with a nasal consonant. This consonant cluster is also anticipated in the phrase *torht ontyned* within the description of *neorxnawang*.

Thus, in *Andreas*, the initial description of the paradise promised to Matthew is aurally enmeshed with the disciples' description of heavenly joys. In his greater reliance on sub-lexical rather than lexical devices, the poet takes a step further the process of identifying the two locations through abstract ideas that we noted in *Guthlac B*. Furthermore, the identification of paradise and heaven is not restricted to these two passages alone, but structurally and thematically integrated into the poem as a whole. The *Andreas*-poet frequently refers to the departure of a member of the holy Trinity upward to the heavenly abode, in statements which are both lexically and structurally formulaic. Each unit includes at least one detail which progressively amalgamates the characteristics of heaven and paradise given in the two descriptions earlier analysed.

The first such reference follows God's promise to Matthew of both *neorxnawang* and Andreas's help:

> Gewat him þa se halga   helm ælwihta,
> engla scyppend,   to þam uplican
> eðelrice.[47]

Here, God's destination is simply the *uplic eðelrice*. There is as yet no lexical identification of this destination with the *neorxnawang* that will constitute Matthew's reward. The next such formulaic unit occurs after God commands Andreas to leave for Mermedonia:

46 *Andreas*, lines 887–8: 'There was pleasure of glory, the throng of warriors, noble action, there was no strife there.'

47 *Andreas*, lines 118–20: 'Then the holy protector of all things, the creator of the angels, departed to the fatherland above.'

Gewat him þa se halga healdend ond wealdend,
upengla fruma, eðel secan,
middangeardes weard, þone mæran ham,
þær soðfæstra sawla moton
æfter lices hryre lifes brucan.[48]

Eðel resonates with the earlier reference to *eðelrice*, while *ham* and *brucan* echo the *hama hyhtlicost* and *brucan* of the *neorxnawang* passage. The qualification for entry and residence in this home makes it clear that it is to be identified as place where the souls of all the faithful go immediately, and permanently, after death. The third use of the departure formula is when Christ reveals himself to Andreas on the shores of Mermedonia:

Gewat him þa se halga heofonas secan,
eallra cyninga cining, þone clænan ham
eaðmedum upp, þær is ar gelang
fira gewhylcum, þam þe hie findan cann.[49]

At this point in the narrative, the disciples have already described their dream to Andreas, and the similarities between their description and that of *neorxnawang* have been established through aural devices. The process of sub-lexical identification is now confirmed on the lexical level as, for the first time, the departure formula brings together the terms *heofonas* and *ham*. *Neorxnawang*, the *hama hyhtlicost*, is thus formally defined as *heofon*. Finally, the sacramental significance of this definition is stated while the poet describes the effects of Andreas's conversion of the Mermedonians:

tireadigra
wenede to wuldre weorod unmæte,
to þam halgan ham heofona rices,
þær fæder ond sunu ond frofre gast
in þrinnesse þrymme wealdeð
in woruld worulda wuldorgestealda.[50]

48 *Andreas*, lines 225–9: 'Then the holy defender and ruler, creator of the angels above, guardian of the earth, departed to seek his homeland, the glorious home where the souls of the righteous may enjoy life after the body's decay.'

49 *Andreas*, lines 977–80: 'Then the holy one, the king of all kings, departed kindly to seek the heavens, the pure home above; there grace belongs to each man, to him who can find it.'

50 *Andreas*, lines 1681–6: 'He instructed an unmeasurable multitude of the blessed to glory, to the holy home of the heavenly kingdom, where Father and Son and the comforting Spirit rule the glorious mansions through the majesty of the Trinity, world without end.'

The importance of this statement is communicated through the aural effects of paronomasia – *þrinness* and *þrym*, *woruld* and *wuldor* – and assonance within *wealdan* and *-geteald*. The poem's concluding reference to heaven reiterates, through the terms *blæd* and *wlitig*, the connection with the initial *neorxnawang* passage (lines 1719–21). Yet, the force of these terms remains abstract, especially as the nouns and adjectives used in the departure formulae are not visually specific: *uplic eðelrice*, *mære ham*, *clæn ham*, *halig ham*, *heofonas* and *heofona rice*. The only specific detail is the insistence on locating this *ham* somewhere above the experiential zone of ordinary humans, as seen in the recurrence of the word *up*.

In *Andreas*, therefore, heaven and paradise, while lexically identified with each other, remain descriptively abstract. However, one image in the poem is inconsistent with this general descriptive policy: that cited at the beginning of this chapter, and which describes the brief vision of trees blossoming wherever Andreas sheds his blood.[51] This image reminds us of Tertullian's declaration that the doors of paradise can be unlocked only through the blood of martyrdom,[52] and indeed we can interpret the blossoming trees as a glimpse of paradise. The diction certainly invites us to make such an association: this is the only place in the narrative which descriptively alludes to the ideal landscape, unqualified by any abstract or metaphorical terms. Thus, nouns denoting vegetation, *bearwas* and *blædas*, combine with participles of growth and regeneration, *geblowen* and *gebroden*. Significantly, the only word these lines have in common with the earlier account of *neorxnawang* is *blæd*; however, even as the proximity to *boldwela* encourages there a primarily non-literal reading of the noun, here the collocation with *bearwas*, *geblowen* and *gebroden* anchors it firmly to its literal sense of 'leaf'. At the same time, the sensory impact of the image retrospectively undercuts the abstract presentation of *neorxnawang* earlier.

The brevity of these lines is important, as we are given only those details which effectively convey the visualisation of paradise. Nevertheless, the poet withholds the term *neorxnawang* from the description. We are reminded of the Vision of Dryhthelm, where Bede describes the flowery meadow as 'not-heaven', and of Ælfric's use of the word *wunung*, along with poetic terms like

[51] See note 1 above.

[52] See above, p. 21, n. 26, and the comments of C. D. Wright, 'The Blood of Abel and the Branches of Sin: *Genesis A*, *Maximus I* and Aldhelm's *Carmen de virginitate*', *ASE* 25 (1996), 7–20, pp. 10–11.

smylt and *grennys* in his own translation of the Vision.[53] Tactics of lexical circumvention and compromise thus appear unchanged in different literary genres from different periods in Anglo-Saxon England. The absence of the term *neorxnawang* from a description that contains its visual essence may be seen as the inverse of the general tendency, extensively analysed in *Andreas* itself, whereby *neorxnawang* is mentioned but the description shifts to a more ideational plane. Can we see the *Andreas*-poet as subverting his own descriptive techniques, and if so, does this subversion extend beyond the lexical to the conceptual level? In other words, do the blossoming trees refer to a paradise distinct from heaven, and are we nudged towards reinterpreting his earlier reference to *neorxnawang* as the interim paradise after all?

We may remain none the wiser about the intention of individual poets, and their intentions may in any case have little to do with how their work was interpreted by subsequent readers and audiences. But the fact that these various questions are raised by a single, sharply focused image confirms that doctrinal constructs were highly susceptible to the force of visual description.

IDEAL LANDSCAPES AND AURAL ABSTRACTIONS: THE INTERIM PARADISE OF *THE PHOENIX*

The *Andreas*-poet is not alone in weaving potentially subversive images into a fabric of aural abstractions. In *The Phoenix*, a more audacious poet transforms that brief glimpse of blossoming trees into an ideal landscape fraught with alternative resonances. As is well known, the source for the first half of this poem is the *Carmen de aue phoenice* attributed to Lactantius.[54] The *Carmen* opens by describing the phoenix's abode as a *locus amoenus* of the type developed by Christian Latin poets in descriptions of Eden.[55] The *Phoenix*-poet superimposes upon the topos of the *locus amoenus* details from two other

[53] See above, p. 46.

[54] S. Brandt, ed., *De aue phoenice*, CSEL 27. 1 (Vienna, 1893).

[55] However, the *Carmen* does not identify this landscape as Eden, even though the identification of the phoenix and Christ had been made by patristic authors such as Ambrose, as pointed out by Blake, ed., *Phoenix*, pp. 21–2, and Appendix ii, pp. 96–7. For the possibility that Lactantius, if the author, wrote the *Carmen* before his conversion, see pp. 17–18. The most recent discussion of the Greco-Egyptian sources of the phoenix myth and their relevance to *The Phoenix* is by C. F. Heffernan, *The Phoenix at the Fountain: Images of Woman and Eternity in Lactantius's Carmen de Ave Phoenice and the Old English Phoenix* (Newark, NJ, 1988).

stylistic categories of Old English poetry: the descriptions of the ideal green landscape and the 'aureate' patterns associated with heavenly joys.[56] The use of three kinds of descriptive technique not only results in the most detailed presentation of an ideal landscape in Old English, but also elicits conflicting interpretations of the landscape itself. Plural significations emerge and recede in the first seventy lines of the poem, extending the richly layered effect from the descriptive to the conceptual level.

The customary opening flourish of Old English verse, *hæbbe ic gefrugnen*, corresponds to the *est locus remotus* introduction of the *Carmen* and sets the tone by announcing the poem's subject as an *æþelest londa*. In lines 7–14, this landscape is idealised through two statements reminiscent of other poetic descriptions of the green landscape: *wlitig is se wong eall, wynnum geblissad* (line 7) and *þæt is wynsum wong, wealdas grene* (line 13). These statements also bracket off details of fragrance and sweet music that belong to the *locus amoenus* topos. Moreover, music pours into this green landscape through the open door of heaven, establishing a spatial distinction between the two places. This image, in fact, bears a striking resemblance to the Vision of Dryhthelm, which describes music from the heavenly kingdom entering the meadow which is its antechamber.

This initial separation of the *wynsum wong* from heaven is followed by a passage that encourages their conflation through a version of the *þær is* syntagm used in descriptions of heaven:

> Ne mæg þær ren ne snaw,
> ne forstes fnæst, ne fyres blæst,
> ne hrægles hryre, ne hrimes dryre,
> ne sunnan hætu, ne sincaldu,
> ne wearm weder, ne winterscur
> wihte gewyrdan, ac se wong seomað
> eadig ond onsund. Is þæt æþele lond
> blotsmum geblowen.[57]

However, the *ne* phrases express not the abstract joys of heaven but details of the clement weather characteristic of the *locus amoenus*, even as the *ac*

[56] The term is used by Roberts, ed., *Guthlac Poems*, p. 63.

[57] *Phoenix*, lines 14–21: 'Neither rain nor snow, nor the breath of frost, nor the blast of fire, nor the falling of hail, nor the descent of rime, nor the heat of the sun, nor unceasing cold, nor warm weather, nor wintry shower, may destroy anything there, but the meadow remains blessed and unspoilt. That noble land is abloom with flowers.'

clause deftly brings the description back to the blossoming meadows of the ideal landscape descriptions.

This trend is continued in lines 21b–27. Another series of *ne* phrases describes the level topography of the area, again a detail echoing the *Carmen*'s account, but the *ac* clause returns to the lexis of the green landscape to reiterate that it is a *æþele feld*, blossoming albeit with joys rather than flowers (lines 26–7). The next five lines (28–32) describe the height of the *torhte lond* as stated in the *Carmen*. If we consider these lines as parallel to the first six lines which introduce the *æþelest londa*, then two passages of roughly equal length form an envelope pattern enclosing three seven-line segments. Within these segments, themselves marked off through vocabulary typical of the ideal landscape, descriptive details suggesting a demarcation between this ideal landscape and heaven mingle with syntactic patterns equally suggestive of their identification.

The next fifty lines of *The Phoenix* reproduce these effects, although the structures become somewhat more fluid. The declaration *smylte is se sigewong* in line 33, and its echo *se æþela wong* ten lines later mark off one section. Within this frame, the entire gamut of vegetation and topography nouns – *sunbearo*, *wuduholt*, *beam*, *blæd* and *leaf* – is used to convey that the landscape *grene stondaþ swa god bibead* (line 36). This statement is then qualified by a lengthy assertion that the phoenix's abode will remain blossoming until Doomsday (lines 43–9). This temporal specification at once recalls the distinction between the interim paradise and heaven, and reinforces the image of the shining meadow separated from the heavenly city until Doomsday.

However, these distinctions are immediately undercut as the poet turns once more to a *þær is* syntagm:

> Nis þær on þam londe   laðgeniðla,
> ne wop ne wracu,   weatacen nan,
> yldu ne yrmðu   ne se enga deað,
> ne lifes lyre,   ne laþes cyme,
> ne synn ne sacu   ne sarwracu,
> ne wædle gewin,   ne welan onsyn,
> ne sorg ne slæp   ne swar leger,
> ne wintergeweorp,   ne wedra gebregd,
> hreoh under heofonum,   ne se hearda forst,
> caldum cylegicelum,   cnyseð ænigne.
> þær ne hægl ne hrim   hreosað to foldan,
> ne windig wolcen,   ne þær wæter fealleþ,

lyfte gebysgad, ac þær lagustreamas,
wundrum wrætlice, wyllan onspringað
fægrum foldwylmum.[58]

This highly formulaic series of *ne* phrases, incorporating typical pairs such as *sacu* and *wracu*, *slæp* and *swar leger*, recalls the descriptions of heavenly joys found in *Andreas*. But while in that poem, internal rhyme, cross alliteration, and syntactic patterning communicate the freedom from bodily constraints experienced in heaven, these ideas in similar rhetorical form are here applied to an ideal landscape. Once again, the poet returns to this landscape through the *ac* clause of the catalogue, which links up the pleasures of heaven to the temperate weather characteristic of the *locus amoenus*.

This catalogue is followed by another passage that mirrors the lexical and conceptual patterns of lines 33–49:

Sindon þa bearwas bledum gehongne,
wlitigum wæstmum, þær no waniað o,
halge under heofonum, holtes frætwe.
Ne feallað þær on foldan fealwe blotsman,
wudubeama wlite, ac þær wrætlice
on þam treowum symle telgan gehladene,
ofett edniwe in ealle tid
on þam græswonge grene stondaþ,
gehroden hyhtlice haliges meahtum,
beorhtest bearwa.[59]

In this section, two references to *bearwas* enclose a series of references to nouns denoting vegetation, qualified by adjectives of brightness, greenness

[58] *Ibid.*, lines 50–64: 'In that land there is no loathsome foe, neither weeping nor anguish, no sign of woe, neither old age nor disease nor painful death, neither loss of life nor advent of the abhorrent, neither sin nor strife nor painful anguish, neither toil of poverty nor need of wealth, neither sorrow nor sleep nor oppressive sickbed, neither wintry turns nor the change to fierce weather under the skies, nor does hard frost oppress anyone with its cold icicles. There neither hail nor rime falls to the ground, nor windy clouds, neither does water fall there, agitated by the breeze, but there wonderfully adorned rivers and wells gush out in lovely springs.'

[59] *Ibid.*, lines 71–80: 'There are groves hung with foliage and bright fruit, there the wood's adornments, blessed under the heavens, never fade away. Flowers, splendour of the trees, never fall faded to the ground there, but always on those trees there with laden boughs, ever-new leaves remain wondrously green on that grassy plain in all seasons, the brightest of groves pleasantly adorned through the powers of holy [God].'

and regeneration. Lines 81–4 then bring the opening description to a close by successively sealing two envelope patterns. The *holt* of line 81 links up with *wuduholt* in line 34, while in the b-verse, *halga stenc* repeats the fragrance mentioned in line 8. The remaining lines reiterate that this landscape will remain green until Doomsday. The poem then moves on to describe the phoenix itself.

The overlapping chiastic patterns of the first eighty-four lines replicate the conceptual overlap that the poet consciously creates through different descriptive techniques and their poetic associations. Fully cognisant of the evocative power of both visual imagery and aural abstraction, he pits one against the other in mutual subversion. The resultant landscape belies the bland assumption, made by most critics, that the poet describes an 'earthly paradise', typologically equivalent to the heavenly kingdom.

Firstly, the poet never calls the phoenix's abode *neorxnawang*, an omission that recalls the techniques of evasion also used by the poet of *Andreas*, Bede and Ælfric. In fact, the sole occurrence of the term *neorxnawang* in the poem (line 397), made in the context of the Fall, differs completely from the opening description in its matter-of-fact tone and near absence of descriptive details. Furthermore, the detail of the *heofonrices duru* (line 12) and the emphasis on the landscape's destruction on Doomsday, align it not to the Garden of Eden but the interim paradise, associated with the same spatio-temporal parameters as is seen in both the Anglo-Latin visions and vernacular prose writings. At the same time, the separation from heaven indicated through both these spatio-temporal specifications and the nature imagery itself is confirmed by the highly visual descriptions of the heavenly city which conclude the poem (lines 590–610). Here, architectural details very similar to those in *Christ and Satan* retrospectively contrast with the ideal landscape of the opening lines, and undercut the typological equation with heaven that the poet himself offers in the second, allegorical part of the poem.

The interpretation which would seem to fit best the opening description is therefore one which would take the opening landscape as a representation of the interim paradise. The phoenix, reborn each millennium, could be interpreted as the good soul which awaits the Second Coming only to be burnt in the Doomsday conflagration before returning to heaven with a new body. The ideal landscape, abode of the phoenix, could then well represent the interim paradise where the good soul waits until Doomsday. As the interim paradise has a celestial location in most of the Anglo-Saxon writings thus far examined, the terrestrial nature of the phoenix's abode could argue against this interpretation. However, the various versions of the 'Theban Legend' exemplum had indicated that the Anglo-Saxon imagination by no means uniformly associated the earthly paradise with the Garden of Eden. The emphasis on the terrestrial nature of the phoenix's abode can be seen as one more instance of the poet's blurring of descriptive associations. Unlike Bede and Ælfric, he does not struggle to reconcile contradictions but embraces them to add to the sparkle of an already multifaceted text.

In fact, the poem progressively exposes this ambivalence as a construct of learned playfulness. In lines 381–92, the poet compares the phoenix and its millennial life-cycle to the blessed and the elect who await the celestial homeland after dark death. However, the inductive leap to equate its abode with the waiting-place itself is prevented by the poet's subsequent declarations. Rather abruptly, he turns instead to the expulsion from Eden, humanity's exile on earth, and the return to the heavenly home after Christ's Advent.

This rapid review of Christian history, ordered along the lines of Augustine's equation of paradise and heaven, is followed by its explicit application to the phoenix's life cycle and abode. This interpretation, moreover, is what 'the learned people have said with words and in writing' (*leorneras weordum secgað ond writu cyþað*, lines 424–5). In other words, the poet consciously affiliates himself with the learned, written tradition at the very moment he articulates the identification of paradise and heaven. He thus aligns himself to learned authority who would seek to correct what they would consider as being unorthodox ideas regarding paradise, even though these are ideas that he has himself incorporated in his opening description. It is precisely the *Phoenix*-poet's learned affiliations, both declared and implicit, which give an extra edge to his subversiveness. Like the poets of *Guthlac B* and *Andreas*, he is aware of the doctrinal implications of visualising paradise and heaven, and, like them, he develops abstract descriptive techniques to theological advantage. Yet, as seen rather more fleetingly in *Andreas*, he enriches the descriptive and conceptual content of his work by also turning to the visual resources of the ideal landscape descriptions which the poems of the Junius manuscript use in their evocations of paradise.

Thus, the influence of learned orthodoxy on poetry does not appear to have restricted individual poetic choice. Rather, it opened up a variety of descriptive options which individual poets utilise according to artistic temperament as well as immediate contextual demands. *The Phoenix* and, to a lesser extent, *Andreas*, reveal that a poet could exercise his craft in the service of orthodoxy and against it. But do these poetic descriptions of *neorxnawang* and *heofon* have any further repercussions on the concept of the interim paradise? How do they fit into the chain of reappropriations that we have been following in this investigation? In answer, and by way of conclusion, I next examine a late vernacular prose response to the *Phoenix*-poet's subversive ambiguities, and point towards the larger context of shifted significations this implies for the interim paradise.

7

From a heavenly to an earthly interim paradise: toward a tripartite otherworld

> Neorxenewange is upprihte on eastewearde þisse wurlde. Nis þær ne hete ne hunger; ne þær niht nefre ne byð, ac simble dæig. Sunne þær scineð seofen siðe brihtlycor þone on þissen earde. Þær wuneð on godes ængles unrim mid þan halgen sawlen oððð domes dæig. Þær wuneð on an fugel fæger Fenix gehaten.[1]

This description of paradise occurs in an anonymous prose text preserved in two manuscripts, Cambridge, Corpus Christi College 198, and London, British Library, Cotton Vespasian D. xiv, and is placed in the second half of the eleventh century by its first editor, F. Kluge, who also pointed out, albeit rather non-committally, that the text focused on the phoenix.[2] N. F. Blake called it the 'Prose Phoenix' and printed it as an appendix to his edition of *The Phoenix*, along with a similar text in Old Norse, but did not address adequately the question of the interrelationships of these texts.[3] Indeed, not only this question but the text itself has been all but ignored by recent scholars, despite its potential interest for investigations into the transmission of Old English verse and prose.[4]

Compelling as these issues are, they are raised here insofar as they shed light on the present investigation. Drawing on recent theories of the composition and transmission of Old English, I argue that the 'Prose Phoenix' represents the reabsorption of the Latinate poetic tradition into a late Anglo-Saxon, vernacular prose text. The question might arise whether such

[1] Warner, ed., *Early English Homilies*, pp. 146–7: 'Paradise is directly to the east of this world. There is neither hate, hunger nor ever night there, but always day. The sun there shines seven times brighter than on this earth. There dwell a countless number of god's angels and holy souls until Doomsday. There dwells a fair bird called the phoenix.'

[2] Kluge, 'Zu altenglischen Dichtungen', p. 475.

[3] Blake, ed., *Phoenix*, Appendix 2, p. 101. This issue is discussed in more detail below, p. 169.

[4] An exception being Yerkes's article, 'The Old Norse and Old English Prose Accounts of the Phoenix', where he argues against the dependence of the Old Norse text on the extant Old English versions.

a late text, preserved in at least one manuscript, Cotton Vespasian D. xiv, from the mid-twelfth century,[5] may be justifiably termed 'Anglo-Saxon' and brought within the scope of this enquiry. However, current scholarly opinion concurs that the influence of Anglo-Saxon culture continued to be felt in a variety of ways well into the twelfth century, with the cut-off point for the 'Anglo-Saxon period' itself being under some revisionist scrutiny.[6] It seems not inappropriate, therefore, to conclude this study of the interim paradise with a glance towards its eleventh- and twelfth-century continuations, and reiterate thereby the importance of the early Middle Ages for the later development of purgatorial doctrine.

In fact, the picture of the interim paradise that emerges from these later documents confirms several of our earlier hypotheses, even while revealing the changes which the concept had undergone towards the end of the Anglo-Saxon period. These claims are borne out by not only the 'Prose Phoenix' but also similar descriptions of the interim paradise in other late Old English texts, namely, several of the other pieces collected in Vespasian D. xiv, and *The Dialogue of Adrian and Ritheus*. The cumulative weight of the evidence will enable us to suggest how the Anglo-Saxon association of paradise and the interim, which we have traced thus far, may be linked to their growing *dis*sociation in the later Middle Ages. In this task of mapping the interim paradise on to the changing otherworlds of the eleventh and twelfth centuries, we shall also be assisted by the testimony of two visions of the otherworld written during this period, the *Visio Tnudgali* and the *Tractatus de purgatorio Sancti Patricii*, as well as the account of interim eschatology provided by a slightly earlier witness to these changes: Honorius Augustodunensis, and the third book of his *Elucidarium*.

THE HALF-HEAVENLY, HALF-EARTHLY PARADISE OF THE 'PROSE PHOENIX'

As Andy Orchard has observed recently, 'Sometimes Anglo-Saxon books speak, and we would do well to listen.'[7] On 'listening' to the 'Prose

[5] In this connection, see Richards, 'Date and Provenance', Handley, 'MS Cotton Vespasian D. xiv', and Scragg, 'Corpus of Vernacular Homilies', pp. 241 and 261.

[6] See, for example, the essays collected by Swan and Treharne, *Rewriting Old English*.

[7] A. Orchard, 'Oral Tradition', in *Reading Old English Texts*, ed. O'Brien O'Keeffe, pp. 101–24, at p. 120.

Phoenix', we can recognise lexical and rhythmic patterns that were earlier encountered in *The Phoenix*'s opening landscape description, but which here freely combine with other beliefs about the interim paradise. Yet, in the absence of manuscript evidence, how do we best explain the similarities between the description of an ideal landscape in an Old English poem and an evocation of the interim paradise in a much later anonymous prose text? Scholars who have considered this question have usually posited in answer the existence of a lost Latin homily, the author of which had translated portions of *The Phoenix*, and which had then come into the hands of the authors of the 'Prose Phoenix' and the Norse 'Phoenix' text.[8]

This hypothesis seems somewhat implausible, as it does not explain satisfactorily the many similarities of vocabulary and phrasing which exist between *The Phoenix* and the 'Prose Phoenix', some of which also reappear in the Old Norse text. It is not totally germane to this particular discussion that we consider in detail whether the following assertions are truly sustainable:

> There is not sufficient correspondence between the vocabulary of *P*[rose] *P*[hoenix] and that of the O[ld] N[orse] versions to warrant the theory that the ON versions were based on an OE original. It should be noted, for example, that where both OE MSS read *cristal*, both ON MSS have the Latinate form *kristallus*.[9]

Suffice it here to say that the difference between these two renderings of 'crystal' is not as great as are their similarities, and that the overall verbal correspondences between the Old Norse and Old English versions are, in fact, quite remarkable. Close comparison between the two texts reveals a consistent level of mild lexical displacement of cognate words and phrases within largely stable syntactic and semantic frames. These features point not so much to the vagaries of written transmission and scribal error as to the techniques of memorial composition and transmission.[10] To argue for memorial transmission from an Old English to an Old Norse environment being beyond the scope of this book, I will concentrate instead on the possibility that memorial transmission could have also been the means by which the author of the 'Prose Phoenix' incorporated material from *The Phoenix* into his eleventh-century text. Particularly helpful for this task are arguments for the memorial transmission of Old English verse, especially

[8] See notes 3 and 4 above. [9] Blake, ed., *Phoenix*, p. 101.

[10] As demonstrated most recently by Teresi, 'Mnemonic Transmission'.

as these favour the circulation of originally written texts within a memorial oral tradition before their re-consignment to written form.[11]

It should be kept in mind, however, that discussions of memorial transmission and transitional literacy have largely developed around the existence of variant versions of Old English poems.[12] Similarities between prose texts, particularly within the homiletic tradition, have usually been analysed within the parameters of source criticism.[13] When the texts in question belong to both prose and verse traditions, the tendency is to discuss the direction of borrowing rather than the mental processes underlying the borrowing itself.[14] Further, many more instances of poetic borrowing from prose texts have been catalogued or suggested thereby, with a recent exception being the discussion generated by the selective, 'cut and paste' use of *Judgement Day II* by the anonymous homilist of Napier XXIX.[15] The 'Prose Phoenix' thus presents us with a rare opportunity to observe how elements from a specific poetic context could be incorporated into a later vernacular prose text. Precisely because of such 'boundary-crossing', however, it is not enough to posit memorial transmission of *The Phoenix*; there must be a plausible reason why a certain section of this particular text was memorised to reappear later in a completely different literary environment.

It is possible that the story of the phoenix's marvellous life cycle and sylvan abode detached itself from the rest of the poem and passed into oral circulation. Not merely the narrative but also signature phrases and key

11 See, in this connection, Jabbour, 'Memorial Transmission', and the more recent extensions of these ideas by O'Brien O'Keeffe in *Visible Song*.

12 See the analyses of Jabbour, 'Memorial Transmission', O'Brien O'Keeffe, *Visible Song*, A. Jones, 'Daniel and Azarias as Evidence for the Oral-Formulaic Character of Old English Poetry', *MÆ* 35 (1966), 95–102, and R. M. Liuzza, 'The Text of the Old English *Riddle* 30', *JEGP* 87 (1988), 1–15.

13 Although there is growing interest in marrying the two methodologies; see, for example, A. Orchard, 'Crying Wolf: Oral Style and the *Sermones Lupi*', *ASE* 21 (1993), 239–64. For a discussion of the methods, assumptions and tasks of source criticism, see D. G. Scragg, 'Source Study', in *Reading Old English Texts*, ed. O'Brien O'Keeffe, pp. 39–58.

14 The most celebrated instance of which is the protracted debate over the shared features between the description of Grendel's mere in *Beowulf* and the descriptions of hell in Blickling XVI and the *Visio Sancti Pauli*, for which see now Wright, *Irish Tradition*, pp. 106–38.

15 See, in this connection, G. D. Caie, 'Text and Context in Editing Old English: the Case of the Poetry in Cambridge, Corpus Christi College 201', in *The Editing of Old English: Papers from the 1990 Manchester Conference*, eds. D. G. Scragg and P. E. Szarmach (Cambridge, 1994), pp. 155–62.

descriptive elements from the written text could have been memorised initially and, in the course of subsequent circulation, less consciously remembered. The regrouping of these elements in the 'Prose Phoenix' suggests that their very selection from the poem and continued currency were prompted by a renewed need to visualise the interim paradise in late Anglo-Saxon England. At the same time, the prose author's unfettered reassembling of phrases, descriptive techniques and even ideas originally from *The Phoenix* recalls the unrestrained descriptions of the interim paradise seen in other anonymous prose texts,[16] and indicates the divergent sensibilities of this author and the *Phoenix*-poet. The Old English poet's learned but subversive response to the interim paradise is thus disambiguated within a less self-conscious tradition, which in turn adds a new inhabitant, the phoenix, to the numbers of the less than perfect and those assumed in the body.

Although the text contains long descriptions of the phoenix's appearance and character, its ostensible subject is not the bird, but St John. The Corpus 198 version of the homily is rubricated *De sancto Iohanne*, and the homily itself opens rather abruptly with a reference to John coming to the end of what seems to be a sea voyage:

> Sanctus Johannes geseh ofer garseg swylce hit an lande wære. Þa genam hine se ængel and gebrohte hine to neorxenewange.[17]

This paradise is then described, beginning with the statement cited at the beginning of this chapter: it is the abode of the souls of the righteous, who remain here until Doomsday, along with God's angels and the phoenix. The significance of these seemingly innocuous statements cannot be overemphasised. Here, in a single late text, we find references to all the functions of the interim paradise that we have noted in the earlier discussion of anonymous prose texts.[18] As in the 'Three Utterances' homilies, Napier XLVI, Redaction XI of the *Visio Sancti Pauli* and even *The Phoenix*, the temporal qualification 'until Doomsday' specifies that the paradise in question is neither the Garden of Eden nor heaven, but the interim paradise. Moreover, as the location to which an angel brings John, this interim paradise appears to offer another instance of the conflation of two originally separate concepts

[16] Another useful analogue here might be C. Lévi-Strauss's concept of mythical thought as intellectual *bricolage*, or a new construction out of pre-existing elements, described in his *La pensée sauvage* (Paris, 1962), especially p. 26.

[17] Warner, ed., *Early English Homilies*, p. 146: 'St John saw across the ocean that it was as if on land. Then the angel took him and brought him to paradise.'

[18] See ch. 3.

– the abode of the corporally assumed and that of good souls – which I demonstrated earlier through the example of Blickling XIII.[19]

It should be recalled that Ælfric had no objections towards recounting the assumption of John, even as he had strenuously objected to the corporal assumption of Mary. I attributed this discrepancy to the fact that the Latin *Transitus* texts available in Anglo-Saxon England describe Mary's corporal assumption into the interim paradise, while there were no texts available which similarly spoke of a corporal assumption of John. Indeed, there seem no versions of the *Metastasis* of John which describe his assumption as anything other than a complete disappearance from this earth.[20] It thus appears that, by the end of the Anglo-Saxon period, this gap had been filled by texts such as the 'Prose Phoenix', in which the bare fact of John's disappearance is converted into a corporal assumption along the lines of that described for Mary in the anonymous homilies. This supposition is strengthened by the following statement from the *Elucidarium*, a compendium of patristic and apocryphal ideas within the framework of a dialogue, and dating from the turn of the eleventh and twelfth centuries:[21]

> Hoc praecessit in Maria et Johanne: Maria, quae recepto corpore post mortem in gloriam est assumpta; Johannes, qui cum corpore raptus et in ipso raptu creditur mortuus et reviviscens.[22]

This point of contact between Vespasian D. xiv and the *Elucidarium* is far from serendipitous. The author of the *Elucidarium*, the somewhat mysterious Honorius Augustodunensis, was closely connected with Canterbury and probably also Worcester, and the *Elucidarium* was in all likelihood written in England.[23] More importantly within the present context, two

[19] See above, p. 59.

[20] See Elliott, *Apocryphal New Testament*, pp. 307–8, Jugie, *La Mort*, p. 708–26, and Clayton, ed., *Apocryphal Gospels*, p. 3.

[21] Various aspects of the *Elucidarium* are discussed by V. I. J. Flint in a series of articles collected in the Variorum reprint, *Ideas in the Medieval West*; see also Lefèvre, ed., *L'Elucidarium* and Gurevich, *Medieval Popular Culture*, pp. 153–75. For the date, see Flint, 'Chronology', p. 227.

[22] Lefèvre, ed., *L'Elucidarium*, p. 455, no. 42: 'This happened in the case of Mary and John: Mary, who when she came back into her body after death was taken up into glory; John, who when he was seized in his body and in the very seizing was believed to be dead and coming to life again.'

[23] Flint, 'The Career of Honorius Augustodunensis', and 'Chronology', p. 219, and her 'The "Elucidarius" of Honorius Augustodunensis and Reform', pp. 180–2, for Honorius's reliance on the works of his teacher, Anselm of Canterbury.

excerpts from the *Elucidarium*, one of which we shall examine shortly, are translated and included within Vespasian D. xiv, representing, in fact, the earliest vernacular adaptation of the *Elucidarium*.

The reference to John's assumption in the *Elucidarium* and the description of John's arrival at a paradise, accompanied by an angel, in the 'Prose Phoenix' provide further evidence for the strong association of corporal assumption with the interim paradise in Anglo-Saxon England. The inclusion of the phoenix among the corporally assumed and the souls of the righteous also brings us back to our claim that the *Phoenix*-poet invites us to interpret his description of the *locus amoenus* as the interim paradise. In the 'Prose Phoenix', at least, we see one acceptance of that invitation. Despite the fact that the poet never uses the term *neorxnawang* in his opening landscape description, and despite his simultaneous evocation of the similarities and dissimilarities between paradise and heaven, the author of the 'Prose Phoenix' has no problem in reading right through these ambiguities and discarding them in his own version of the phoenix's abode. The 'Prose Phoenix' ends with a reminder of the phoenix's thousand-year life cycle that ends on its funeral pyre. In an environment which is clearly non-heavenly, this detail can only further the phoenix's identification with the good soul waiting in the interim paradise until the regenerating fire of Doomsday.

The paradise of the 'Prose Phoenix' is, moreover, non-heavenly in two senses: it is not only distinct from heaven but also semi-terrestrial in nature. After the opening reference to John, the author goes on to state:

> Neorxenewange nis naðer ne on heofene ne on eorðe. Seo boc sægð þæt Noes flod wæs feowrtig fedmen heh ofer þa hegesta dunen þe on middenearde synden, and neorxenewang is feowrtig fedme herre þone Noes flod wæs; and hit hangeð betwonen heofone and eorðen wunderlice, swa hit se Eallwealdend gescop, and hit is eall efenlang and efenbrad.[24]

This rather bizarre idea can be explained, at least partially, as an attempt to mediate between the usual celestial location of the interim paradise, and the terrestrial location of the phoenix's abode as described in the poem. As we noted in connection with Book II of Julian's *Prognosticon*, Isidore's initial

[24] Warner, ed., *Early English Homilies*, p. 146: 'Paradise is neither on heaven nor on earth. The book says that Noah's flood reached forty fathoms above the highest mountains which are on earth, and paradise is forty fathoms higher than Noah's flood was; and it hangs wondrously between heaven and earth, just as the ruler of all created it, and it is equally long and equally wide.'

definition of the interim paradise, modified later by Julian, hinges on the difference between an earthly Garden of Eden and the celestial waiting-place of good souls.[25] Of the Anglo-Saxon references discussed in the previous chapters, all of which are earlier than the 'Prose Phoenix', only the 'Theban Legend' homilies and *The Phoenix* speak of a terrestrial location.[26] In the 'Theban Legend', however, it is not a heavenly antechamber for good souls which is explicitly described, but a paradise qualitatively subordinated to heaven, and *The Phoenix* is deliberately all-inclusive in its ambiguous characterisation of the landscape.

Both the 'Theban Legend' and *The Phoenix* signal the terrestrial character of their paradise through a reference to its eastern location and also through details of topography. The 'Theban Legend' mentions a mountain of beaten gold and *The Phoenix* describes in detail the level plateau on which the landscape is situated. Interestingly, all these details reappear in the 'Prose Phoenix'. It is to the east of the world, higher than the highest mountain, and *efenlang and efenbrad*. The author even uses the latter phrase to introduce a negative *ðær is* syntagm, which describes the plateau in terms seemingly remembered from *The Phoenix*:

> nis ðær naðer ne dene ne dune. Ne þær ne bið ne forst ne snaw ne hagol ne reign, ac þær is fons vite, þæt is lifes welle.[27]

While each *ne* phrase is culled from a different catalogue in the poem, the *ac* clause somewhat crudely replicates the poet's effortless movement from the general pleasures of open-air habitation to the actual features of the landscape.[28]

Other details from the opening description of *The Phoenix* are similarly recalled and reassembled. Like the *wuduholt wynlic* of *The Phoenix*, the island is a *fæger wudeholt*, but one called *Radionsaltus* (p. 146). This puzzling word can be deciphered as a garbled recollection of the Latin phrase *radians saltus*, 'shining valley', which could have been a phrase that had remained in the author's mind because of its learned sound.[29] Each tree in this wood is higher than those here on earth, again, a detail which assimilates the

[25] See above, pp. 44 and 93. [26] See above, pp. 71 and 165.

[27] Warner, ed., *Early English Homilies*, p. 146: 'There is neither valley there nor mountain, neither is there snow nor frost nor hail nor rain, but the *fons vite*, the well of life, is there.'

[28] As analysed above, p. 163.

[29] See the similar explanation of the otherwise puzzling *intimphonis* in *Adrian and Ritheus*, discussed below, p. 181.

Phoenix-poet's frequent mention of trees and his statement that the plateau is more even than any found here on earth. Another *ac* clause describing the wood's unchanging greenness replicates the idea reiterated through the poet's description of the landscape, using, in the process, two of the adjectives most preferred by the *Phoenix* poet:

Ne fealleð þær næfre leaf of, ac heo byð singrene, wlitig and wynsum, welena unrim.[30]

Along with these details from *The Phoenix*, which derive from a combination of the Latinate *locus amoenus* tradition and the green landscapes of Old English poetry, we find a statement which belongs squarely to the apocryphal tradition: that the sun here shines seven times more brightly than on earth.[31] This qualification of shining 'seven times brighter' occurs in the *Visio*'s account of the *terra repromissionis*, as well as in several *Transitus Mariae* texts to describe Mary's soul; it is, in fact, applied to the good soul in the Junius 'Three Utterances' homily.[32]

What can we conclude from this eclectic assortment of details from different sources and the half-heavenly, half-earthly location? I would argue that we see here a witness to the changing signification of the interim paradise. As a result of the different dialectics in operation throughout the Anglo-Saxon period, and observed in the previous chapters, the interim paradise undergoes certain conceptual transformations which are registered on the descriptive level. Before suggesting what these transformations may have been, however, it should be noted that the 'Prose Phoenix' is by no means their sole witness; other texts from the late Anglo-Saxon period testify to not only these newer ideas regarding the interim paradise, but also their coexistence with alternative and earlier beliefs.

ENOCH, ELIJAH AND VARIETIES OF THE INTERIM PARADISE IN VESPASIAN D. XIV

It is characteristic of medieval attitudes towards authorship and authority that the compiler of Vespasian D. xiv should have brought together in the

[30] Warner, ed., *Early English Homilies*, p. 146: 'A leaf never falls there, but it is always green, splendid and joyous, of immeasurable riches.' [31] Cited above, n. 1.

[32] See above, pp. 20 and 51, and also Clayton, ed., *Apocryphal Gospels*, p. 259, ch. 25. The 'shining seven times brighter' topos is being investigated by T. N. Hall in '"Their Souls Will Shine Seven Times Brighter than the Sun": An Eschatological Motif and Its Permutations in Old English', article in progress.

same manuscript the 'Prose Phoenix' and Ælfric's translations of the visions of Furseus and Dryhthelm, including his prefatory condemnation of the *Visio Sancti Pauli*, and followed by Old English translations of Gregory's Vision of a Soldier and Bede's Vision of Ymma.[33] The thematic connections between these different otherworldly visions and the 'Prose Phoenix' are thus recognised and underscored through their compilation into the same manuscript, although one wonders what Ælfric would have made of this new context given to his own carefully edited accounts, and of the fact that his very rejection of the *Visio* and other apocrypha as 'heretical lies' is here juxtaposed with an account of the interim paradise as imaginative and eclectic as any apocryphal work he could have been aware of. In fact, two other texts in Vespasian D. xiv provide further testimony to the compiler's interest in different aspects of the interim paradise, and, even more specifically, to its role as the place into which Enoch and Elijah were assumed in the body and preserved from death thereby.[34]

Vespasian D. xiv includes an Old English homiletic version of the *Gospel of Nicodemus A*, which also occurs in two earlier manuscripts.[35] In *Nicodemus A*, those people under the Old Law who are released from hell after the Harrowing enter a paradise which is clearly celestial but not identical to heaven. Here, they encounter not only Enoch and Elijah in their bodies but also the Good Thief.[36] These inhabitants of paradise affiliate *Nicodemus A* to a nexus of beliefs and interpretations which hinge on the separation of paradise and heaven, and bring it in conflict with exegetical arguments for their synonymy. The association of Enoch and Elijah with paradise is, for example, vigorously circumlocuted by Ælfric, and Augustine's interpretation of Christ's promise to the Good Thief held that the paradise which he was meant to enter was either hell or the same place as heaven.[37] These are precisely the stances taken by that version of the *Gospel of Nicodemus* known as *Nicodemus B*. This version, which was also available in Anglo-Saxon England and translated into Old English, mentions neither Enoch, Elijah nor paradise, and the Good Thief enters hell briefly before ascending with

33 Warner, ed., *Early English Homilies*, pp. 109–16.

34 See above, pp. 18 and 37.

35 Warner, ed., *Early English Homilies*, pp. 77–87. The other versions, in Cambridge, University Library, Ll. 2. ii, and London, British Library, Cotton Vitellius A. xv, are edited by Hulme, 'Old English Version of the *Gospel of Nicodemus*'.

36 See Tischendorf, ed., *Evangelia Apocrypha*, p. 384.

37 See above, pp. 26–7.

the patriarchs to heaven.[38] The Vespasian compiler's choice of the *A* over the *B* version of *The Gospel of Nicodemus*, with its reference to Enoch and Elijah's preservation in paradise rather than in heaven, points once again to his interest in the interim paradise.

Furthermore, the second reference to Enoch and Elijah in Vespasian D. xiv presents yet another variation to the theme of their preservation from death: the belief that they were kept in an earthly (as opposed to heavenly) paradise until Doomsday. This reference occurs in the second of the manuscript's two translated excerpts from the *Elucidarium*. The excerpt begins by asking where Christ dwelled for forty days after he arose from death, and provides the following reply:

Swa swa we gelefeð, he wunede on þære eorðlicen neorxenewange mid Helian and Enoche, and þa þa mid him arisen of deaðe.[39]

This detail of the earthly paradise, as indeed the entire excerpt, is derived directly from the source.[40] It is likely that Honorius had in mind here the Irish descriptions of the island abodes of Enoch and Elijah.[41] During the Middle Ages, the paradise of Enoch and Elijah was placed on earth most

[38] See p. 152 for its use by the poet of *Christ and Satan*, and Tischendorf, ed., *Evangelia Apocrypha*, p. 407. Hulme, 'The Old English *Gospel of Nicodemus*', edits the Old English version of *Nicodemus B* from Cambridge, Corpus Christi College 41, also preserved in Cambridge, Corpus Christi College 303. Note that these manuscripts contain the relatively orthodox versions of the Assumption and the *Life of Margaret* respectively. For a history of the two *Nicodemus* traditions and their Old English transmission, see Morey, 'The Gospel of Nicodemus'.

[39] Warner, ed., *Early English Homilies*, p. 144: 'As we believe, he dwelled in the earthly paradise with Enoch and Elijah and those who arose with him from death.'

[40] Lefèvre, ed., *L'Elucidarium*, p. 391, no. 166: 'In terreno paradiso, ut creditur, cum Elia and Enoch et cum his qui cum eo surrexerunt'. See further p. 390, no. 160, notes 1 and 2, for variations between 'caelestem paradisum' and 'caelestem Hierusalem, id est paradisum', and the additional affiliations to the paradise of the Good Thief, in answer to the question, 'Quo ivit anima eius (Christ's) post mortem?'

[41] Especially as he may himself have been Irish, as argued by R. W. Southern, *St Anselm and his Biographer* (Cambridge, 1963), p. 216, and R. E. Reynolds, 'Further Evidence for the Irish Origins of Honorius Augustodunensis', *Vivarium* 7 (1969), 1–8. However, Flint discards this possibility: 'No good evidence of an association between Honorius and Ireland has yet been found.' ('Career', p. 84). If Honorius did not himself have direct acquaintance with Irish beliefs concerning Enoch and Elijah, he could well have come across versions mediated through Anglo-Saxon England, as in the example from *Adrian and Ritheus*, discussed below on pp. 180–2.

regularly within Irish texts, which describe Enoch and Elijah on an island weeping while they wait for the arrival of Antichrist prior to Doomsday.[42] In 'The Two Sorrows of the Kingdom of Heaven', Enoch and Elijah preach to souls under a tree, itself reinterpreted here as the tree of life in paradise.[43] The souls are in the form of giant birds which beat their wings and share in their sadness – quite different from the usual rejoicing that is imagined as taking place within the interim paradise in the Anglo-Saxon accounts. Towards its conclusion, the *Fís Adamnán* also refers to the sorrow of Enoch and Elijah in paradise, which they convey to the other righteous souls who dwell there in the form of birds.[44] The tenth-century *Immram Snégdusa ocus Maic Riagla* provides another variation on this theme.[45] The voyager clerics encounter Elijah and a group of 'men from Ross' on an island, and are told that Enoch remains in a secret dwelling-place until the arrival of Antichrist. It is possible, however, that an island they visit earlier is this secret abode, as it describes a flock of sorrowing birds under a tree being preached to by another bird, which could represent Enoch himself.[46]

In the Irish texts, therefore, the spotlight is on Enoch and Elijah and their sorrow, rather than on good souls in general, and the concept of the interim paradise remains ancillary to their specific condition. When the location of this paradise is mentioned, it is more often than not an island. In the Anglo-Saxon texts we have discussed thus far, in contrast, the interim paradise has a far wider range of functions, only one of which is the housing of Enoch, Elijah and others assumed in the body. Furthermore, while the Anglo-Saxon visionary and homiletic material we examined earlier did not place the interim paradise on an island, the texts collected in Vespasian D. xiv give more prominence to both the island location of this paradise and its connection with Enoch and Elijah. In fact, these Irish versions of the Enoch and Elijah story possibly also underlie the fact that in the 'Prose Phoenix' John is brought to what appears to be an island-paradise, although Enoch and Elijah are not mentioned in this text.[47] As I stated in an earlier

42 See Seymour, 'Notes on Apocrypha in Ireland', pp. 110–11, Dumville, 'Biblical Apocrypha', pp. 309–10, and McNamara, *Apocrypha in the Irish Church*, pp. 25–7.

43 See Dottin, ed., 'Les Deux Chagrins'.

44 Boswell, trans., *An Irish Precursor of Dante*, p. 46, ch. 33.

45 Stokes, ed., 'The Voyage of Snégdus and Mac Riagla', pp. 22–3.

46 *Ibid.*, p. 21.

47 In the Norse 'Phoenix' text (Blake, ed., *Phoenix*, Appendix 2, p. 102) however, the Good Thief is placed within the band of righteous souls, angels and the phoenix, thus pointing to a partial assimilation there to an interim eschatology similar to that of *Nicodemus A*.

chapter, Anglo-Saxon concepts of the interim paradise could well have influenced coexisting Irish beliefs, in this case, those concerning Enoch and Elijah.[48] Equally, these beliefs could have fed back into later Anglo-Saxon accounts of the interim fate of souls, resulting in texts such as those collected in Vespasian D. xiv. When the texts involved are as numerous and difficult to date as those we have been examining, and when two cultures have been in contact over a prolonged period, we can at best acknowledge an ongoing process of mutual influence, with shifting directions of borrowing at any given moment coexisting alongside independent responses to influential texts such as the *Visio Sancti Pauli*.[49]

THE FRAGMENTED INTERIM PARADISE OF THE *DIALOGUE OF ADRIAN AND RITHEUS*

Another example of a composite picture of the interim paradise, very similar to that gained collectively through the various texts of Vespasian D. xiv, is found in the *Dialogue of Adrian and Ritheus*.[50] This late Old English text is, like the *Elucidarium*, an example of a *Ioca monachorum* dialogue – a list of questions and answers which relay information about liminal aspects of human history and geography culled from apocryphal lore and extremely literal-minded biblical exegesis.[51] Such lists were very popular throughout the medieval period and especially in Anglo-Saxon England, which

[48] See above, p. 92.

[49] A case in point is the reference to Enoch and Elijah dwelling on a golden mountain to the east of the world and beyond the ocean, made within the twelfth-century *Pantheon* of Godfrey of Viterbo. On the basis of its similarities to the *Navigatio Sancti Brendani*, Esposito, 'An Apocryphal "Book of Enoch and Elias"', claimed that their common source was a lost apocryphal book of Enoch and Elijah. For a refutation of this hypothesis, see Dumville, 'Biblical Apocrypha', pp. 310–11, especially his observation on p. 311: 'We seem to have here a Latin version of a local ecclesiastical legend which was itself an adaptation of an apocryphon to the story-types of Celtic literature.' This possibility is further complicated by the similarities between this account and the 'Theban Legend' exemplum (see above, p. 71, n. 70), as well as the different texts collected in Vespasian D. xiv itself.

[50] Preserved in London, British Library, Cotton Julius A. ii. For the date and manuscript details, see Cross and Hill, eds., *Adrian and Ritheus*, p. 14.

[51] For a succinct introduction to the genre, see Cross and Hill, eds., *Adrian and Ritheus*, pp. 3–13. Extant Latin lists are printed and discussed by W. Suchier and L. W. Daly, eds., *Altercatio Hadriani Augusti et Epicteti Philosophi*, Illinois Studies in Language and Literature 24 (Urbana, IL, 1939).

furnishes two of their earliest vernacular examples, *The Prose Dialogue of Solomon and Saturn* and *Adrian and Ritheus*.[52]

While nearly all *Ioca monachorum* texts include questions about the assumption of Enoch and Elijah, the Latin texts appear more interested in their escaping death thereby. The ninth-century *pseudo-Bede Collectanea*, for instance, contains the following question and response: *Qui sunt nati et non sunt mortui? Enoch et Elias*.[53] In *Adrian and Ritheus*, in contrast, the following exchange concerning Enoch and Elijah betrays a greater interest in their post-assumption arrangements:

> Sæge me, hwæt sint þa twegen men on neorxnawang and þas gelomlice wepað and beoð unrote.
> Ic þe secge, enoc and helias; hi wepað for þam ðe hi sceole cuma on ðisne middangeard and beon deade þeah hy ær þone deað longe yldon.[54]

This allusion to Enoch and Elijah's weeping and their ultimate return to this earth recalls Irish versions of the legend, discussed above. Unlike the Irish versions, but like the Vespasian D. xiv texts, *Adrian and Ritheus* specifies that this abode is paradise, a connection which is reiterated in the next question and its answer:

> Saga me hwær wuniað hy.
> Ic þe secge, Malifica and Intimphonis; þæt is on simfelda and on sceanfelda.[55]

[52] See Cross and Hill, eds., *Adrian and Ritheus*, p. 8. Later vernacular lists, including some from Middle English, are printed by Suchier in *L'Enfant sage: das Gespräch des Kaisers Hadrian mit dem Klagen Kinde Epitus*, Gesellschaft für romansiche Literatur 24 (Dresden, 1910). For an early Insular, Hiberno-Latin example, possibly from the ninth century, see Bayless and Lapidge, eds., *Collectanea pseudo-Bedae*. Wright, 'Apocryphal Lore', pp. 137–9, notes that two Latin *Ioca monachorum* lists are found in St Gallen, Stiftsbibliothek 908 and St Gallen, Stiftsbibliothek 913, both manuscripts with Anglo-Saxon connections. Interestingly, St Gallen 908 also contains a Hiberno-Latin 'Three Utterances' sermon; see p. 51, n. 5.

[53] Bayless and Lapidge, eds., *Collectanea pseudo-Bedae*, p. 122: 'Who are born and are not dead? Enoch and Elijah.' As the editors note before providing other parallels from the *Ioca monachorum* lists, p. 202: 'This is one of the most common questions of the *Ioca monachorum*, usually paired with the riddle which appears as *Collectanea* no. 123, on Adam, who died and was never born.'

[54] Cross and Hill, eds., *Adrian and Ritheus*, p. 37, no. 19: 'Tell me who are the two men in paradise, and these continually weep and are sorrowful. I tell you, Henoch and Helias. They weep because they must come into this world and die, although hitherto they have long delayed death' (trans. Cross and Hill).

[55] *Ibid.*, no. 20: 'Tell me where they live. I tell you, *Malifica* and *Intimphonis*, that is in Simfelda and in Sceanfeld' (trans. Cross and Hill).

The recent editors postulate a complicated but nevertheless plausible explanation for this puzzling reply. In *De uirginitate*, Aldhelm refers to Enoch and Elijah's assumption into a paradise that he defines as *in tempis*; this classical allusion is glossed as *scenfelda*. Thus *Intimphonis/sceanfelda* (shining fields) is a garbled remembrance of this gloss, and elaborates upon *neorxnawang*.[56] *Malefica/simfelda*, emended to *sinfelda*, similarly refers to a parallel abode for the sinful, and an intervening question introducing these sinful inhabitants must have dropped out.[57] This reconstruction corresponds neatly to the contrast between a paradise for the righteous and the assumed, and a penal region for the wicked, that operates within the four-part otherworld.

It could well be that the term *neorxnawang* is a reflex of Anglo-Saxon conceptions of the interim paradise, which are here welded together with the Irish tradition of Enoch and Elijah's sorrow. Both influences are also discernible in the answer to an earlier question:

Saga me hwær scyne seo sunne on niht.
Ic þe secge, on þrim stowum: on ærest þæs hwales innoðe þe is cweden leuiathan and on oðre tid heo scynð on helle and þa ðridda tid heo scynð on þam ealond þæt is glið nemned, and þar restað haligra manna saula oð domesdæig.[58]

The reference to the place where the souls of holy men rest until Doomsday recalls the near-identical statement in the Hatton 'Three Utterances' homily, though there, of course, there was no mention of an island named *glið*. While the term *glið* remains inexplicable,[59] the detail of the island provides a further correspondence between *Adrian and Ritheus* and the island-paradises of Irish voyages and visions. Moreover, this question itself and a variety of answers occur in several Irish or Irish-influenced texts.[60] The most elaborate answer to it, for example, is supplied by *In Tenga Bithnua* ('The Evernew Tongue'), also dating, most probably, from the ninth century; according to this text, the sun shines in twelve and possibly fourteen places, one of which is 'Adam's paradise'.[61] The parallels between the list of places in *In Tenga* and

[56] A similarly confused recollection of a gloss has been postulated already for the term *radionsaltus* in the 'Prose Phoenix' (p. 174).

[57] For details of this argument, see Cross and Hill, eds., *Adrian and Ritheus*, pp. 143–5.

[58] *Ibid.*, pp. 35–6, no. 6: 'Tell me where the sun shines at night. I tell you, in three places, first on the belly of the whale which is called Leviathan, and, in the second period, it shines on Hell, and the third period it shines on the island which is called *glið*, and the souls of holy men rest there until Doomsday' (trans. Cross and Hill).

[59] *Ibid.*, pp. 133–4. [60] Discussed by Carey, 'The Sun's Night Journey', pp. 16–20.

[61] For this discrepancy in number, see *ibid.*, pp. 14–15 and n. 4.

the series of islands visited by travellers in the *Immram* tradition are as interesting as is the contrast afforded by the three places visited by the sun in *Adrian and Ritheus*. It should also be noted that although the questions about Enoch and Elijah and the sun's disappearance at night are standard inclusions in the *loca monachorum* lists, their corresponding answers in *Adrian and Ritheus* have no exact parallels in dialogue literature.[62]

What is the precise impetus behind the fragmented, unprecedented evocation of these ideas in *Adrian and Ritheus*, whereby various functions of paradise are separated, combined with allusions to Irish tradition, and assigned to different questions? Perhaps, as the generic title could indicate, it was part of a monastic joke.[63] Or, perhaps the author wished to dissociate Enoch and Elijah's paradise from the interim abode, and identify it instead with the Garden of Eden, also referred to as *neorxnawang* in the first question of the dialogue.[64] At the same time, this reference to the sun shining on three, rather than four, places suggests a change in the four-part otherworld also alluded to in the reply to the Enoch and Elijah question.

The persistence of older beliefs about the interim paradise alongside the new encapsulates the concept's history during the Anglo-Saxon period, even while suggesting that it did not so much disappear as change shape in subsequent centuries. Under the influence of Bede and Boniface, Anglo-Saxon witnesses to the interim paradise incorporate it into a four-part cosmology, where the interim paradise is paralleled by a provisional hell or 'proto-purgatory'. As all these locations are celestial, the interim paradise remains conceptually and descriptively distinct from the earthly Garden of Eden. From the twelfth century onwards, however, medieval literature describes a very different kind of otherworld, and it will be fitting to end this investigation by looking forward to this difference as it emerges in three highly influential works from this period.

THE SPLINTERED LANDSCAPES OF THE TWELFTH-CENTURY OTHERWORLD

While characterising the twelfth century as a period of 'certainty and hesitation' regarding purgatorial doctrine, Le Goff finds in the *Elucidarium* of

[62] For examples from other lists, see Cross and Hill, eds., *Adrian and Ritheus*, pp. 131–2 and 142–3. [63] See *ibid.*, p. 6, for the editors' comments on the title *loca monachorum*.
[64] *Ibid.*, p. 35.

Honorius a 'typical example of this early confusion' but also asserts that Honorius himself 'did indeed have original ideas about the otherworld'.[65] In his subsequent summary of a passage from Book III of the *Elucidarium*, however, Le Goff seems not to have noticed the close dependence of much of Honorius's thinking on earlier Anglo-Saxon ideas of the interim paradise, especially the Vision of Dryhthelm. This passage consists of some questions and answers relating to interim eschatology, and provides us with a complete backdrop against which we may place the fragmented references to the interim paradise which we have discussed above.

Book III of the *Elucidarium* (*De futura uita*) begins with a reference to the soul which, on exiting its body, is taken with sweet music, immense light and the sweetest of fragrances *ad caeleste palatium in spiritualem paradisum*.[66] The disciple asks whether this paradise is a corporal place (*locus corporeus*); in answer, Honorius declares that it is, on the contrary, a spiritual mansion of the blessed (*spiritualis beatorum mansio*), where one can view God face to face. Only the souls of the perfect (*animae perfectorum*) are brought here: these are martyrs, monks and virgins, in whom Christian precepts are fully realised. The souls of the just (*animae iustorum*), on the other hand, are dispersed in certain other mansions. The difference between the just and the perfect is then expounded by focusing on their respective post-mortem fates.

The just, who are those who have narrowly missed being perfect, are taken after death to an earthly paradise (*terrenus paradisus*); the adjective *terrenus* recalls the use of the same adjective earlier for the paradise of Enoch and Elijah, in that section of the *Elucidarium* which appears in Vespasian D. xiv. The fate of those in this paradise is far from stable. A certain group of the just (*quidam ordo iustorum*), who will definitely join the company of the angels after Judgement Day, are retained until then in a most pleasant abode (*amoenissima habitacula*). However, they may be promoted to greater joy even before the Day of Judgement through the supplications of the saints and the alms of the living. Alternatively, they may be dragged off at any given moment by demons for purgation (*ad purgandum*) like the erring son given over to the servant for flogging; again, it is only masses, alms, prayers and pious works on the part of the living, which can prevent this fate.

[65] *Birth of Purgatory*, p. 136 and passim.

[66] Lefèvre, ed., *L'Elucidarium*, p. 443, no. 1: 'To the celestial palace in the spiritual paradise.' The following discussion refers to pp. 443–5, nos. 1–7.

We can recognise here the simultaneous presence of several different stages in the Anglo-Saxon development of the interim paradise. Firstly, there is a vestigial reference to the belief in two paradises, propagated from Isidore onwards, whereby the celestial paradise was the interim place of waiting and the terrestrial paradise simply the Garden of Eden. Here, in keeping with the general shift of ideas we have postulated, the terrestrial paradise becomes the interim abode. Secondly, as in the Vision of Dryhthelm, this place is still where the souls of the just, the nearly perfect, wait for Judgement Day.[67] Thirdly, however, and in keeping with the two-part supplication we noted in prayers from the ninth-century prayer-books,[68] the inhabitants of the interim paradise also appear susceptible to the effect of alms-giving, masses and pious deeds, which are now needed to prevent them lapsing into the horrors of the provisional hell.

What is new, then, is the insistence that the interim paradise has a terrestrial location, and the emphasis on purgatorial fire (*ignis purgatorius*), which Honorius subsequently describes as either bodily afflictions suffered here on earth, including death, or the excesses of fire and ice as a type of punishment after death.[69] This passage is seen by Le Goff as Honorius's most notable contribution to the development of the doctrine of Purgatory, but its greater significance seems to lie in its coexistence with earlier schemes of interim eschatology, within which the interim paradise had been pivotal. In fact, Honorius's view of interim eschatology affords a clear picture of how the beneficial effects of alms, prayers and masses, initially seen as needed only by those in the provisional hell gradually became important for those in the interim paradise as well. By the twelfth century, consequently, it had become possible to subject the entire body of souls consigned to some form of interim existence to a gigantic game of purgatorial snakes and ladders.

It cannot be overemphasised that the interim paradise, which contributed in large measure to the development of this vast mechanism, did not disappear overnight to leave a neat, tripartite scheme of heaven, hell and purgatory. Just as the concept coexists alongside a greater awareness of the *ignis purgatorius* in the *Elucidarium*, the visual equivalent of this coexistence is found in the splintered, multi-comparmentalised otherworlds of two enormously popular, much-translated visions of the otherworld from the

[67] See above, p. 89. [68] See above, p. 127.

[69] Lefèvre, ed., *L'Elucidarium*, pp. 445–6, no. 8.

twelfth century, *Visio Tnudgali* and *Tractatus de purgatorio sancti Patricii*. The Irish connections of these works and their clear dependence on the Vision of Dryhthelm confirms our earlier suggestions concerning the Anglo-Saxon influence on Irish interim eschatology. In fact, these visions seem to visualise the abstract ideas of the *Elucidarium* in much the same way as the Anglo-Latin visions, five centuries ago, mapped the interim eschatology of Julian's *Prognosticon* on to a four-fold otherworld.

In 1149 AD, an Irish monk named Marcus, resident in Germany, reported a detailed vision of the otherworld seen by a wealthy knight, known variously as *Tnúthgal*, *Tondale*, *Tundale*, or, as in the Latin of this original version, *Tnudgalus*.[70] The otherworldly topography of *Visio Tnudgali* draws upon the conventions established during the first flourishing of the visionary genre four centuries earlier, but it also reflects the changing conceptualisation of the otherworld at the very moment of the so-called 'birth of purgatory'.[71] Led by the mandatory angelic guide, Tnúthgal wanders through an astonishing series of purgatorial and infernal regions. He stumbles across monstrous beasts which differ from each other only in physical detail, experiences the alternation of extreme heat and cold in varying guises,[72] and witnesses a variety of purgatorial mechanisms which encompass older motifs and new. More interesting for our purposes is the vision's equally burgeoning repertoire of joys for the blessed, which range from the blasé to the baroque. The *campus laetitiae*, by now familiar to us as the resting-place for the *non ualde boni*, is reminiscent of the meadows described by Bede, Boniface and Gregory, and, as in the 'Prose Phoenix', is watered by a *fons uitae*.[73] This *campus* is followed by five different zones for increasingly blessed categories of souls.[74] The first two zones are marked off

[70] To these numerous medieval spellings has been added the metathesised Latin version 'Tnugdalus,' apparently created and perpetrated by modern scholarship; cf. the titles cited below, notes 71 and 73. To avoid confusion, I use the Irish version 'Tnúthgal'; all references to the Latin vision in the body of the text will retain the unmetathesised form, 'Tnudgalus', for which see J. V. Kellcher, ed., *Corpus Genealogiarum Hiberniae*, I, 2nd edn. (Dublin, 1976), p. 743.

[71] For the different versions and aspects of the 'Vision of Tnúthgal', see Palmer, ed., '*Visio Tnugdali*', Picard, trans., *The Vision of Tnugdal*, Kren, ed., *The Visions of Tondal*, and Carozzi, 'Vision de Tnugdal'.

[72] For which, see, of course, the Vision of Dryhthelm, *HE*, V, ch. 12, pp. 488–99, and also *Fís Adamnán*, Boswell, *Irish Precursor*, p. 40. Some medieval Welsh parallels are discussed by Vendryes, 'L'enfer glacé'.

[73] Wagner, ed., *Visio Tnugdali*, p. 41.

[74] *Ibid.*, pp. 42–53.

by walls of silver and gold; the third is a splendid series of pavilions, the fourth is a verdant, fruit-bearing tree under the shade of which are numerous monastic cells made of gold and ivory, and the fifth and most spectacular zone is cordoned off by a wall of precious stones and gold mortar.

This summary of the pleasant regions described in the *Visio Tnudgali* is, unfortunately, too curtailed to afford more than a brief glimpse of the author's imaginative use of traditional topoi, especially those for which he appears heavily indebted to the Vision of Dryhthelm. However, it does provide some indication of his descriptive methods – the permutations, combinations and multiplications of the traditional hierarchy between natural and architectural imagery that he indulges in to convey the full range of joys available to his categories of the blessed. Similar processes of splintering and multiplication are seen in the somewhat later *Tractatus de purgatorio Sancti Patricii* (c. 1180–4 AD), which purports to be an account of the Knight Owein's travels through the otherworld.[75]

To give a flavour of the even more elaborate visionary topography of the *Tractatus*, I cite from one of its opening chapters, which summarises the contents of the vision:

> Raptas etiam et iterum ad corpora reductas uisiones quasdam et reuelationes sibi factas narrare dicit siue de tormentis impiorum seu de gaudiis iustorum et in hiis tamen nichil nisi corporale uel corporibus simile recitasse: flumina, flammas, pontes, naues, domos et nemora, prata, flores, homines nigros uel candidos, et cetera qualia in hoc mundo solent uel ad gaudium amari uel ad tormentum timeri; se quoque, solutas corporibus, manibus trahi, pedibus duci, collo suspendi, flagellari, precipitari et multa huiusmodi, que nostre minime repugnant narrationi. . . . Et quod paradysus in oriente et in terra sit, narratio ista ostendit, ubi fidelium anime, a penis purgatoriis liberate, dicuntur aliquandiu morari iocunde. Dicit uero beatus Augustinus animas defunctorum post mortem usque ad ultimam resurrectionem abditis receptaculis contineri, sicut unaqueque digna est, uel in requiem uel in erumpnam.[76]

[75] See Easting, ed., *St Patrick's Purgatory*, p. lxxxiv for the date, and pp. lxxxv–xc for the details of manuscripts and transmission history.

[76] *Ibid.*, pp. 121–2: 'He says that certain visions and revelations made to him tell how [souls] are actually snatched and brought back to the body again whether [he is talking] about the tortures of sinners or about the joys of the righteous and in these he says they recounted nothing that was not to do with the body or similar to human bodies: rivers, flames, bridges, ships, houses and groves, meadows, flowers, men black and white, and other kinds of things which in this world are accustomed either to be loved for their enjoyment or to be feared for their torment; and also that they may be freed from their

Avoiding once again the potential distractions of the elaborate purgatorial mechanisms, I note instead the two aspects of the above citation which are most significant in the present context. Firstly, the interim paradise is still the temporary abode of good souls and those who are released from the pains of purgatory, very much in the manner of the four-fold otherworld of the Vision of Dryhthelm. However, it is firmly identified with the paradise of Eden through the eastern and terrestrial location. Even more interesting is the citation of Augustine's originally cautious statement from *Enchiridion*.[77] With this example of yet another author using Augustine to justify speculations on a topic which Augustine himself had avoided through that very statement, this investigation comes full circle.

'THE BIRTH OF PURGATORY' OR 'THE DEATH OF THE INTERIM PARADISE'?

It is now possible, perhaps, to offer some revisions of Le Goff's claims for the spectacular 'birth of purgatory' during the twelfth century. It is apparent that as the four-part otherworld expanded and fragmented in the twelfth century, the interim paradise still remained as one of its compartments, although identified more and more strongly with the earthly paradise.[78] At the same time, an increasing number of texts describe the rediscovery of the earthly paradise by intrepid travellers, assimilating this paradise on the eastern fringes of the earth to other 'Wonders of the East'.[79]

bodies, dragged down by their hands, led along by their feet, hung from their neck, whipped, cast down, and many other things of this kind, which are not at all contradictory to our tale . . . And that account demonstrates that there is a paradise in the east and on earth, where faithful men's souls, which have been freed from the punishments of purgatory, are said on some occasions to linger pleasantly. Indeed the blessed Augustine says that the souls of the departed are preserved after death right up to the final resurrection in hidden retreats, according to each one's deserts, either for peace or for hardship.'

77 As noted by Easting, 'Purgatory and the Earthly Paradise', p. 29.

78 A similar contention is made by Easting, 'Purgatory and the Earthly Paradise', as part of a larger refutation of Le Goff's claims for the *Tractatus* as the earliest witness to the tripartite otherworld. While he remarks on the dependence of the *Tractatus* and of the *Visio Tnudgali* on the four-fold otherworld of the Vision of Dryhthelm, he does not note the significance of their insistence that this paradise is terrestrial. He also seems unaware of the corresponding developments within late Old English texts and in the *Elucidarium*, although he cites this latter work for its reference to a purgatorial fire (*ibid.*, p. 35).

79 See, in this context, Scafi, 'Mapping Eden', and I. M. Higgins, ed., *Writing East: the 'Travels' of Sir John Mandeville* (Pennsylvania, PA, 1997).

A detailed discussion of such texts is beyond the scope of this investigation, as is an enquiry into the opening up of geographical and other horizons which catalysed their development. But we can nevertheless see, in the eleventh- and twelfth-century texts we have examined, the bridge between the four-part cosmology of the Anglo-Saxon period proper, and the later medieval tripartite scheme.

Learned authorities such as Bede and Ælfric had accepted the interim paradise because of its innate usefulness in linking together Church and laity through the fortunes of the dead. In fact, as my analysis of the Anglo-Latin visions had suggested, the older hierarchy between the interim paradise and heaven had been used to fashion a similar hierarchy between hell and an interim penal region. However, once the connection between intercession, mass and the interim condition had been established, two intermediate locations must have appeared conceptually superfluous. This superfluity is evident as early as the Anglo-Latin prayers, in which the inhabitants of paradise require the same treatment as those of the purgatorial region during the interim period. Logically, therefore, there would have remained little need for the Church to continue supporting the idea of the interim paradise. This is indeed what happens in the thirteenth century: even as the idea of purgatory became enshrined in doctrine, the University of Paris declared in 1240 AD that the idea of an interim abode for the righteous was heretical.[80]

However, the imagination did not as easily relinquish the concept of an interim abode. It is my contention that the increase in learned objections to the interim paradise towards the later Anglo-Saxon period, as ascertained through the later language of liturgy and prayer, was accompanied by its transmutation into an earthly location. Precedent for this change would be found in accounts like the 'Theban Legend', that did describe an earthly paradise which was neither Eden and nor heaven, and in ambiguous poems like *The Phoenix*, while twelfth-century eschatological schemes reveal its earliest clear manifestations. The pressure to do away with the interim paradise thus led to the transfer of its emotive and conceptual freight onto another idea, related through the term paradise itself: the Garden of Eden, which broadened its own resonances in the process.

Thus, the loss of a four-part otherworld consisting of two penal and two pleasant regions did not merely involve its replacement by the three regions

80 Delumeau, *Un histoire du paradis*, I, p. 56.

of hell, purgatory and paradise/heaven, but also the supplementing of this tripartite cosmology by a more accessible earthly paradise. This process is already glimpsed in the simultaneous reference to three places where the sun shines and Enoch and Elijah's paradise in *Adrian and Ritheus*. The half-celestial, half-earthly interim paradise of the 'Prose Phoenix' thus captures for posterity but one transitional phase in a series of larger changes, which would culminate in a world-view that could document, on the one hand, the earthly paradises of Mandeville and Prester John as easily as it could produce Dante's *paradiso*, synonymous with heaven, on the other. Only our continued recognition of the paradise that stands *oð domesdæg* during the Anglo-Saxon period can make this a fair exchange.

Select bibliography

Amat, J., *Songes et visions: l'au-delà dans la littérature latine tardive* (Paris, 1985).

Amos, T. L., 'Monks and Pastoral Care in the Early Middle Ages', in *Religion, Culture and Society*, eds. Noble and Contreni (1987), pp. 165–80.

Andrieu, M., ed., *Les 'Ordines Romani' du haut moyen âge*, 5 vols., Spicilegium sacrum Lovaniense 11, 23, 24, 28, 29 (Louvain, 1931–61).

Banting, H. M. J., ed., *Two Anglo-Saxon Pontificals*, HBS 104 (London, 1989).

Barnard, L. W., 'Bede and Eusebius as Church Historians', in *Famulus Christi*, ed. Bonner (1976), pp. 106–24.

Bayless, M. and M. Lapidge, eds., *Collectanea Pseudo-Bedae* (Dublin, 1998).

Bazire, J. and J. E. Cross, eds., *Eleven Old English Rogationtide Homilies*, Toronto Old English Series 7 (Toronto, 1982).

Becker, E. J., *A Contribution to the Comparative Study of the Medieval Visions of Heaven and Hell, with Special Reference to the Middle English Versions* (Baltimore, MD, 1899).

Beeson, C. H., 'The *Ars Grammatica* of Julian of Toledo', in *Miscellanea Francesco Ehrle* I, Studi e testi 37 (Rome, 1924), pp. 50–70.

Bestul, T. H., 'Continental Sources of Anglo-Saxon Devotional Writing', in *Sources of Anglo-Saxon Culture*, ed. Szarmach (1986), pp. 103–26.

Biggs, F. M., T. D. Hill and P. E. Szarmach, eds., *Sources of Anglo-Saxon Literary Culture: a Trial Version*, Medieval and Renaissance Texts and Studies 74 (Binghamton, NY, 1990).

Birch, W. De G., *An Ancient Manuscript of the Eighth or Ninth Century, Formerly Belonging to St Mary's Abbey, or Nunnaminster, Winchester* (London, 1889).

Bishop, E., 'Liturgical Note', in *The Book of Cerne*, ed. Kuypers (1902), pp. 234–83.

Liturgica Historica: Papers on the Liturgy and Religious Life of the Western Church (Oxford, 1918).

Blair, J. and R. Sharpe, eds., *Pastoral Care before the Parish* (Leicester, London and New York, 1992).

Blake, N. F., ed., *The Phoenix*, rev. edn. (Exeter, 1990).

Bonner, G., ed., *Famulus Christi: Essays in Commemoration of the Thirteenth Centenary of the Birth of the Venerable Bede* (London, 1976).

Boswell, C. S., trans., *An Irish Precursor of Dante: A Study on the Vision of Heaven and Hell ascribed to the Eighth-Century Irish Saint Adamnán* (London, 1908).

Botte, B., '*Prima resurrectio*: un vestige de milleniarisme dans les liturgies occidentales', *Recherches de théologie ancienne et médiévale* 15 (1948), 5–17.

Brown, A. K., '*Neorxnawang*', *NM* 74 (1973), 610–23.

Brown, M. P., *The Book of Cerne: Prayer, Patronage and Power in Ninth-Century England* (London and Toronto, 1996).

Brown, P., 'Vers La Naissance du purgatoire: amnistie et pénitence dans le christianisme occidentale de l'Antiquité tardive au Haut Moyen Age', *Annales: économies, sociétés, civilisations* 52 (1997), 1247–61.

Bullough, D. A., 'Burial, Community and Belief in the Early Medieval West', in *Ideal and Reality*, ed. Wormald (1983), pp. 177–201.

'Alcuin and the Kingdom of Heaven', in *Carolingian Essays: Andrew W. Mellon Lectures in Early Christian Studies*, ed. U.-R. Blumenthal (Washington, DC, 1983), pp. 1–69.

Burke, P., *Popular Culture in Early Modern Europe*, rev. repr. (London, 1994).

Cabrol, F., 'Le *Book of Cerne*: les liturgies celtiques et gallicanes et la liturgie romaine', *Revue des questions historiques* 76 (1904), 210–22.

Campbell, J. J., ed., *The Advent Lyrics of the Exeter Book* (Princeton, NJ, 1959).

Capelle, B., 'L'antienne *In paradisum*', in his *Travaux liturgiques de doctrine et d'histoire*, III (Louvain, 1967), pp. 252–67.

Carey, J., 'The Otherworld in Irish Tradition', *Éigse* 19 (1982–3), 36–43.

'The Sun's Night Journey: a Pharaonic Image in Medieval Ireland', *Journal of the Warburg and Courtauld Institutes* 57 (1994), 14–34.

Carozzi, C., 'Structure et fonction de la vision de Tnugdal', in *Faire croire: modalités de la diffusion et de la réception des messages religieux du XIIe au XVe siècle: table ronde, Rome, 22–23 juin 1979*, ed. A. Vauchez, Collection de l'École Française de Rome 51 (Rome, 1981).

'La Géographie de l'au-delà et sa signification pendant le haut moyen âge', *SettSpol* 29 (1983), 423–81.

Le Voyage de l'âme dans l'au-delà: d'après la littérature latine (Ve–VIIIe siècle) (Rome, 1994).

Casey, R., 'The Apocalypse of Paul', *JTS* 34 (1933), 1–32.

Chadwick, N. K., *Celt and Saxon: Studies in the Early British Border* (London, 1961).

Charles, R. H., ed., *Apocrypha and Pseudepigrapha of the Old Testament*, 2 vols. (Oxford, 1913).

Chartier, R., 'Culture as Appropriation: Popular Cultural Uses in Early Modern France', in *Understanding Popular Culture*, ed. Kaplan (1984), pp. 229–53.

Ciccarese, M. P., 'La *Visio Baronti* nella tradizione letteraria delle *Visiones* dell' aldilà', *Romanobarbarica* 6 (1981–2), 25–52.

'Le più antiche rappresentazioni del purgatorio, dalla *Passio Perpetuae* alla fine del IX sec.', *Romanobarbarica* 7 (1982–3), 33–76.

'Le visioni di S. Fursa', *Romanobarbarica* 8 (1984–5), 231–303.

ed., *Visioni dell' aldilà in occidente: fonti, modelli, testi* (Florence, 1987).

Clayton, M., 'Blickling Homily XIII Reconsidered', *LSE* ns 17 (1986), 25–40.

The Cult of the Virgin Mary in Anglo-Saxon England, CSASE 2 (Cambridge, 1990).

ed. and trans., *The Apocryphal Gospels of Mary in Anglo-Saxon England*, CSASE 26 (Cambridge, 1998).

Clayton, M. and H. Magennis, eds. and trans., *The Old English Lives of St Margaret*, CSASE 9 (Cambridge, 1994).

Clemoes, P. A. M., 'Cynewulf's Image of the Ascension', in *England before the Conquest*, eds. Clemoes and Hughes (1971) pp. 293–304.

ed., *Ælfric's Catholic Homilies: the First Series: Text*, EETS ss 17 (Oxford, 1997).

Clemoes, P. A. M. and K. Hughes, eds., *England before the Conquest: Studies in Primary Sources presented to Dorothy Whitelock* (London, 1971).

Colgrave, B., 'Bede's Miracle Stories', in *Bede Essays*, ed. Thompson (1935) pp. 201–29.

Colgrave, B. and R. A. M. Mynors, eds. and trans., *Bede's Ecclesiastical History of the English People* (Oxford, 1991).

Constable, G., 'Monasteries, Rural Churches, and the *cura animarum* in the Early Middle Ages', *SettSpol* 28 (1982), 349–95.

Cross, J. E. and T. D. Hill, eds. and trans., *The 'Prose Solomon and Saturn' and 'Adrian and Ritheus': edited from the British Library Manuscripts with Commentary*, McMaster Old English Studies and Texts 1 (Toronto, Buffalo, NY, and London, 1982).

Crouzel, H. and M. Simonetti, eds., *Origène: traité des principes, livres I et II*, SC 252 (Paris, 1978).

Curtius, E. R., *European Literature and the Latin Middle Ages*, trans. W. R. Trask (London, 1953).

Daniélou, J., 'Terre et paradis chez les Pères de l'Eglise', *Eranos Jahrbuch* 22 (Zurich, 1954), 433–72.

De Bruyne, D., 'Fragments retrouvés d'apocryphes priscillianistes', *RB* 24 (1907), 318–35.

Delumeau, J., *Une Histoire du paradis*, 2 vols. (Paris, 1992).

Deshusses, J., *Le Sacramentaire grégorien: ses principales formes d'après les plus anciens manuscrits*, Spicilegium friburgense 16 (Fribourg, 1971, 1979, 1982).

Diaz y Diaz, M. C., 'La Cultura de la España visigótica del siglo VII', *SettSpol* 5 (1958), 813–44.

Dinzelbacher, P., *Vision und Visionsliteratur im Mittelalter*, Monographien zur Geschichte des Mittelalters 23 (Stuttgart, 1981).
Doane, A. N., ed., *Genesis A: a New Edition* (Madison, WI, 1978).
The Saxon Genesis (Madison, WI, 1991).
Dombart, B. and A. Kalb, eds., *Sancti Aurelii Augustini de ciuitate Dei*, CCSL 47 8 (Turnhout, 1953).
Dottin, G., 'Les Deux Chagrins du royaume du ciel', *RC* 21 (1900), 349–87.
Dumville, D. N., 'Liturgical Drama and Panegyric Responsory from the Eighth Century: a Re-Examination of the Origin and Contents of the Ninth-Century Section of the Book of Cerne', *JTS* 23 (1972), 374–406.
'Biblical Apocrypha and the Early Irish: a Preliminary Investigation', *PRIA* 73C (1973), 299–388.
'*Echtrae* and *Immram*: Some Problems of Definition', *Ériu* 27 (1976), 73–94.
'Towards an Interpretation of *Fís Adamnán*', *SC* 12–13 (1977–8), 62–77.
'Two Approaches to the Dating of the *Navigatio Sancti Brendani*', *SM* 29 (1988), 87–102.
Dutton, P. E., *The Politics of Dreaming in the Carolingian Empire* (Lincoln, NA, and London, 1994).
Dwyer, M. E., 'An Unstudied Redaction of the *Visio Pauli*', *Manuscripta* 32 (1988), 121–38.
Easting, R., 'Purgatory and the Earthly Paradise in the *Tractatus de Purgatorio Sancti Patricii*', *Cîteaux: Commentarii Cisterciensis* 37 (1986), 23–48.
ed., *St Patrick's Purgatory: Two Versions of 'Owayne Miles' and 'The Vision of William of Stranton', together with the Long Text of the 'Tractatus de purgatorio Sancti Patricii'*, EETS os 298 (1991).
Elliott, J. K., *The Apocryphal New Testament: a Collection of Apocryphal Christian Literature in an English Translation* (Oxford, 1993).
Esposito, M., 'An Apocryphal "Book of Enoch and Elias" as a Possible Source of the *Navigatio Sancti Brendani*', *Celtica* 5 (1960), 192–206.
Evans, E., ed., *Sancti Aurelii Augustini enchiridion ad Laurentium de fide et spe et caritate*, CCSL 46 (Turnhout, 1969), pp. 48–114.
Evans, J. M., *'Paradise Lost' and the Genesis Tradition* (Oxford, 1968).
Flint, V. I. J., 'The Original Text of the *Elucidarium* of Honorius Augustodunensis from the Twelfth-Century English Manuscripts', *Scriptorium* 17 (1964), 91–4 (*Ideas*, VIII).
'The Career of Honorius Augustodunensis: Some Fresh Evidence', *RB* 82 (1972), 75–80 (*Ideas*, V).
'The "Elucidarius" of Honorius Augustodunensis and Reform in Late Eleventh-Century England', *RB* 85 (1975), 178–89 (*Ideas*, X).
'The Sources of the "Elucidarius" of Honorius Augustodunensis', *RB* 85 (1975), 190–8 (*Ideas*, X).

Ideas in the Medieval West: Texts and their Contexts, Variorum Reprint (London, 1988).

Frank, H., 'Die älteste *Ordo defunctorum* der römischen Liturgie und sein Fortleben in Totenagenden des frühen Mittelalters', *ALW* 7 (1962), 360–415.

Fritzsche, C., 'Die lateinischen Visionen des Mittelalters bis zur Mitte des 12. Jahrhunderts', *Romanische Forschungen* 2 (1886), 247–79 and 3 (1887), 337–69.

Gardiner, E., *Visions of Heaven and Hell before Dante* (New York, 1989).

Medieval Visions of Heaven and Hell: a Sourcebook (New York and London, 1993).

Gatch, M. McC., 'Eschatology in the Anonymous Old English Homilies', *Traditio* 21 (1965), 117–65.

'Old English Literature and the Liturgy: Problems and Potential', *ASE* 6 (1977), 239–48.

'Poetry and Liturgy in the Old English *Vision of Leofric*', in *Words, Texts and Manuscripts*, ed. Korhammer (1992), pp. 159–80.

Preaching and Theology in Anglo-Saxon England: Ælfric and Wulfstan (Toronto and Buffalo, NY, 1977).

'Two Uses of Apocrypha in Old English Homilies', *Church History* 33 (1964), 379–91.

Geary, P. J., *Living with the Dead in the Middle Ages* (Ithaca, NY, and London, 1994).

Gneuss, H., 'Liturgical Books in Anglo-Saxon England and their Old English Terminology', in *Learning and Literature*, eds. Lapidge and Gneuss (1985), pp. 91–142.

Godden, M. R., 'The Development of Ælfric's Second Series of Catholic Homilies', *ES* 54 (1973), 209–16.

'Ælfric's Saints' Lives and the Problem of Miracles', *LSE* ns 16 (1985), 83–100.

'Experiments in Genre: the Saints' Lives in Ælfric's *Catholic Homilies*', in *Holy Men and Holy Women: Old English Prose Saints' Lives and their Contexts*, ed. P. E. Szarmach (Albany, NY, 1996), pp. 261–88.

ed., *Ælfric's Catholic Homilies: the Second Series: Text*, EETS ss 5 (London, 1979).

Goldbacher, A., ed., *Sancti Aurelii Augustini epistulae* IV, CSEL 57 (Vienna, 1911).

Grant, R. J. S., ed. and trans., *Three Homilies from Cambridge, Corpus Christi College 41: the Assumption, St Michael and the Passion* (Ottawa, 1982).

Grégoire, R., *Les Homéliaires du moyen âge: inventaire et analyse des manuscrits*, Rerum ecclesiasticarum documenta, Series maior, Fontes 6 (Rome, 1966).

Gretsch, Mechthild, *The Intellectual foundations of the English Benedictine Reform*, CSASE 25 (Cambridge, 1999).

Grimm, R. R., *Paradisus coelestis, paradisus terrestris*, Medium ævum, philologische Studien 33 (Munich, 1977).

Gurevich, A. J., 'Popular and Scholarly Medieval Cultural Traditions: Notes in the Margin of Jacques Le Goff's Book', *JMH* 9 (1983), 71–90.

Medieval Popular Culture: Problems of Belief and Perception, trans. J. M. Bak and P. A. Hollingsworth (Cambridge, 1988).

Haibach-Rheinisch, M., ed., *Ein neuer 'Transitus Mariae' des Pseudo-Melito* (Rome, 1962) [repr. in Clayton, ed., *Apocryphal Gospels* (1998), pp. 234–43].

Hall, D., 'Introduction', in *Understanding Popular Culture*, ed. Kaplan (1984), pp. 5–18.

Handley, R., 'British Museum MS Cotton Vespasian D. xiv', *N&Q* 21 (1974), 243–50.

Healey, A. DiP., ed., *The Old English Vision of St. Paul*, Speculum Anniversary Monographs 2 (Cambridge, MA, 1978).

Healey, A. DiP. and R. L. Venezky, eds., *A Microfiche Concordance to Old English* (Toronto, 1980).

Hill, C. E., *Regnum Caelorum: Patterns of Future Hope in Early Christianity* (Oxford, 1992).

Hill, J., 'Reform and Resistance: Preaching Styles in Late Anglo-Saxon England', in *De l'Homélie au sermon: histoire de la prédication médiévale: actes du colloque international de Louvain-la-Neuve (9–11 Juillet 1992)*, eds. J. Hamesse and X. Hermand (Louvain-la-Neuve, 1993), pp. 15–46.

Hillgarth, J. N., 'St Julian of Toledo in the Middle Ages', *Journal of the Warburg and Courtauld Institutes* 21 (1958), 7–26.

'Fuentes de San Julián de Toledo', *Anales Toledanos* 3 (1971), 97–122.

Visigothic Spain, Byzantium and the Irish, Variorum Reprint (London, 1985).

ed., *Libri prognosticorum futuri saeculi*, in *Sancti Iuliani Toletanae sedis episcopi opera I*, CCSL 115 (Turnhout, 1976), pp. 10–126. (in the footnotes, I have referred to *Libri prognosticorum* as *Prognosticon* and the collection as *Juliani opera*.)

Himmelfarb, M., 'The Temple and the Garden of Eden in Ezekiel, the Book of Watchers and the Wisdom of Ben Sira', in *Sacred Places and Profane Spaces: Essays in the Geographics of Judaism, Christianity and Islam*, eds. J. S. Scott and P. Simpson-Housley (Westport, CT, 1991), pp. 63–78.

Hohler, C. E., 'Some Service-Books of the Later Saxon Church', in *Tenth-Century Studies: Essays in Commemoration of the Council of Winchester and Regularis Concordia*, ed. D. Parsons (London, 1975), pp. 60–84.

Holdsworth, C. J., 'Visions and Visionaries in the Middle Ages', *History* 48 (1963), 141–53.

Hughes, K., 'Some Aspects of Irish Influence on Early English Private Prayer', *SC* 5 (1970), 48–61.

'Evidence for the Contacts between the Churches of the Irish and the English from the Synod of Whitby to the Viking Age', in *England before the Conquest*, eds. Clemoes and Hughes (1971), pp. 49–67.

Hulme, W. H., 'The Old English Version of the *Gospel of Nicodemus*', *PMLA* 13 (1898), 471–515.

'The Old English *Gospel of Nicodemus*', *MP* 1 (1903–4), 11–36.

Hume, K., 'The Concept of the Hall in Old English Poetry', *ASE* 3 (1974), 63–74.

Hurst, D., ed., *Bedae venerabilis opera, pars III: opera homiletica*, CCSL 122 (Turnhout, 1955).

Jabbour, A., 'Memorial Transmission in Old English Poetry', *Chaucer Review* 3 (1969), 174–90.

Jones, C. W., ed., *Bedae venerabilis opera, pars II: opera exegetica: libri quatuor in principium Genesis*, CCSL 118A (Turnhout, 1967).

Jugie, M., *La Mort et l'assomption de la Sainte-Vierge: étude historico-doctrinale,* Studi e testi 114 (Rome, 1944).

Kaplan, S. L., ed., *Understanding Popular Culture: Europe from the Middle Ages to the Nineteenth Century*, New Babylon: Studies in the Social Sciences 40 (Berlin, New York and Amsterdam, 1984).

Kluge, F., 'Zu altenglischen Dichtungen', *Englische Studien* 8 (1884–5), 472–9.

Knowles, D., *The Monastic Order in England: a History of its Development from the Times of St Dunstan to the Fourth Lateran Council, 943–1216*, 2nd edn (Cambridge, 1963).

Korhammer, M., ed., with K. Reichl and H. Sauer, *Words, Texts and Manuscripts: Studies in Anglo-Saxon Culture presented to Helmut Gneuss* (Woodbridge and Rochester, NY, 1992).

Krapp, G. P. and E. V. K. Dobbie, eds., *The Anglo-Saxon Poetic Records*, 6 vols. (New York, 1931–42).

Kren, T., ed., *Margaret of York, Simon Marmion, and the Visions of Tondal* (Malibu, 1992).

Kuypers, A. B., ed., *The Prayerbook of Aedeluald the Bishop, commonly called the Book of Cerne* (Cambridge, 1902).

Laistner, M. L. W., 'The Library of the Venerable Bede', in *Bede Essays*, ed. Thompson (1935), pp. 237–66.

Lapidge, M., 'Surviving Booklists from Anglo-Saxon England', in *Learning and Literature*, eds. Lapidge and Gneuss (1985), pp. 33–89.

Lapidge, M. and H. Gneuss, eds., *Learning and Literature in Anglo-Saxon England: Studies presented to Peter Clemoes* (Cambridge, 1985).

Lefèvre, Y., ed., *L'Elucidarium et les lucidaires* (Paris, 1954).

Le Goff, J., *The Birth of Purgatory*, trans. A. Goldhammer (London, 1984).

'The Learned and Popular Dimensions of Journeys to the Otherworld in the Middle Ages', in *Understanding Popular Culture,* ed. Kaplan (1984), pp. 19–37.

Levison, W., 'Bede as Historian', in *Bede Essays*, ed. Thompson (1935), pp. 111–51.

'Die Politik in Jenseitsvisionen des frühen Mittelalters', in his *Aus Rheinischer und Frankischer Frühzeit* (Düsseldorf, 1948), pp. 229–46.

ed., 'Visio Baronti Monachi Longoretensis', in his *Passiones uitaeque sanctorum aeui merouingici*, MGH SRM 5 (Hanover and Leipzig, 1910), pp. 368–94.

Luiselli Fadda, A. M., ed., *Nuove omelie anglosassoni della rinascenza benedettina*, Filologia germanica, testi e studi I (Florence, 1977).

Madoz, F., 'Fuentes teologico-literarias de San Julián de Toledo', *Gregorianum* 33 (1952), 399–417.

Magennis, H., *Images of Community in Old English Poetry*, CSASE 18 (Cambridge, 1996).

Manuel, F. E. and F. P. Manuel, *Utopian Thought in the Western World* (Oxford, 1979).

Marstrander, C., 'The Two Deaths', *Ériu* 5 (1911), 120–5.

McClain, J. P., *The Doctrine of Heaven in the Writings of St Gregory the Great* (Washington, DC, 1956).

McClung, W. A., *The Architecture of Paradise: Survivals of Eden and Jerusalem* (Berkeley and Los Angeles, CA, and London, 1983).

McDannell, C. and B. Lang, *Heaven: a History* (New Haven, CT, and London, 1988).

McNally, R. E., '*In nomine Dei summi*: Seven Hiberno-Latin Sermons', *Traditio* 35 (1979), 121–43.

McNamara, M., *The Apocrypha in the Irish Church* (Dublin, 1984).

Milik, J. T., ed., *The Books of Enoch: Aramaic Fragments of Qumrân Cave 4* (Oxford, 1976).

Miller, T., ed., *The Old English Version of Bede's Ecclesiastical History of the English People*, 2 vols., EETS os 95 and 110 (London, 1890–8).

Morey, J. H., 'The Gospel of Nicodemus', in *Sources of Anglo-Saxon Literary Culture*, eds. Biggs, Hill and Szarmach (1990), pp. 45–9.

Morgan, A., *Dante and the Medieval Other World* (Cambridge, 1990).

Morin, G., ed., *Sancti Caesarii Arelatensis sermones*, CCSL 103–4 (Turnhout, 1953).

Morris, R., ed., *The Blickling Homilies of the Tenth Century*, EETS os 58, 63, 73 (London, 1874–80, repr. as one volume, 1967).

Morrish, J., 'Dated and Datable Manuscripts Copied in England during the Ninth Century: a Preliminary List', *MS* 50 (1988), 512–38.

Moussy, C. and C. Camus, eds., *Les Louanges de Dieu, livres I et II: Dracontius, oeuvres I* (Paris, 1985).

Muir, B. J., *A Pre-Conquest English Prayerbook (BL MSS Cotton Galba A. xiv and Nero A. ii (fols. 3–13))*, HBS 103 (London, 1988).

Napier, A. S., ed., 'An Old English "Vision of Leofric", Earl of Mercia', *TPS* (1907–10), 180–8.

Wulfstan: Sammlung der ihm zugeschriebenen Homilien nebst Untersuchungen über ihre Echtheit I (Berlin, 1883, repr. with appendix by K. Ostheeren, Dublin, 1967).

Noble, T. F. X. and J. J. Contreni, eds., *Religion, Culture and Society in the Early Middle Ages: Studies in Honor of Richard E. Sullivan*, Studies in Medieval Culture 23 (Kalamazoo, MI, 1987).

Nodes, D. J., ed., *Avitus: the Fall of Man: de spiritalis historiae gestis libri I-III* (Toronto, 1985).

Ntedika, J., *L'Evocation de l'au-delà dans la prière pour les morts: étude de patristique et de liturgie latine (IVe–VIIIe s)* (Louvain, 1971).
O'Brien O' Keeffe, K., *Visible Song: Transitional Literacy in Old English Verse*, CSASE 4 (Cambridge, 1990).
ed., *Reading Old English Texts* (Cambridge, 1997).
Palmer, N. F., ed., *'Visio Tnugdali': the German and Dutch Translations and their Circulation in the Later Middle Ages* (Munich, 1982).
Patch, H. R., *The Other World according to Descriptions in Medieval Literature* (Cambridge, MA, 1950).
Paxton, F. S., *Christianizing Death: the Creation of a Ritual Process in Early Medieval Europe* (Ithaca, NY, and London, 1990).
Pearsall, D. and E. Salter, *Landscapes and Seasons of the Medieval World* (London, 1973).
Peiper, R., ed., *Cyprianus Gallus: Heptateuchos*, CSEL 23 (Vienna, 1891).
Picard, J.-M., trans., with an introduction by Y. de Pontfarcy, *The Vision of Tnugdal* (Blackrock, 1989).
Piehler, P., *The Visionary Landscape: a Study in Medieval Allegory* (London, 1971).
Pope, J. C., ed., *Homilies of Ælfric: a Supplementary Collection*, EETS os 259–60 (London, 1968).
Pulsiano, P., 'Hortatory Purpose in the Old English *Visio Leofrici*', *MÆ* 44 (1985), 109–16.
Rankin, S., 'The Liturgical Background of the Old English Advent Lyrics: a Reappraisal', in *Learning and Literature*, eds. Lapidge and Gneuss (1985), pp. 317–41.
Ray, R. D., 'Bede, the Exegete, as Historian', in *Famulus Christi*, ed. Bonner (1976), pp. 125–140.
Raynes, E. M., 'MS. Boulogne-sur-Mer and Ælfric', *MÆ* 26 (1957), 65–73.
Richards, M. P., 'On the Date and Provenance of MS Cotton Vespasian D. xiv, Folios 4–169', *Manuscripta* 17 (1973), 31–5.
Roberts, J., 'A Preliminary Heaven Index for Old English', *LSE* ns 16 (1985), 208–19.
ed., *The Guthlac Poems of the Exeter Book* (Oxford, 1979).
Robinson, F. C., 'The Devil's Account of the Next World', *NM* 73 (1972), 362–71.
Rousseau, A., L. Doutreleau and C. Mercier, eds., *Irénée de Lyon: contre les hérésies, livre V*, SC 153 (Paris, 1969).
Rowland, C., *The Open Heaven: a Study of Apocalyptic in Judaism and Christianity* (London, 1982).
Russell, D. S., *The Method and Message of Jewish Apocalyptic: 200 BC–AD 100* (London, 1964).
Russell, J. B., *A History of Heaven: the Singing Silence* (Princeton, NJ, 1997).
Scafi, A., 'Mapping Eden: Cartographies of the Earthly Paradise', in *Mappings*, ed. D. Cosgrove (London, 1999), pp. 50–70.

Schenkl, C., ed., *De paradiso*, in *Sancti Ambrosii opera pars prima*, CSEL 32.i (Vienna, 1896), pp. 264–336.

Schmitt, J.-C., '"Religion populaire" et culture folklorique', *Annales: économies, sociétés, civilisations* 31 (1976), 941–53.

'Les Traditions folkloriques dans la culture médiévale: quelques réflexions de méthode', *Archives de sciences sociales des religions* 52 (1981), 5–20.

Scragg, D. G., 'The Corpus of Vernacular Homilies and Prose Saints' Lives before Ælfric', *ASE* 8 (1979), 223–77.

'The Devil's Account of the Next World Revisited', *American Notes and Queries* 24 (1986), 107–10.

'Source Study', in *Reading Old English*, ed. O'Brien O'Keeffe (1996), pp. 39–58.

ed., *The Vercelli Homilies and Related Texts*, EETS os 300 (London, 1992).

Seymour, S. D., 'The Eschatology of the Early Irish Church', *ZCP* 14 (1923), 179–211.

'Notes on Apocrypha in Ireland', *PRIA* 37C (1927), 107–17.

Irish Visions of the Otherworld: a Contribution to the Study of Medieval Visions (New York, 1930).

Sicard, D., *La Liturgie de la mort dans l'Eglise latine des origines à la réform carolingienne*, Liturgiewissenshäftliche Quellen und Forschungen 63 (Münster, 1978).

Silverstein, T., 'The "Vision of Leofric" and Gregory's Dialogues', *RES* 9 (1933), 186–8.

ed., *Visio Sancti Pauli: the History of the Apocalypse in Latin together with Nine Texts*, Studies and Documents 4 (London, 1935).

Silverstein, T. and A. Hilhorst, eds., *Apocalypse of Paul: a New Critical Edition of Three Long Latin Versions* (Geneva, 1997).

Simon, U., *Heaven in the Christian Tradition* (London, 1958).

Sims-Williams, P., *Religion and Literature in Western England, 600–800*, CSASE 3 (Cambridge, 1990).

'Some Celtic Otherworld Terms', in *Celtic Language, Celtic Culture: a Festschrift for Eric P. Hamp*, eds. A. T. E. Matonis and D. F. Melia (Van Nuys, CA, 1990), pp. 57–81.

Sisam, K., 'An Old English Translation of a Letter from Wynfrith to Eadburga (AD 716–17) in Cotton MS Otho. C', in his *Studies in the History of Old English Literature* (Oxford, 1953), pp. 199–224.

Skeat, W., ed., *Ælfric's Lives of Saints*, EETS os 94 and 114 (London, 1966).

Sleeth, C. R., *Studies in 'Christ and Satan'*, McMaster Old English Texts and Studies 3 (Toronto, Buffalo, NY, and London, 1982).

Sparks, H. F. D., ed., *The Apocryphal Old Testament* (Oxford, 1984).

Stevenson, J., 'Ascent through the Heavens, from Egypt to Ireland', *CMCS* 5 (1983), 21–35.

Stokes, W., ed., 'The Voyage of Snégdus and Mac Riagla', *RC* 9 (1888), 14–25.
Stone, M. E., 'The Metamorphoses of Ezra: Jewish Apocalypse and Medieval Vision', *JTS* ns 33 (1982), pp. 1–18.
Stuiber, A., *Refrigerium interim: die Vorstellungen vom Zwischenzustand und die frühchristliche Grabekunst*, Theophaneia 11 (Bonn, 1957).
Swan, M. and E. M. Treharne, eds., *Rewriting Old English in the Twelfth Century*, CSASE 30 (Cambridge, 2000).
Szarmach, P. E., ed., *Sources of Anglo-Saxon Culture* (Kalamazoo, MI, 1986).
Tangl, M., ed., *Die Briefe des heiligen Bonifatius und Lullius*, MGH, Epistolae Selectae 1 (Berlin, 1916).
Teresi, 'Mnemonic Transmission of Old English Texts in the Post-Conquest Period', in *Rewriting Old English*, eds. Swan and Treharne (2000), pp. 98–116.
Thompson, A. H., ed., *Bede: his Life, his Times and Writings: Essays in Commemoration of the Twelfth Centenary of his Death* (Oxford, 1935).
Thorpe, B., ed., *Homilies of the Anglo-Saxon Church: the First Part, containing the Sermones Catholice, or Homilies of Ælfric* (London, 1844).
Tischendorf, C., ed., *Apocalypses Apocryphae Mosis, Esdrae, Pauli, Iohannis, item Mariae Dormitio* (Leipzig 1866).
Evangelia Apocrypha, 2nd edn. (Leipzig, 1866).
Tristram, H. L. C., 'Stock Descriptions of Heaven and Hell in Old English Prose and Poetry', *NM* 79 (1978), 102–13.
Turner, D. H., ed., *The Claudius Pontificals (From MS Cotton Claudius A. iii in the British Museum)*, HBS 97 (London, 1964).
Usener, H., ed., 'S. Marinae et S. Cristophori', in *Festschrift zur fünften Säcularfeier der Carl-Ruprechts-Universität zu Heidelberg*, presented by the Rector and Senate of the Rheinische Friedrich-Wilhelms-Universität (Bonn, 1886), pp. 1–80.
Vendryes, J., 'L'Enfer glacé,' *RC* 46 (1927), 134–42.
Vogel, C., 'Deux Conséquences de l'eschatologie grégorienne: la multiplication des messes privées et les moines-prêtres', in *Grégoire le Grand*, eds. J. Fontaine, R. Gillet and S. Pellistrandi (Paris, 1986), pp. 267–76.
Medieval Liturgy: an Introduction to the Sources, rev. and trans. W. G. Storey and N. K. Rasmussen (Washington, DC, 1986).
Vogüé, A., ed., *Grégoire le Grand: Dialogues*, 3 vols., SC 251, 260 and 265 (Paris, 1978–80).
Wack, M. F. and C. D. Wright, 'A New Latin Source for the Old English "Three Utterances" Exemplum', *ASE* 20 (1991), 187–202.
Wagner, A., ed., *Visio Tnugdali lateinisch und altdeutsch* (Erlangen, 1882).
Ward, B., 'Miracles and History: a Reconsideration of the Miracle Stories used by Bede', in *Famulus Christi*, ed. Bonner (1976), pp. 70–7.

Warner, R. D.-N., ed., *Early English Homilies from the Twelfth-Century MS Vespasian D. XIV*, EETS os 152 (London, 1917).

Warren, F. E., ed., *The Leofric Missal: as used in the Cathedral of Exeter AD 1050–72* (Oxford, 1883).

The Antiphonary of Bangor: an Early Irish Manuscript in the Ambrosian Library at Milan, HBS 4 and 10 (London, 1893).

Waszink., J. H., ed., *De anima*, in *Tertulliani Opera: Pars II: Opera Montanistica*, CCSL 2 (Turnhout, 1954), pp. 779–869.

Watkins, C., 'Doctrine, Politics and Purgation: the Vision of Tnúthgal and the Vision of Owein at St Patrick's Purgatory', *JMH* 22 (1996), 225–36.

Weber, R., with B. Fischer and J. Gribimont, eds., *Biblia Sacra iuxta Vulgatam versionem*, 2 vols. (Stuttgart, 1975).

Wenger, A., 'Ciel ou paradis: le séjour des âmes, d'après Philippe le Solitaire, *Dioptra*, livre iv, chapitre x', *Byzantische Zeitschrift* 44 (1951), 560–9.

L'Assomption de la très Sainte Vierge dans la tradition byzantine du VIe aux Xe siècle: études et documents, Archives de l'orient chrétien 5 (Paris, 1955).

Willard, R., 'The Address of the Soul to the Body', *PMLA* 50 (1935), 957–83.

Two Apocrypha in Old English Homilies, BeP 30 (Leipzig, 1935).

'On Blickling Homily XIII: "The Assumption of the Virgin": the Source and the Missing Passages', *RES* 12 (1936), 1–17.

'Latin Texts of the Three Utterances of the Soul', *Speculum* 12 (1937), 147–66.

'The Two Accounts of the Assumption in Blickling Homily XIII', *RES* 14 (1938), 1–19.

Willems, R., ed., *Sancti Aurelii Augustini in Iohannis evangelium tractatus cxxiv*, CCSL 36 (Turnhout, 1954).

Wilmart, A., 'L'Ancien Récit latin de l'Assomption', in *Analecta reginensia: extraits des manuscrits latins de la Reine Christine conservés au Vatican*, Studi e testi 59 (Rome/Vatican City, 1933), pp. 325–57.

Wormald, P., 'Bede and Benedict Biscop', in *Famulus Christi*, ed. Bonner (1976), pp. 141–69.

ed., *Ideal and Reality in Frankish and Anglo-Saxon Society: Studies presented to J. M. Wallace-Hadrill* (Oxford, 1983).

Wright, C. D., 'Apocryphal Lore and Insular Tradition in St Gall, Stiftsbibliothek MS 908', in *Irland und die Christenheit*, eds. Ní Chatháin and Richter (1987), pp. 124–45.

'Some Evidence for an Irish Origin of Redaction XI of the *Visio Pauli*', *Manuscripta* 34 (1990), 34–44.

The Irish Tradition in Old English Literature, CSASE 6 (Cambridge, 1993).

Wright, W., *Contributions to the Apocryphal Literature of the Old Testament* (London, 1865).

The Departure of My Lady Mary from this World (London, 1965).

Yerkes, D., 'The Old Norse and Old English Prose Accounts of the Phoenix', *Journal of English Linguistics* 17 (1984), 24–8.

Zycha, J., ed., *Sancti Aurelii Augustini de Genesi ad litteram*, CSEL 28.i (Vienna, 1894).

Index

Lightning Source UK Ltd.
Milton Keynes UK
UKOW051634040713

213235UK00002B/117/A

9 780521 030601